Tourism in the Pacific Rim

To the Wandering Islands and One of the Best Ones

Je pense que je pourrais me passer de toi

Si je n'avais pas le choix

Mais s'il te plaît ne t'organise jamais pour que j'aie à le faire

Ça m'a pris tout ce temps pour te trouver

Tourism in the Pacific Rim

Development, Impacts, and Markets

Colin Michael Hall

Longman Cheshire

WILEY HALSTED PRESS

Longman Cheshire Pty Limited
Longman House
Kings Gardens
95 Coventry Street
Melbourne 3205 Australia

Offices in Sydney, Brisbane, Adelaide and Perth, and associated
companies throughout the world.

Copublished in the Western Hemisphere, United Kingdom
and Europe by Halsted Press: an Imprint of
John Wiley & Sons, Inc.
New York Toronto Chichester

Edited by Robin Bower
Designed by Rob Cowpe
Set in 10/12pt New Baskerville
Produced by Longman Cheshire Pty Ltd
through Longman Malaysia, LWP

National Library of Australia
Cataloguing-in-Publication data

Hall, Colin Michael, 1961– .
    Tourism in the Pacific Rim : development, impacts and
    markets.

    Includes index.
    ISBN 0 582 91343 8.

    1. Tourist trade - Pacific Area. I. title.

338.47919

Library of Congress Cataloging-in-Publication Data

Hall, C. M. (C. Michael)
    Tourism in the Pacific Rim: development, impacts, and
markets/
    Colin Michael Hall.
    p. cm.
    Includes bibliographical references and indexes
    ISBN 0-470-23375-3
    1. Tourist trade–Pacific Area. I. Title.
    G155.P25H35 1994
    338.4'791091823–dc20   93-45950
                                                 CIP

Contents

Tables and figures

Tables

viii   Tables and Figures

Figures

Acknowledgements

Tourism is a major industry in the Pacific region and contributes substantially to economic development and employment generation as well as having significant socio-cultural and environmental impacts. Western nations such as Australia, Canada, New Zealand and the USA increasingly look towards Asia and the Pacific Rim for trading partners and their economic futures. However, despite the growing importance of tourism within the Pacific Rim and, in turn, the Asia–Pacific region within the global economy, students have had access to only a very limited number of texts and reference materials on tourism in the region. Therefore, the purpose of this book is to bring together a series of national and regional accounts of the tourism industry within the framework of a number of issues that run through tourism development in the region. Although a comprehensive account of tourism in all the nations of the Pacific Rim is beyond the scope of the present work, it is hoped that this book will go some way towards explaining the dynamic nature of the tourism industry in the region and its future prospects.

Many people and organisations have contributed to the writing of this book. Information and assistance has been gratefully received from various government tourism organisations throughout the Pacific region including the Australian Bureau of Tourism Research; Fiji Ministry of Tourism; Fiji Visitors Bureau; Hawaii Visitors Bureau; Hong Kong Tourism Association; Indonesian Directorate General of Tourism, Department of Tourism, Post and Telecommunication; Japan Travel Bureau; the Kiribati Visitors Bureau; National Tourism Administration of the People's Republic of China; National Tourism Office of Vanuatu; New Zealand Tourism Board; Singapore Tourist Promotion Board; Tourism Bureau, Ministry of Transportation and Communications, Republic of China; and the Tourist Development Corporation Malaysia. Massey University Library, New South Wales Tourism Commission Library, New Zealand Tourism Board Library and Visitor Management (New Zealand Ltd) have all been most helpful in supplying information and inter-library loans, while special mention must also be made of *Asia Travel Trade* and the *Far Eastern Economic Review* for their excellent reporting of tourism and relevent political, economic and social events in the Pacific Rim without which the writing of this book would have been made much more difficult.

A number of people have also provided invaluable information, advice and assistance while gathering material for this book, although the interpretation of their comments is, of course, my own. I would particularly like to thank Mariella Bates, Inga Batterham, Nicole Beasley, Steve Britton, Dick Butler, Joanne Cheyne-Buchanan, Stuart Christopherson, Claire Clark, Jody Cowper, Dave Crag, Rachel Gatumia, Bill Hanning, Keith Hollinshead, John Jenkins, Geoff Kearsley, Brian King, Neil Leiper, Virginia Long, Doug Marshall, Simon McArthur, Treve McCarthy, Morag McDowell, Dave Mercer, Tony Molloy, Doug Pearce, Christine Peterson, Brenda Rudkin, Valene Smith, Penny Spoelder, Brian Springett, Delyse Springett, Geoff Wall, Betty Weiler, Josette Wells, and Emma Willson. *Indigo Girls, This Mortal Coil,* Bruce Cockburn, Paul Kelly, Keith Jarrett, and David Sylvian provided much needed inspiration. Many thanks must also go to my students in Pacific Rim Tourism and my graduate students for the opportunity to throw ideas at them and to have ideas given in return. Sandra Haywood and Treve McCarthy provided excellent research assistance in preparing the final copy of the manuscript and in proofreading.

I have been extremely fortunate to have received assistance from Massey University and the University of Canberra in undertaking research for this book. A Canadian Airlines International Canadian Studies Award was also invaluable in gaining a North American perspective on Pacific Rim tourism issues. I would also like to give special mention to Ron Harper of Longman Cheshire for his continued support of the project and to Robin Bower for her cheerful editing efforts. Finally, I must give special thanks to my friends for their continued love and support in all my endeavours.

Browns Bay
January 1993

1 The Pacific age: the development of the Pacific Basin and its implications for tourism

> The Pacific era has dawned. Today the region in and around the Pacific Basin—the largest of the world's oceans—holds most of the human and natural resources and is the most dynamic and prosperous area of the world (Kim 1987: 165).

Introduction

The Orient has long had a place in the Western tourist imagination. Romantic images of sandy beaches, blue skies, tropical climates, palm trees, busy markets, rickshaws, women in native dress and 'exotic' Asian and Pacific cultures are all elements of the promotion of the region's tourism resources. Tourism has been a component of economic development of the Asia–Pacific since the early 1960s and is an important source of foreign exchange for many of the countries in the region. However, tourism development has not been without its unwanted effects. How much do Westerners know about what lies behind the classic popular images of smiling happy people in the 'sun, sand, sea and surf' of the Pacific?

Eastern Asia has had the longest sustained period of economic growth in modern history. The Pacific Rim is the world's fastest growing tourism market. The region's rapid economic growth has been accompanied by significant increases in per capita incomes and available leisure time, the impacts of which on travel patterns and tourism investment are only now beginning to be recognised.

This book is designed to provide an account of the world's most dynamic tourism region. As Urry (1990: 48) observed, the 'internationalisation of tourism means that we cannot explain tourist patterns in any particular society without analysing developments taking place in other countries'. Contemporary international tourism and its future global develop-

1

ment cannot be understood without reference to the changing economic environment and travel patterns of the Pacific Rim. However, despite the undoubted economic, social, political and environmental significance of tourism in the Pacific, and in Eastern Asia in particular, it is only in recent years that comprehensive attempts have been made to address tourism development issues in the region (Pye & Lin 1983; Richter 1989). Therefore, this book seeks to provide an overview of tourism in the Asia–Pacific region and identify the key problems and issues that face tourism in the 1990s and beyond.

The economic growth which the Pacific Rim has experienced has undoubtedly been a major factor in contributing to the expansion of outbound travel. Furthermore, tourism has also contributed much of that economic growth. However, the significance of tourism as an economic contributor to host communities cannot be separated from the broader social, political, economic, and environmental milieu in which tourism management and policy-making occurs. Similarly, regional and national economic development, and tourism as a component of that development, cannot be fully understood if it is seen in isolation from other events within the Pacific Rim. Therefore, in order to gain an appreciation of why the Pacific Rim has developed as it has, we need to understand the major factors which determine tourism trends.

Figure 1.1: Factors in the determination of tourism trends

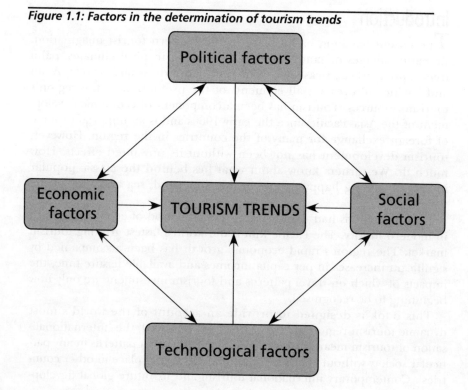

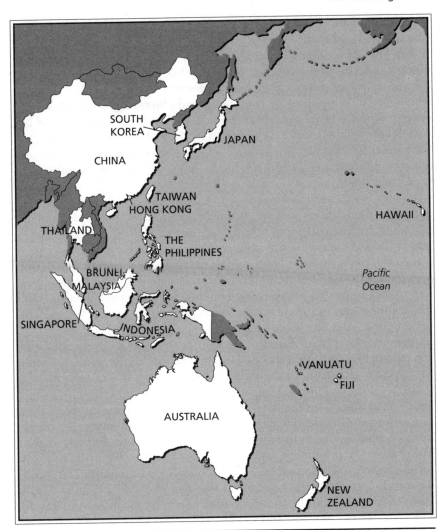

Figure 1.2: The Pacific Basin

Tourism trends are determined by four interrelated factors: economic, political and social environments, and technology (Figure 1.1). The level of economic development will determine the availability of tourism infrastructure in a destination and the capacity of individuals to travel in a generating region. Economic growth also leads to changing spending patterns and shifts in social behaviour. As Martin and Mason (1987: 112) observed, 'Social change has a major influence on the shape of the tourism market. Shifts in population structure, and changing social values and lifestyles, will combine with increased leisure time and disposable incomes to determine the amount and nature of holidays and travel in the 1990s'. The interaction of different cultures and societies will also have substantial impacts on host communities and travellers alike.

The level of economic development and consumer demand is also significant in terms of the creation of new technology in travel and tourism. Technological advances are especially important in the aviation sector in which the development of long-haul, wide-bodied jets has allowed a greater number of passengers to be transported longer distances at less cost. Similarly, transport developments in the rail and road sectors allow for greater accessibility of destinations while improvements in computer and communications technology mean that it is easier for consumers to book their travel.

Politics is also an important factor in determining travel patterns. The appeal of destinations may be drastically reduced by political instability including such occurrences as political protest, human rights violations, and civil war. In addition, the ability of consumers to travel also has a political dimension. Countries may prohibit nationals from certain other countries from entering because of fears of foreign ideologies and political values or because of diplomatic disagreements. Similarly, the rights and abilities of individuals to travel from or within a country may also be restricted for economic or political reasons.

As noted above, the impact of the four factors affecting tourism trends are cumulative and interrelated. The four factors combine to determine the appeal of destinations, the ability of tourists to get there, the economic, social, political and physical impacts of tourists, and the long-term sustainability of tourism. This first chapter provides an overview of some of these factors within a Pacific-wide context. The first section examines the dimensions of economic growth in the region which provides the government justification for promoting tourism and also provides the economic base for the rapid growth in outbound travel over the past decade. The second section discusses the development of the idea of a Pacific Rim or Pacific Basin community and the transformation of the Pacific from a geographic to an economic, political and social entity. The third section notes the tourism growth which the region has experienced over the past two decades and the broad implications which this has had for travel patterns and tourism investment. The final section provides an outline of the remainder of the book.

It is impossible for any text to adequately cover all aspects of such a dynamic industry as tourism, particularly in such a large area as the Pacific. Instead, this book examines the tourism phenomenon in the regions and nations that are generally recognised as comprising the Pacific economic community (Figure 1.2) and which are major generators or receivers of tourism and particularly within the rapidly developing nations of Eastern Asia. Therefore, for the purposes of this text, the Pacific Rim is defined as constituting the countries of North East Asia (China, Hong Kong, Japan, South Korea and Taiwan), the Association of South East Asian Nations (ASEAN) (Brunei, Indonesia, Malaysia, the Philippines, Singapore and

Thailand), Australia, New Zealand, and the microstates of the South Pacific (e.g. Fiji and Vanuatu). Canada and the USA are also important members of the Pacific community; however, apart from a discussion of tourism in Hawaii, their significance for the Pacific region is examined primarily in terms of visitor flows and investment rather than in separate chapters. The countries of Central America and South America have also been excluded from the above definition of the Pacific Rim because their economies are not as well integrated with other Pacific nations nor do they play a major part in tourist flows to the same extent as that of other Pacific nations such as Australia and New Zealand. Although the approach to defining Pacific Rim has meant that an examination of tourism development in some of the region's developing nations such as Vietnam, Cambodia, and Laos are not covered in this text, problems of tourism development in microstates are discussed in Chapter 7. Indeed, it is intended that this book will help encourage students of tourism to think about some of the main issues that surround tourism development not only in the Pacific but elsewhere in the world also.

Each chapter provides an account of inbound and outbound travel and tourism development in the nations of the Pacific economic community and the issues which have emerged during the development process. Thus it is hoped that the reader will not only be aware of the contemporary scene but will also be in a position to critically assess future options and directions. However, before the individual nations of the Pacific community are examined, I would like to discuss some of the broader trends in Pacific tourism.

The age of the Pacific

The signing of the peace treaty on the USS *Missouri* in 1945 to end the war in the Pacific marked the end of one era and heralded the beginning of another—the age of the Pacific. The defeat of Japan's imperial ambitions in Asia and the Pacific led, paradoxically, to the development of Japan as an economic superpower, the decline of the European colonial powers in the Pacific, the further assertion of American interests in the region, and the emergence of Asian and Pacific nationalism.

Economic growth in the Pacific Rim, and in North East Asia and ASEAN in particular, has been the most dynamic in the world over the past forty years (Bollard, Holmes, Kersey & Thompson 1989; Garnaut 1990). The last decade has seen economic growth in East Asia average well over 6 per cent per annum and stay above the rest of the world by around 1 per cent per annum on average (Rowley 1992a). The rapid economic growth of East Asia has been associated with increased ratios of foreign trade to output, rapid structural change in response to changing economic conditions, and strong specialisation in export and production in keeping with international comparative advantage (Garnaut 1990). The countries of the Pacific region owe less than 20 per cent of the world's developing country debt, compared with over 50 per cent in Latin America. The debt-to-service ratio is the lowest of any region, under 16 per cent, and the debt-to-export ratio, nearly 80 per cent, was the best in the world in the mid-1980s (Kim & Conroy 1987: 2).

The growth of the economies of East Asia has also led to a major shift in the balance of world trade. For example, the North American international economic outlook has shifted from Europe to Japan and Asia. Canada has switched its attention from west to east (Holmes 1982), and 'since 1978 the United States has traded more with the Asian and Pacific nations than with her traditional trading partners of the Atlantic' (Kuroda 1982: 94). Similarly, Australia and New Zealand, who traditionally traded with the UK, Europe and North America, have had their trading patterns shift north towards Asia (Bollard *et al.* 1989; Garnaut 1990).

Japan, the first of the Asian countries to industrialise, is regularly taken as the model for Asian development. Japan has undergone significant structural change in the past four decades. Up until the early 1980s, the Japanese economy was primarily led by export growth. However, in the late 1980s and early 1990s, economic expansion has been more a result of domestic demand. In addition, the economy has been marked by increased competition from imports as a consequence of a higher yen and strong consumer demand, greater openness to foreign participation, and a gradual liberalisation of tariff barriers. Nevertheless, the imbalance between Japan's import and export income and protectionary measures, particularly in agricultural goods, has led to substantial international disquiet and tensions concerning the economic relationship with the Japanese (Ross 1982; Castle & Findlay 1988; Wevers 1988; Bollard *et al.* 1989; Garnaut 1990).

One of the key points to emerge from the economic growth of eastern Asia in the past decade is that trade is becoming increasingly Asian-centred. Demand in Asia is compensating for the effects of the recessionary American and European economies and leading to high rates of economic growth (Table 1.1). For example, for 1993 the Asian Development Bank has predicted an average GDP growth of 7.2 per cent for its 25 member countries compared to 6.9 per cent in 1992. Japan's Nomura Research Institute has forecast that real GDP in North East Asia (Hong Kong, South Korea and Taiwan) should grow by 6.4 per cent in 1993, up from an estimated 5.6 per cent in 1992; while the ASEAN economies should grow an average 6.3 per cent, against 5.6 per cent in 1992, and China by 9.2 per cent. In contrast, the American investment bank Salomon Brothers has forecast that the European economies will grow by less than 1 per cent on average in 1993 with the German economy being likely to contract, and the USA will have only moderate growth over the coming years of between 2.5 per cent and 4 per cent on average (*Far Eastern Economic Review* 1992a; Rowley 1992a).

According to Chi Hung Kwan of the Nomura Research Institute, 'the impact on Asia from the global economy has become very small. Asian economies are now less dependent upon the rest of the world and have become larger absorbers of exports from within the region' (cited in Rowley 1992a: 53). Intra-Asian trade now far exceeds trade with the USA.

Economic growth is clearly a significant factor in tourism development. However, it is significant in a number of ways. First, greater disposable income per capita makes it easier for people to engage in leisure activities including travel for pleasure. Second, economic development generates significant business-oriented travel. Third, economic growth provides a basis for public and private investment in tourism infrastructure and the development of tourist product. Nevertheless, the relationship between economic growth and tourism is not all one way. As we shall see, tourism is itself a major contributor to economic growth and regional development in the Asia–Pacific in terms of both domestic and inbound travel (Pye & Lin 1983; Mak & White 1988, 1992). As Chew (1987: 84) noted 'with the centres of production shifting from the Western nations to the developing countries. The focus of international trade will thus shift to the Asia–Pacific region and along with it increases in business and leisure travel to the region'.

Economic growth is only one element in tourism development. To state that economic growth leads to tourism growth is an over-simplification of a complex story. In attempting to understand why tourism has become such an important part of the economies of the Pacific Rim and its impacts on the nations of the region, it is essential to understand the interrelationship of economic growth and tourism with other factors such as political stability,

Table 1.1: Economic growth in the Pacific Rim

Country	Average GDP Growth 1985–89 %	1992 GDP % Estimate	1993 GDP % Forecast
Australia	3.7	2.1	2.7
China	11.6	11-12	8-9
Hong Kong	8.9	5.2	5.7
Indonesia	5.13	5.5	5.9
Japan	4.52	2.1	1.6
Malaysia	*7.6	8.5	8.0
New Zealand	0.8	2.2	1.5
The Philippines	2.81	-0.5	1-2
Singapore	6.0	5.1	6.0
South Korea	10.4	5.4	6.3
Taiwan	9.99	6.7	7.0
Thailand	9.95	6.1	7.1

* 1989 estimate only

Source: Malik 1991; *Far Eastern Economic Review* 1992a: 58.

the social and natural environment, and technology. Furthermore, in the examination of the development of tourism in the Pacific, the process of integration is also an important factor which underlines the growth of tourism in the region.

The emergence of a Pacific community?

A new tide is running in the Pacific: the tide of interdependence (Morley 1987: 11).

Despite the enormous diversity to be found in the countries of the Asia–Pacific, 'the search for stability... has been a remarkable trend in the time frame of the last half century' (Delworth 1982: 4). The emergence of the phrases 'Pacific Community', 'Pacific Rim' and 'Pacific Basin' in the 1970s, indicated the development of a new set of international relationships that reflect a common outlook on the Pacific Ocean. The growth of the Japanese and other Asian economies, the reorientation of Australia and New Zealand to their northern neighbours, and the shift of North American trade from Europe to the Orient has led to the development of a series of interdependent economic and political relationships between the various countries of the Pacific Rim. According to Morley (1987: 11):

only a new form of regional cooperation can ease the vulnerabilities and relieve competitive strains to which each is being subjected... [the] 'Pacific Basin Movement'... while not yet an effective political force, may well portend a future development of truly historic importance.

The big five free market nations of the Pacific (Australia, Canada, Japan, New Zealand, and the USA) have been the strongest advocates of the Pacific Rim concept in its various forms. Japan has probably been foremost in providing leadership in the development of strong linkages between the nations of the Pacific Rim. 'Japan has the most at stake in preserving free trade and promoting economic cooperation in the region. *Thus despite the term "Pacific", the concept is essentially Asia-centered, and primarily trade oriented'* (Quo 1982: x) [my emphasis]. Indeed, 'the key factor in the dynamic growth of the Asia–Pacific region is the increasing reliance by most countries in the region on market mechanisms and market principles' (Bollard *et al.* 1989: 173).

The origins of the Pacific Rim idea are to be found in Tokyo, Japan, in the early 1960s when Sebro Okita, an economist, proposed that the five most advanced countries in the Pacific—the USA, Canada, New Zealand, Australia and Japan—form a Pacific Free Trade Area (PAFTA). The proposal did not find acceptance at the government level; however, the idea did have some intellectual impact in both academic and diplomatic circles. Perhaps most prominent of the impacts was the establishment of the Australia–Japan project with the support of the Australian Government and Japanese Government at the Australian National University (ANU), Canberra, in October 1972. The project has led to the development and publication of a large number of research studies on Australian–Japanese relations and the broader questions of Pacific trade and integration. In effect, the project has been one of the intellectual engines which has provided the momentum for the idea of a Pacific community.

In May 1981, the Special Committee on Pacific Cooperation (SCPC) defined the concept of Pacific Basin Cooperation as follows:

1 The Pacific Basin Cooperation concept is an idea to secure and promote the present trend of interdependence amongst countries in the region, thus viewing into the 21st century.
2 In order to implement the idea, it is desirable to create a network of non-governmental forums with the blessing of each government concerned.
3 Its purpose is not to create an economic sphere of influence dominated by the 'haves', or politically-oriented exclusive regional bloc, but to promote cooperative relationships based on interdependence and mutual understanding among the countries in the region (cited in Quo 1982: ix).

In many ways, the conditions for the concept of Pacific Basin Cooperation have been met. As discussed above, the Asia–Pacific region has an increasing amount of intraregional trade which reinforces interdependence between nations. It is true that regional interdependence and intraregional trade is far less developed in the East Asian region than in the European Community (Lorenz 1989). Nevertheless, intraregional trade as a per cent of exports has almost doubled since 1986 and is continuing to grow (Rowley 1992a) and a network of non-government forums is being created to deal with trade and other issues. For example, the Association of South East Asian Nations (ASEAN) has started to develop a structure for the formal reduction of tariffs between member states (see Chapter 4) while other international organisations such as the Asia–Pacific Economic Cooperation Council (APEC) meet on a regular basis (Malik 1991). The latter organisation in particular, which provides a forum for dialogue between the major Pacific nations, has had a substantial impact on the development of greater understanding on Pacific trade issues.

In addition to the issue of interdependence discussed above, another crucial element in the increasing integration of the Asia–Pacific region is the reduction in superpower conflict and the effect that this has had on political stability (Crosbie 1987). The end of the (former) Soviet Union–USA rivalry—unthinkable a decade ago—provides for substantial reallocation of economic resources and a lowering of political tensions. In addition to a decline in United States and Japanese fears of Soviet expansionism, the 'new' Russia seeks to become actively engaged in Pacific trade and investment. Mikhail Gorbachev's Vladivostok initiative on 28 July 1986, signalled the renewed interest of Russia in the Pacific region in economic terms: '... the Soviet Union is also an Asian and a Pacific country... Asia provides a living legacy that makes up one of the important fundamentals of the current political realities in this part of the world' (*Pravda*, 29 July 1986: 3). Similarly, China has reoriented itself to the non-socialist world and has actively sought foreign investment under the 'four modernizations' since the late 1970s (see Chapter 5). Although the restructuring of former communist states, which the World Bank refers to as 'socialists in transition', is not without domestic political instability, the international political tensions of the 1950s to early 1980s are fading rapidly. However, as the World Bank has noted, 'No country has yet proved that a smooth transition from socialism to market economics is possible' (Rowley 1992a: 53). Nevertheless, as we shall see, the general improvement in political stability has been a critical factor in the development of a climate favourable for tourism in the region.

The development of the concept of a Pacific community is not simply a resort to protectionist measures and political pressure against trading partners in the present world-wide economic recession. As noted above, the concept has a history which goes back over almost three decades. The notion of the Pacific Rim is a reaction to the increased economic and political interdependence within East Asia and the Pacific. The Pacific is therefore becoming transformed from a geographic to an economic, political and social entity.

Tourism has an enormous part to play in the transformation process. Through improvements in transport, tourist destinations and generating regions are becoming ever closer. Therefore, the vast distances of the Pacific are diminishing with corresponding increases in intra-Pacific travel. Tourism is also contributing to economic growth and interdependence through both investment and higher tourism flows. Tourism has also been touted as a force for peace. While this book does not necessarily support such a proposition, the following chapters do indicate that political stability is extremely important for tourism development and that tourism and politics are inextricably linked.

The growth of tourism in the Pacific

...for the next few years it seems inevitable that the Asia/Pacific will be the most dynamic in the world's international travel trade (Economist Intelligence Unit 1992: 92).

The Asia–Pacific area is the world's fastest growing tourism region. According to the World Tourism Organization (1991), the East Asia–Pacific region has grown from 0.75 per cent of world tourist arrivals in 1950 to 11.48 per cent in 1991 (Table 1.2). At the same time, the East Asia–Pacific share of international tourism receipts grew from 1.43 per cent in 1950 to 14.69 per cent in 1991, double the share in 1980 (World Tourism Organization 1991: 12).

As may be expected given the economic development of the region, the rate of tourism growth over the last decade has been extremely rapid. From 1981 to 1991 visitor arrivals to the Pacific Asia Travel Association (PATA) region, which covers nearly all of the East Asia–Pacific area, grew at an average rate of 7.69 per cent per annum. Growth was only interrupted in the early 1980s by a global recession and in 1989 and 1990 by the

Table 1.2: Regional share of international tourist arrivals, 1950–1991 (%)

Region	1950	1960	1970	1980	1991
Africa	2.07	1.08	1.51	2.54	2.90
Americas	29.61	24.11	22.95	21.32	21.50
East Asia–Pacific	0.75	0.98	3.04	6.82	11.48
Europe	66.60	72.66	70.76	65.55	61.84
Middle East	0.78	0.91	1.17	2.98	1.58
South Asia	0.19	0.26	0.57	0.79	0.71

Source: World Tourism Organization 1991

impacts of the political instability in China and the Gulf War. Table 1.3 indicates the visitor arrivals to PATA destinations in 1981–1991, while Table 1.4 shows the origin of visitor arrivals over the same period.

Growth is occurring in both long- and short-haul travel to and from the region. The traditional European and North American markets to Asia have expanded rapidly. This is due to a number of factors. First, the deregulation of the aviation industry in North America and Europe has meant greater competition between carriers. Therefore, carriers have demanded more efficient aircraft in terms of fuel usage and costs, and greater passenger comfort for all classes of traveller, which in turn leads to the opening up of new markets throughout the world including the Asia–Pacific region (Shackleford 1987). According to Chew (1987: 84):

To the Europeans, airfares to the Asia–Pacific region have become more attractive than South America. In fact, Asia is now the second most popular long-haul destination for Europeans after the USA. The air passenger travel markets in Europe and the USA are gradually losing their world shares to the faster-growing Asia–Pacific region... In fact, the International Civil Aviation Organization... has forecast that by 1995 the growth of international scheduled passenger traffic in the Asia–Pacific region will be 30% higher that the world average. The region's share of the world traffic will also increase to 32.8%, exceeding North America's share of 21.4%.

Accompanying the shift in the nature of the international air passenger travel market, and in particular the long-haul market, will be changes in the nature of the traveller. The new travellers to the Asia–Pacific region will also be older travellers and may also be a part of the rapidly growing incentive market segment. The size of the 'mature traveller' market is enormous (Frechtling 1987) and as Lickorish (1987: 94) has commented, 'While they can go, they will go'. In addition, special interest tourism has become a major feature of travel to the region with growing emphasis being given to cultural and heritage tourism, eco- or nature-based tourism, and marine tourism (Weiler & Hall 1992).

Table 1.3: Visitor arrivals to PATA destinations, 1981–1991

Year	Number (millions)
1981	23.2
1982	24.3
1983	24.9
1984	26.1
1985	27.5
1986	30.0
1987	33.8
1988	38.9
1989	42.6
1990	47.7
1991	48.0

Source: Pacific Asia Travel Association (PATA) 1992: 7

Table 1.4: Origin of visitor arrivals to PATA regions, 1981–1991 (including Hawaii)

	1981	1991	Average per annum growth rate (%)
North America	4 951 481	8 942 026	6.1
Europe	3 648 950	6 689 567	6.2
Asia	11 127 277	26 560 505	9.1
Pacific	1 982 499	3 902 049	7.0
Other	1 443 715	1 908 751	2.8
Total	**23 153 922**	**48 002 898**	**7.6**

Source: Pacific Asia Travel Association (PATA) 1992: 8

Short-haul short-stay intraregional travel within East Asia and the Pacific is also rapidly increasing. Intraregional tourism, including ethnic Chinese, accounted for 73 per cent of total arrivals in the region in 1990 (World Tourist Organization 1991). The expansion of intraregional travel is a reflection of greater disposable income, increased leisure time, a reduction in government restrictions on travel, and improved transport networks and tourism infrastructure. The Japanese are the single largest generating market and account for a greater number of arrivals in the region than all European Community countries combined (see Chapter 2). However, the highest rates of outbound travel to the region during the late 1980s and early 1990s have been recorded by South Korea and by the

Republic of China (Taiwan) (see Chapter 3). (Economist Intelligence Unit 1990a)

Although most countries in the Asia–Pacific are actively seeking greater inbound tourism, Taiwan and China are promoting outbound travel. The Japanese Government (through such measures as the 'ten million project') and Taiwanese Government have been encouraging their nationals to travel abroad in order to correct the balance of trade that they have with many countries. The potential of the Japanese market, for example, is enormous. *The Economist* (15 April 1989) reported that while 30 per cent to 40 per cent of Europeans travel abroad each year, the figure for Japan was only about 7 per cent and increasing.

Travel flow goes hand-in-hand with investment patterns. For example, 'growth in Japanese tourist travel in the region is accompanied by Japanese investment in hotels, local transport and tourist consumer products' (Bollard *et al.* 1989: 53). The growth in international travel in the region has also been matched by increased foreign investment in the tourism industry. In the search for continued economic growth, Japan and other industrialising countries of Asia are passing through a succession of stages of economic development and foreign investment. The first stage concentrated on investment in the extraction of primary resources in order to secure a firm base for the development of value-added product. The second stage of investment has been marked by the shifting of manufacturing capacity off-shore in order to benefit from lower labour costs. The third stage of investment is in service industries such as finance and banking, telecommunications and tourism (Garnaut 1990), with the latter probably constituting the most rapidly growing area of foreign direct investment in the service sector (Bollard *et al.* 1989). Nevertheless, despite the need of many countries for foreign investment in the development of tourism infrastructure, there is often a great deal of resistance to overseas investment because of a perception that there is a loss of control to foreigners and outsiders (Hall 1991). Nowhere is this more the case in the Asia–Pacific region than in the case of Japan.

The economic policies of Japan are instrumental in the wider economic performance of the region. As the World Bank noted, 'Japan is quietly replacing the U.S. as the key partner in the development of East Asia in aid, trade and investment' (cited in Rowley 1992a: 53). Since 1986 the proportionate amount of Japanese direct foreign investment in the service sector, and in tourism in particular, throughout Eastern Asia and the Pacific has increased substantially (Bollard *et al.* 1989). However, 'Japan has frequently been a convenient scapegoat when acrimony over economic and political issues reach the boiling point' (Scalapino 1989: 141). Therefore, one of the key issues which needs to be addressed in any assessment of tourism development in the Pacific region is the implications of Japanese investment in the tourism industry for the long-term development of tourism, particularly with respect to its economic and social impacts.

Economic growth in the Pacific community is not evenly spread, neither is the pattern of travel or tourism investment. Despite its potential economic benefits, not all effects of tourism have been positive. Tourism has been instrumental in causing social dislocation and community breakdown, damaging the environment, and reinforcing social and economic inequalities. Increasingly, the negative impacts of tourism development are being addressed by government in the fear of slower growth or decline. Therefore, the search for appropriate forms of tourism is also a common concern throughout the region. Indeed, the issue of sustainability is probably the central issue in Pacific tourism. As this section has illustrated, tourism growth and development in the East Asia–Pacific region is extremely dynamic. However, as each of the following chapters will illustrate, the maintenance or expansion of inbound tourism without further damage to the social and physical environment is problematic.

Outline of the book

Tourism has been a key component of economic development of the Pacific Rim and of the East Asian nations in particular. However, the growth of the Asian economies has also created the base for substantial outbound travel in the Pacific in conjunction with other social, political and technological factors. This first chapter has outlined some of those trends and has also discussed the significance of economic growth and provided a portrait of the emergence of a Pacific community. The following chapters will examine individual nations and regions in the light of the broader issues raised in this first chapter.

Chapter 2 discusses the largest outbound travel market, Japan, and also examines some of the implications of the growth of Japanese tourism for investment patterns and the integration of the Pacific economies. The chapter will also note the often ignored, yet still economically significant, domestic and inbound tourism markets.

Chapter 3 examines tourism in the three other developed economies of North East Asia: Korea, the Republic of China (Taiwan), and Hong Kong. Tourism in all three countries has been deeply affected by questions of political stability and this factor is set to dominate both inbound and outbound travel in the region for the remainder of the decade.

Chapter 4 also uses a regional approach to examine tourism in the Association of South East Asian Nations (ASEAN) region. The countries which comprise ASEAN are Brunei, Indonesia, Malaysia, the Philippines, Thailand and Singapore. Apart from Brunei, tourism is a major source of foreign exchange and a factor in economic development in all the nations. Despite the growth of intra-ASEAN travel and continued increases in inbound travel, substantial social, environmental and infrastructural constraints are beginning to emerge which must be addressed if tourism development is to be sustained.

The economic and political dimensions of tourism are paramount in

Chapter 5 which discusses tourism in the Peoples' Republic of China. As with many nations of the region, China has used inbound tourism to gain much needed foreign exchange. However, the transformation of a centralist economy has meant major problems have emerged in the appropriate provision of tourism infrastructure, while the political stability of the country is set to be the determinant in releasing the potential of tourism in the world's largest country.

Chapter 6 examines tourism in Australia and New Zealand, two nations with predominantly European cultures which are increasingly turning towards Asia and the Pacific Rim for their economic futures. Both countries are transforming from being predominantly tourist generating regions to becoming major destinations. The economic restructuring of Australia and New Zealand has meant that tourism is increasingly seen as a means to overcome balance-of-payments problems in securing export earnings. Furthermore, the development of the Closer Economic Relations (CER) agreement between the two countries has substantial implications for aviation and tourism, and is perhaps a precursor for other economic and travel agreements within the Pacific Rim.

Chapter 7 discusses tourism development in the South Pacific. Although, not a part of the Pacific economic community, the islands of the South Pacific are often dependent on tourism for economic development and on external aid from the Pacific Rim powers such as Australia, New Zealand, the USA and, increasingly, Japan. As the chapter demonstrates, the Pacific island microstates face enormous difficulties in managing tourism development in a manner which does not damage their social and physical environment, and ensures their financial and political independence. Yet, in the face of a lack of natural resources, many of the islands are forced to develop tourism as there are few alternatives.

Chapter 8 draws together the major issues which the book has raised and examines the future of tourism in the Pacific. The chapter examines the role of the Japanese in tourism in the Pacific and notes the negative perceptions that are often associated with Japanese investment. In addition, the chapter discusses the role of tourism in economic development in the Pacific and the role of free trade. Finally, it addresses questions regarding the future of tourism in the Pacific and the search for sustainable forms of tourism development.

Tourism is a major component in the economies of the Pacific. It has also had substantial impacts on host communities and the natural environment. However, despite the economic, political, social and environmental significance of tourism, our understanding of the implications of tourism development in the Pacific, even at a general level, is only beginning. It is recognised that this book is only a first step in examining the complexities of tourism in the region, but it is hoped that the ideas and reactions it generates will help achieve a greater appreciation of the place of tourism in modern society and the means by which its benefits can be maximised.

Suggestions for further reading

Several useful books and reports are available on the economic development of the Pacific and the growing interdependence of the Pacific economies. Students should refer to Ariff (1991) *The Pacific Economy: Growth and External Stability*, and Castle & Findlay (eds) 1988, *Pacific Trade in Services*. Bollard (*et al.*) (1989) *Meeting the East Asia Challenge: Trends, Prospects and Policies*, and Garnaut (1990) *Australia and the Northeast Asian Ascendency* serve as two extremely good examples of the recognition of the importance of Asia–Pacific trade, including tourism, for New Zealand and Australia respectively.

Relatively little material is available on the importance of tourism to the Pacific Rim as a whole. The two most significant books are Richter (1989) *The Politics of Tourism in Asia*, and Hitchcock, King & Parnwell (1992) *Tourism in South-East Asia.* The content of Pye & Lin (1983) *Tourism in Asia: The Economic Impact*, is now somewhat dated, but it is still useful as a guide to the state of tourism in the region in the early 1980s. The Economist Intelligence Unit (1990) publication of *Far East and Pacific Travel in the 1990's*; the Pacific Asia Travel Association (PATA) (1992), *Annual Statistical Report 1991*, and the World Tourism Organization (1991) report on *Tourism Trends Worldwide and in East Asia and the Pacific 1950–1991*, provide a very comprehensive overview of industrial statistics and trends. Harrison (ed.) (1992) *Tourism and the Less Developed Countries* also contains much valuable information on tourism development in the Pacific region. A useful overview of tourism in the Pacific is also to be found in Mak & White (1988) 'Tourism in Asia and the Pacific', and a 1992 article by the same authors, 'Comparative tourism development in Asia and the Pacific'.

Students seeking to update their knowledge of tourism in the Pacific should consult the major journals in the tourism field (*Annals of Tourism Research, Journal of Travel and Tourism Marketing, Journal of Travel Research, Journal of Sustainable Tourism, Tourism Management, Tourism Recreation Research, Tourist Review*), while the *Journal of Tourism Studies*, published at James Cook University in Australia, tends to contain much research of relevance to tourism in the Pacific. *Asia Travel Trade* is by far the best trade journal which contains information on tourism issues in the Asia–Pacific region, while the *Far Eastern Economic Review* provides a regular update on economic, social, political and environmental issues in the region. The *Review* also publishes an annual yearbook which should be consulted by students wanting a quick introduction to the geo-political situation in the countries of the eastern Pacific Rim.

Discussion and review

This section will appear at the end of each chapter to assist students in discussing and reviewing some of the key concepts and questions that emerge in the study of tourism in the Pacific.

Key concepts
Economic development, economic growth, social values and lifestyles, technology, political stability, Pacific Basin, Pacific Rim, Pacific Community, balance of world trade, tariff barriers, intraregional trade, interdependence, Pacific Basin Cooperation, world tourist arrivals, international tourism receipts, long-haul travel, short-haul aviation, the 'mature traveller', special interest tourism, incentive market, tourism investment, service sector, social dislocation, negative impacts.

Questions for review and discussion
1 What are the major factors which determine tourism trends?
2 How might social change influence the shape of the tourism market?
3 How have changes in transport influenced the development of travel both to and within the Pacific region?
4 How might politics determine travel patterns?
5 In what ways has the Pacific been transformed from a geographic to an economic, political and social entity?
6 What evidence exists to suggest that the focus of international trade is shifting towards the Pacific region?
7 '...despite the term "Pacific", the concept is essentially Asia-centered, and primarily trade oriented' (Quo 1982: x). Discuss in relation to the development of the Pacific Rim concept.

2 Japan: tourism superpower of the Pacific

> The significance of promoting overseas travel goes beyond the simple attempt to reduce Japan's surplus in the international balance of trade. It must essentially be seen in the wider context of globalization, and in this sense, it is an important factor for Japan to adopt a more independent position in international society.
>
> Overseas travel lets the tourist experience the 'richness of leisure' and gain hands-on contact with a different, foreign culture, thus acquiring an empirical knowledge which alone creates the breadth of mind that is capable of making cross-cultural and cross-human contacts. (Japan Travel Bureau 1991: 68)

An understanding of the growth, development and nature of Japanese tourism is essential to understanding tourism in the Pacific. Japan is not only the dominant economic power of the Pacific but in tourism terms it is the largest inbound market for many of the countries of the region; Japanese tourists are usually the largest per capita spenders per day; Japan is a major source of investment funds in the tourism industry; and a substantial provider of international aid for tourism related development projects. Furthermore, the involvement of the Japanese in tourism, whether as tourist or investor, is still growing and will continue to be a major factor in Pacific Rim tourism until the turn of the century and beyond. See Figure 2.1.

This chapter will examine a number of factors which give rise to the significance of the Japanese tourism industry in the Asia–Pacific region. The chapter is divided into five sections. The first section discusses the role of tourism in the Japanese economy and its significance as a policy issue. The second section notes the growth of inbound tourism in recent years and the focus on convention and business travel in keeping with Japan's desire

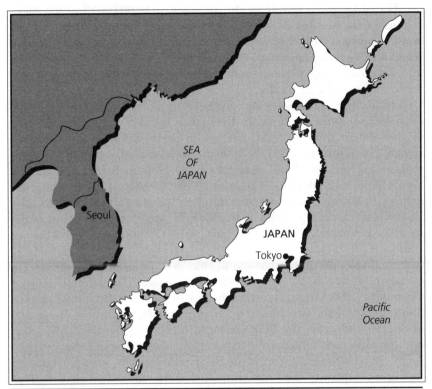

Figure 2.1: Japan

to be recognised as an economic power. The third section discusses the growth of Japanese outbound travel and the spending power of Japanese tourists. The growth of outbound travel has gone hand-in-hand with overseas investment and the fourth section notes the role of tourism-related foreign investment and overseas development assistance in the Asia–Pacific region. The final section discusses the future of Japanese tourism and notes the significance of domestic leisure trends and foreign acceptance of Japanese tourists and investments for the future growth of Japanese travel.

Japanese tourism: economic significance and policy issues

Unlike many other countries in Asia and the Pacific, tourism is not an important item in Japan for economic development and the generation of foreign exchange. This function was important during the 1960s but was rapidly eclipsed by other export industries and by the country's strong domestic economy. Instead, outbound tourism is encouraged by government as a means of reducing trade imbalances with other nations in the region and to serve broader educative, diplomatic and political goals.

Travel-related expenditures are the third largest import category in Japan behind mineral fuels and machinery and equipment. In 1990 the number of Japanese travelling abroad reached 10.997 million travellers, ensuring that the plan to increase overseas travel known as the 'Ten Million Programme' launched in 1987 had reached its target a year ahead of schedule. The Programme was designed by the Ministry of Transport as a means to reduce Japan's large trade surplus thereby avoiding the potential for conflict with major trading partners such as the USA and the European Union. Table 2.1 indicates the Japanese trade balance and the travel-related expenditures balance. In 1989 Japan became the country with the highest deficit travel account balance in the world ahead of Germany (Japan Travel Bureau 1991). In 1990 the travel trade balance of payments (balance of total travel and passenger fares) had a deficit of US$27.3 billion, a figure equivalent to 43 per cent (US$63.5 billion) of the total trade surplus. In 1990 Japanese overseas travellers spent an average of US$2270, US$60 less than the previous year. However, in yen terms, each traveller spent approximately ¥328 000, an increase of ¥7000 (Japan Travel Bureau 1991).

A good example of the changed significance of tourism in Japanese Government thinking is the shift in roles for the Japan National Tourist Organization (JNTO). Originally established in 1959 as the marketing organisation responsible for attracting foreign tourists to Japan and the promotion of domestic tourism, the JNTO has also been charged, since 1979, with offering services to facilitate the travel of Japanese overseas. Japan has used promotional schemes, for example the Ten Million Programme, changes to tax exemptions for corporate travellers, increases in duty-free allowances, and development assistance to destinations in order to encourage increased outbound travel.

Table 2.1: Japanese trade and travel-related expenditures balance, 1980–1990 (US$m)

Year	Trade Balance	Travel-Related Expenditures Balance
1980	2 125	-4 913
1981	19 967	-5 046
1982	18 079	-4 518
1983	31 454	-4 756
1984	44 257	-4 952
1985	55 986	-4 981
1986	92 827	-7 416
1987	96 386	-11 356
1988	95 012	-19 468
1989	76 917	-24 416
1990	63 528	-27 339

Source: The Bank of Japan in Japan Travel Bureau 1991: 3

Despite the images provided in the popular media of hordes of Japanese tourists advancing throughout the world, the proportion of the population which travels overseas is relatively low by OECD standards. Domestic tourism dominates the Japanese tourism industry with domestic travel accounting for 60 per cent to 70 per cent of total business for Japan's three largest travel agencies: Japan Travel Bureau (JTB), Kinki Nippon Tourist (KNT) and Nippon Travel Agency (NTA) (*Asia Travel Trade* 1990c). Inbound tourism earned US$300 million for Japanese travel agents, representing only 0.8 per cent of their total 1989 revenue of US$33.1 billion. In comparison, outbound travel generated US$13.6 billion (41.2 per cent of total revenue) and domestic tourism accounted for US$19.2 billion (58 per cent) of travel agents' earnings (Jeffrey 1991).

Domestic travel has grown substantially in Japan over the past decade. In 1990 the total volume of domestic overnight travel was estimated at 363 million person-nights, an increase of 46 million person-nights on the previous year, while the total volume of person-trips was 190 million in 1990 compared to 174 million in 1989 (trips must be greater than 24 hours to be included). Pleasure-oriented travel accounts for approximately 80 per cent of all domestic tourism in Japan. The average per capita expenditure on domestic tourism was ¥67 100 in 1990, a 16.1 per cent increase from 1989. Total domestic tourism expenditure was ¥8290 billion in 1990, an increase of ¥1170 billion over 1989 (Ministry of Transport 1991).

A good example of the significance of Japanese domestic tourism and the involvement of government in the tourism sector is the 1987 Law for Development of Comprehensive Resort Areas commonly known as the Resort Act (*Asia Travel Trade* 1990b). The Act was directed towards the promotion of effective use of leisure time, the stimulation of domestic demand for touristic activities, and was also intended to encourage private sector investment in resort projects by the availability of tax breaks, low-interest loans and other government incentives including infrastructure development. The Act was motivated by a desire to ease overseas pressure on Japan to reduce its reserve holdings through investment in tourism properties and as relief for industries suffering from recession. According to Kimitaka Fujino, director of the development division in the tourism department of the Ministry of Transport:

> There is new demand for resorts, because people are now more active, and leisure time is lengthening. Secondly, local governments in Japan want more development in their areas, but there are environmental problems with development of heavy industries, and hi-tech industries are not so labour intensive. Tourism is ideal for creating jobs, and also, there is a lot of national land in Japan (cited in *Asia Travel Trade* 1990b: 44).

According to McCormack (1991) so many local government authorities were seeking 'resort area' designation that 19.2 per cent of the country's land area was involved, with 646 projects underway and 205 at planning stage. Many of the resort projects under the Act are large-scale integrated resort developments which include marinas and golf courses (*Asia Travel Trade* 1990b). Given the size of many of the projects under the Act, the scheme has served to benefit large corporations such as construction companies, banks, real estate developers, and trading companies (Fujiwara 1991). Furthermore, considerable opposition has emerged to some of the projects on environmental grounds and because of lack of community support in some instances (AMPO 1991; Inoue 1991; Mackie 1992).

In order to guide the future development of the tourism industry the Japanese Government has developed a policy statement, 'Tourism Action Programme in the 90s' (TAP '90s), which plans to maintain outbound growth, develop a tourism consciousness among the Japanese (both domestic and outbound) and promote new destinations. The programme seeks to 'internationalise' regions of Japan and would:

- provide more holiday time and relax rules governing sick leave
- promote Japan as an international convention and business destination
- expand tourism services for foreign visitors
- develop new domestic tourism destinations and encourage resort development. (*Asia Travel Trade* 1990a)

Given the content of TAP '90s, it is readily apparent that the Japanese Government will continue to utilise tourism as a mechanism not only to meet domestic social and economic aspirations but also to strengthen Japan's position within the Asia–Pacific region. As the next section discusses, inbound tourism has no substantial foreign exchange function, but it can be utilised by government to justify domestic public expenditure on infrastructure development and to develop business and cultural relations with the Pacific Rim.

Inbound tourism

My aim is for foreigners to gain an understanding of Japan, not how much revenue is earned—Tsuneaki Iki, Executive Vice-President, JNTO (cited in Jeffrey 1991: 34).

Although the focus of international attention on Japanese tourism is on the outbound market, inbound travel to Japan is substantial and is also expanding. In 1990 Japan received over three million visitors (Table 2.2). The increase in inbound travel has occurred primarily because of the removal of restrictions for outbound travel in Korea and Taiwan with both countries becoming major inbound markets. For example in 1990, 21 per cent of inbound tourists came from Korea (*Asia Travel Trade* 1990a). Nevertheless, for countries outside the North East Asian region the promotion of Japan is difficult because of perceptions that it is an expensive destination (Jeffrey 1991).

Koreans, Taiwanese and Americans make up the major inbound tourists. The increasing strength of the Asian economies and the removal of travel restrictions in several countries of the region is indicated by the growing market share of Asian visitors in inbound arrivals (Table 2.3). In addition, it is interesting to note that the growth of market share for Korean and Taiwanese travellers has been at the expense of the United States market (Table 2.4), and is indicative of general economic trends in the Pacific Rim.

Despite the relative economic insignificance of inbound travel, government is still interested in its broader international political dimensions. The government policy of 'Two-way Tourism 21' was launched in 1991 with the goals of education, international understanding and balanced travel. Unlike many other countries in the Asia–Pacific region, Japan does not rely on the revenue to be gained through inbound tourism. There will be no 'Visit Japan' year. In order to boost inbound tourism the government has developed a 'Five Million Programme', but unlike the high profile '10 Million Programme' for outbound travel, the inbound campaign is low-key and focuses on niche markets such as incentive and convention travel rather than leisure-oriented travel (*Asia Travel Trade* 1990a). The Government has projections of 3.9 million arrivals in 1992, 5 million in 1995, and 10 million in 2000 (Stuart 1992). However, substantial infrastructure problems emerge for inbound tourism in terms of accommodation, transport, and the availability of seats on inbound flights (*Asia Travel Trade* 1990b; Economist Intelligence Unit 1990b; Jeffrey 1991). The value of the yen also has a substantial impact on inbound travel. For example, in 1986 a sharp appreciation of the yen led to a fall in the number of arrivals from 2.3 million in 1985 to 2 million in 1986. In the same period, the

Table 2.2: Visitor arrivals in Japan, 1965–1990

Year	Number ('000)	% Growth	Year	Number ('000)	% Growth
1965	367	3.9	1978	1 039	1.0
1966	433	18.1	1979	1 113	7.1
1967	477	10.1	1980	1 317	18.3
1968	519	8.9	1981	1 583	20.2
1969	609	17.3	1982	1 793	13.3
1970	854	40.4	1983	1 968	9.8
1971	661	-22.7	1984	2 110	7.2
1972	724	9.5	1985	2 327	10.3
1973	785	8.4	1986	2 062	-11.4
1974	764	2.6	1987	2 155	4.5
1975	812	6.2	1988	2 355	9.3
1976	915	12.7	1989	2 835	20.4
1977	1 028	12.4	1990	3 236	14.1

Source: Compiled by the Japan National Tourist Organization on data furnished by the Ministry of Justice in Ministry of Transport 1991

Table 2.3: Foreign visitors to Japan by region, 1988–1990 ('000s)

Region	1988			1989			1990		
	Number	%Change	%Share	Number	%Change	%Share	Number	%Change	%Share
Asia and Middle East	1 257	19.9	53.4	1 637	30.2	57.8	1 919	17.2	59.3
Europe	401	5.2	17.0	455	13.6	16.1	516	13.4	16.0
Africa	11	5.3	0.4	12	13.1	0.4	12	2.1	0.4
North America	590	-5.3	25.0	605	2.6	21.3	633	4.7	19.6
South America	32	17.5	1.4	49	52.7	1.7	78	59.8	2.4
Oceania	62	0.3	2.6	74	19.3	2.6	75	0.9	2.3

Source: Compiled by the Japan National Tourist Organization on data furnished by the Ministry of Justice in Ministry of Transport 1991

Table 2.4: Major inbound markets to Japan by nationality, 1988–1990 ('000s)

Region	1988			1989			1990		
	Number	%Change	%Share	Number	%Change	%Share	Number	%Change	%Share
USA	516	-6.2	21.9	532	3.0	18.8	555	4.4	17.1
Taiwan	411	7.2	17.5	528	28.4	18.6	608	15.1	18.8
Korea	341	57.7	14.5	610	78.7	21.5	740	21.4	22.9
UK	155	4.2	6.6	177	14.7	6.3	214	21.0	6.6
China	109	56.0	4.6	97	-10.2	3.4	106	8.8	3.3
UK (Hong Kong)	66	N.A.	3.0	84	26.5	3.0	112	34.0	3.5

Source: Compiled by the Japan National Tourist Organization on data furnished by the Ministry of Justice in Ministry of Transport 1991

number of people who travelled to Japan for purposes other than pleasure (such as business, incentives, visiting friends and relatives) steadily increased from 1986 onwards due to fluctuations in the exchange rates. Tourists accounted for 58.7 per cent of all arrivals in 1984; by 1988, they made up only 47.4 per cent (Jeffrey 1991: 37).

As well as promotional strategies to meet inbound arrival targets, the Government has also created assistance packages to help develop tourism infrastructure. For example, in 1986 the Ministry of Tourism designated fifteen areas as 'New Sites of Discovery' covering fifteen prefectures and a total of 153 cities, towns and villages that were designed to appeal to foreign visitors. The sites needed to fulfil certain planning criteria such as Western style accommodation, good public transport systems, tourist attractions, information centres and local support. In addition, the Ministry of Transport arranges loans through the Japan Development Bank for investment in new accommodation and restaurants at the site (Ministry of Transport 1986). However, while the policy implications of inbound tourism have been given a higher profile in recent years, Government attention has, and will continue to be, focused primarily on outbound travel.

The outbound market: have yen will travel

Japanese outbound travel has been one of the most spectacular tourist success stories of the modern era. Since the restriction on outbound travel was lifted in 1964, Japanese travel overseas has shown continued high growth apart from 1973–1974 (first oil crisis), 1980 (second oil crisis), 1991 (Gulf War and recession) (Tamao 1980; Leiper 1984; Inoue 1991) (Table 2.5). The growth in outbound travel closely followed a surge in the strength of the yen and increasing allowances on the amount of foreign currency available for tourist use. However, the 8.9 per cent of the population which travelled overseas in 1990 is still considerably short of the United States figure of 16.8 per cent, signifying further potential outbound travel growth (Stuart 1992).

The major destination for Japanese travellers, the USA, experienced substantial growth in 1990 (Table 2.6). Korea, Hawaii, Hong Kong and Singapore are the most popular short-haul destinations, with the European countries of France, Germany, and Italy being the most popular of the long-haul destinations after the USA. The only country to experience a decline in Japanese arrivals in 1990 was Taiwan which dropped 5 per cent from the previous year. The reason for the decline was a switching of Japanese travel back to mainland China in 1990 following the decline in 1989 after the events at Tiananmen Square. In 1990 China had a 28.1 per cent increase on its 1989 figures.

Of the 10.997 million Japanese overseas travellers in 1990, 67.7 per cent were travelling for pleasure and 18.7 per cent for business. Males conducted the major portion of business travel, but it should also be noted

Table 2.5: Japanese outbound travel, 1964–1991

Year	Number ('000)	%Growth	Year	Number ('000)	%Growth
1964	128	-	1978	3 525	12
1965	159	24	1979	4 006	15
1966	212	33	1980	3 909	-3
1967	268	26	1981	4 038	2
1968	344	28	1982	4 086	2
1969	493	43	1983	4 232	4
1970	663	35	1984	4 659	10
1971	961	45	1985	4 948	6
1972	1 392	45	1986	5 516	11
1973	2 289	64	1987	6 829	24
1974	2 336	2	1988	8 427	23
1975	2446	6	1989	9 663	15
1976	2853	16	1990	10 997	14
1977	3151	10	1991	10 623	-3

Source: Ministry of Justice in Japan Travel Bureau 1991: 1; PATA Annual Statistical Report in New
Zealand Tourism Board 1992a: 8

that males outnumber females in the total figure by a ratio of six to four. A
significant characteristic of Japanese outbound travel is the reliance on
package tours. Package tours were used by 77.8 per cent of pleasure travellers. 'The greatest number of those utilizing package tours (1.256 million), were women in their twenties. In total, 73.7 per cent of all men and
81.6 per cent of all women used package tours' (Japan Travel Bureau 1991:
9). Package tours have been a popular mode of overseas travel for Japanese
travellers for a number of reasons: time restraints, safety, degree of integration of Japanese travel companies (90 per cent of overseas travellers used a
travel agency), mechanism for overcoming language and cultural difficulties, and a gentle introduction to overseas travel. However, the increasing
number of repeat travellers, the growth of Japanese who can speak English, and the desire for more 'independent' travel among the young traveller means that the proportion of Japanese using package tours is decreas-
ing with 'more demand for individual travel and greater use of small sub-
agents who provide only air tickets or skeleton packages' (*Asia Travel Trade*
1990c: 45). As the Japan Travel Bureau (1991: 65) commented: 'As the
repeater segment grows, and personal initiative and ambition to make
individual foreign travel plans become stronger, there will be more people
with the originality of mind to want to venture out on their own'.

Since 1985 there has been a substantial shift in the profile of Japanese
outbound travellers with large increases in those under twenty years of age,
children, and women in their thirties and forties (Ministry of Transport

Table 2.6: Number of Japanese visitors by destination, 1989–1990 ('000s)

Destination	1990	1989	% increase
USA (mainland)	1 605	1 005	33.2
Korea	1 460	1 380	5.8
Hawaii (USA)	1 440	1 319	9.2
Hong Kong	1 332	1 176	13.4
Singapore	972	841	15.6
Taiwan	914	962	4.9
France*	840	631	33.1
Germany*	762	661	15.3
Italy*	720	385	87.0
Malaysia	665	281	136.6
Thailand	636	520	22.3
Guam (USA)	635	556	14.2
UK*	499	381	31.0
Switzerland	498	472	5.5
Canada	474	463	2.4
China	460	359	28.1
Australia	432	350	23.4
Northern Marianas	330	249	32.5
Indonesia	263	190	38.4
Spain	244	217	12.4
Austria	236	192	22.9
The Philippines*	216	182	18.7
New Zealand	108	97	11.3

*Refers to 1989 and 1988 figures respectively

Source: Japan Travel Bureau 1991: 10

1986). In 1990 the largest percentage of travellers were women in their twenties (15.8 per cent of market) and men between the ages of twenty five and fifty-four (43.4 per cent). The Japan Travel Bureau (1991) has categorised the Japanese overseas travel market into fourteen market segments (Table 2.7). Europe was the main destination for students followed by the West Coast of the USA. A high proportion of male students also visited East Asian destinations. The main destination for female office workers and single, unemployed women was Hawaii, followed by Europe, East Asia, and South East Asia. Housewives visited short-haul destinations such as Hawaii, Guam, Saipan (Marianas), East Asia and South East Asia. Males favoured

Table 2.7: Japanese outbound travel market segments

Segment	%
Children	0.3
Male students	0.9
Female students	2.0
Female office workers (18–29)	10.7
Female office workers (30–44)	3.5
Single, unemployed women (18–44)	1.5
Honeymooners	7.0
Working housewives (18–44)	4.9
Housewives (18–44)	2.8
Single men (18–44)	5.2
Married men (18–44)	16.3
Middle-aged group (45–59)	19.6
Elderly group (60+)	7.6
'Full Moon' travellers (couples, 45+)	10.7

Source: Japan Travel Bureau Foundation 1991 in Japan Travel Bureau 1991: 12

East Asia and South East Asia, while the elderly and the middle-aged visited East Asia. The honeymooners' main destinations were Hawaii, Oceania and Europe. The 'full moon' couples primarily visited Europe, East Asia, Southeast Asia and Hawaii. In the period 1985 to 1990 Malaysia and Australia have had the largest growths in market share, with Australia, Hawaii, Canada, Switzerland and China being the preferred destinations in terms of future travel across the various market segments.

The growth in outbound travel over the past decade has been extremely rapid, and given the continued strength of the yen and the development of the single female market, this growth would seem set to continue. However, perhaps the most critical point in terms of future growth is not the money to travel, but as we shall discuss below, the time to travel and the availability and receptiveness of destinations to Japanese tourists.

Japanese overseas tourism investment and development assistance

Japan is a major overseas investor, with tourism becoming an increasingly important component of the overseas investment mix in recent years. Indeed, Wevers (1988: 1) has argued that the substantial trade surplus which Japan has had in recent years has led to major off-shore investment which 'will alter global patterns of output and ownership' (Wevers 1988: 1).

To a great extent, this is already true. Japanese capital is the third wave of foreign investment in the Asia–Pacific region after that of the UK and the USA (Edgington 1990). Japan is the dominant investor in much of South East Asia and has much influence in the region through its foreign investment programmes and associated aid packages, replacing much of the previous United States post-war economic dominance. However, whereas Japanese companies used to regard ASEAN and the newly industrialised countries of South Korea, Taiwan, Hong Kong and Singapore 'as off-shore production bases, they now see them as important markets' (Rowley 1992a: 53).

Since 1985 Japanese overseas investment has shifted markedly to encompass more service industries such as tourism. Japanese companies are now investing in tourism development projects, not only to take advantage of the enormous growth in Japanese outbound travel but also to capitalise on the broader increase in intra-Asian tourism.

The investment strategy of Japanese transnational corporations in the Asia–Pacific region involves the vertical integration of travel and tourism related services in the generating region, in transit, and in the tourist destination (Dunning & McQueen 1982a, b). The aims of such a strategy appear fourfold and relate to penetrating new markets, increasing profits and providing appropriate returns on investments, controlling product quality, and using tourism related investments as a base from which to diversify into non-tourism areas in the host country. Foreign investment by transnational corporations often gives rise to fears of foreign domination and control. According to Leiper (1984: 26), 'The consequences for the destination country is that ownership and control of local resources passes into foreign hands, and much of the expenditure by visiting tourists does not remain in that country, but passes back to the traveller generating country'. However, Japanese transnationals have shown a preference for joint venture operations rather than the wholly owned subsidiaries which characterise many Western transnationals (Edgington 1990). Therefore, much Japanese investment should be characterised as strategic rather than controlling investment.

As noted above, Japanese investment in the tourism sector of several of the countries of the region has gone hand-in-hand with the growth of Japanese outbound travel. For example, in the early 1970s about one-third of Japanese investment in the Philippines went into the finance and service-oriented segments of the Philippine economy with the 'acquisition of hotels for the accommodation of Japanese tourists' (Schollhammer 1978: 146). Unfortunately, much of the early growth in travel was associated with sex tourism and this has served to cast a shadow over the benefits of much of the investment of the 1970s (Hall 1992a). Furthermore, the differences between Japanese private investment and public aid also remains blurred, leading to often substantial mistrust as to the rationale of Japanese development assistance to countries in the Asia–Pacific region.

The political economy of golf

Substantial amounts of private Japanese investment has gone into the development of golf courses and associated tourist infrastructure in South East Asia, the South Pacific, Australia and New Zealand. Kuji (1991) has described the issues which arise out of the relationship between Japan and the countries in which golf courses are constructed, as the 'political economy of golf'. Development of Japanese golf-related tourism developments throughout the Pacific Rim has occurred for a number of reasons. First, the popularity of the game in Japan and its growth as a leisure activity and status symbol has created demand for golfing holidays. Second, the expense of developing Japanese golf courses means that with their far lower land and construction costs, clubs in South East Asia and the Pacific will have substantially lower membership fees than in Japan (Inoue 1991; Ling 1991). 'As a consequence, even with air fares and accommodation costs, it may still be cheaper to play golf in Malaysia or the Philippines than an élite club in Japan' (Mackie 1992: 79). Third, the development of golf courses in Japan is often opposed on environmental grounds, primarily because of pesticide and fertiliser use and negative impacts on fauna and flora. Therefore, golf course development in developing countries may be a mechanism to bypass environmental considerations (AMPO 1991; McCormack 1991).

Aid

Japan is a major overseas aid donor and is the greatest donor of economic aid in Asia. In the absence of an ability to establish an independent defence security, aid becomes a mechanism to establish economic security. In 1988 Japan's net disbursement of overseas development assistance totalled US$9134 million and ranked as the OECD's Development Assistance Committee's second largest donor after the USA (Rix 1990). Japan's overseas aid programme is an integral component of its foreign policy measures and has been used to help build up goodwill in the Asia–Pacific region. The focus of the Japanese aid programmes has been on the ASEAN nations, particularly Indonesia, Thailand and the Philippines, while China has been a major recipient of assistance since 1980.

Japan uses the term 'economic co-operation' to describe its aid policy. As Rix (1990: 4–5) commented: 'Japan's aid has always been based on the premise of "cooperation" between donor and recipient; a two-way process of interaction, not a one-way gift without return or recognition.' Therefore, aid is regarded as a key element in the development of strengthening Japan's economic and political influence in the Asia–Pacific region (Orr 1990; Rix 1990).

Japan's aid programme consists of a mixture of multilateral assistance through such organisations as the World Bank and the International Development Agency, loans, bilateral grants, and technical assistance. In Asia, bilateral aid has been used by the Japanese to develop resource reserves, establish infrastructure, and encourage the development of export oriented industries. Tourism has been regarded as an industry suitable for aid assistance and the Japanese, through such bodies as the Japanese International Cooperation Agency, have been active in engaging in tourism development projects. For example, as part of the Japanese Government's international finance co-operation programme, Japan and the ASEAN countries established the ASEAN Promotion Centre on Trade, Investment and Tourism in 1981 for the purpose of promoting exports from the ASEAN countries to Japan, accelerating the flow of investment from Japan to ASEAN nations, and increasing traffic from Japan to ASEAN (Ministry of Transport 1986). Indeed, *Asia Travel Trade* (1990a: 33) has suggested that in order to continue fostering outbound travel from Japan, and hence contribute to more balanced trade, 'Japan may need to bankroll tourism development in other nations'. Kimitaka Fujino, director of the development division in the tourism department of the Ministry of Transport, comments: 'Japan [government] has to assist foreign countries, not only financially but with planning, research, feasibility studies, and information on financing [large-scale tourism related projects]' (cited in *Asia Travel Trade* 1990a: 33).

Japan has been a major contributor to tourism-related development assistance projects in ASEAN countries. For example, in 1990 Japan's Overseas Economic Cooperation Fund (OECF) granted the Tourism Authority of Thailand a loan worth 3000 million baht (US$120 million) to help Thailand promote and develop tourism during the period of Thailand's seventh National Economic and Social Development Plan (1992–1996). The loan was the second from the OECF, which had previously granted the TAT a loan for tourism projects between 1989 and 1991. The first loan financed 61 projects at a cost of approximately 1265 million baht (US$50.6 million) and included construction of roads and water supply systems as well as assistance for marketing and promotion. The loans carry a 3 per cent annual interest rate and have a thirty year repayment period with no payment required in the first ten years (Corben 1990f).

However, while national governments have been keen to secure Japanese aid and investment, substantial disquiet has appeared at the community level and from members of the intelligentsia over the level of Japanese control over development projects. As Murakami (1976: 243) has commented, 'it is impossible to discuss the experience of Japan as a large source of investment without paying due consideration to... anti-Japanese sentiment in small host countries'. Undoubtedly, much of the opposition to Japanese investment stems from the international division of labour, whereby the capital and knowledge aspects of tourism are controlled in the tourist generating country, with the host country providing the labour (Britton 1982b). Nevertheless, Japan is often singled out for attention because of the memories of the Second World War and concerns that Japan is trying to establish its economic dominance over the region (for example, Hong 1985). Japan is extremely sensitive to trade and general economic issues in the Pacific region; indeed, Japan's tourism policy has been greatly influenced by concerns over trade balances and appropriate investment strategies. Nevertheless, the legacy of the Second World War and subsequent fears of Japanese intentions in the region will probably take another generation to diminish to an extent where they do not influence trade relations.

The future of Japanese tourism

There has been no improvement in the ratio of the number of days leave granted by companies and the number of days actually taken as holiday by the worker over the years. Thus the current situation is that only 50% of all workers take their leave entitlement (JapanTravel Bureau 1991: 64).

Although the Japanese economy will continue to remain strong by world standards for the remainder of the century, the key issue in terms of continued outbound tourism growth will be the availability of leisure time rather than the level of disposable income. In addition, infrastructure and policy issues will also have a bearing on the future of Japanese tourism.

Surveys of quality of life indicators have indicated that since 1983, leisure and free time has been the highest priority of Japanese people (Prime Minister's Office cited in Japan Travel Bureau 1991). However, while leisure has been the most important factor in the quality of life, the average total actual working hours (statutory hours plus overtime) in a year had dropped by only 56 hours between 1980 and 1990. Indeed, according to the Japan Travel Bureau (1991: 63), 'The five-day week with Saturday and Sunday off has been adopted in its complete form by only 9.6% of all companies, and for only 36.9% of the nation's working population' and went on to observe, 'The complete introduction of the five-day work week and the practice of workers using their full paid-leave entitlement will be a key factor for future increases in overseas travel by the Japanese' (Japan Travel Bureau 1991: 64). 'Despite the low number of holidays taken by the Japanese, leisure already is a multi-trillion yen business equal to more than 16 per cent of nominal gross national product. By the year 2000, it will probably equal 30 per cent of Japan's GNP' (*Asia Travel Trade* 1990b: 42).

In order to meet the aspirations of the Japanese people and to continue to lower the trade surplus, the twelfth five-year plan of the official Economic Planning Agency published in mid-1992 has aims which include: fewer hours at work, greater spending on public infrastructure and social services, housing improvements, and a better environment (Rowley 1992b). The desire for greater leisure time, combined with a forecast 3.5 per cent annual real economic growth through to 1997, will mean continued expansion of the outbound travel market. Instead, 'concerns about the impact of Japan's economic condition center almost exclusively on business travel' (Stuart 1992: 30). Before the 1991–1992 recession, the Ministry of Transport (MOT) predicted a 3 per cent to 4 per cent annual growth in Japanese outbound travel through to the year 2000 resulting in 20 to 25 million annual departures. More recently, Japan's *Travel Journal* survey of industry predicted 15.15 million outbound in 1996 and 19.82 million by 2001. For 1992 the Japan Travel Bureau predicted 12 million overseas travellers (Stuart 1992).

The Japanese Tourist Bureau Foundation has forecast that by the year 2001, 22 to 24 million Japanese might be travelling overseas with an equivalent value of ¥11 500 billion. Table 2.8 indicates the forecast growth on a regional basis with over 30 million Japanese estimated to be travelling overseas by 2001. Given the construction of suitable infrastructure in both Japan and at the various destinations, growth will occur in all markets with the most substantial occurring in Oceania and the South Pacific and in Australia in particular (Japan Travel Bureau 1991).

Although the yen remains strong in relative terms, the slightly weaker yen of 1991–1992 has encouraged the growth of inbound travel, especially from Korea and Taiwan. The continued economic development of East Asia and the growth of intra-Asian tourism will also substantially contribute to the number of inbound visitors. Nevertheless, given that other economic and political factors remain constant, it would appear likely that the Japanese Government will continue to see inbound travel primarily in diplomatic and cultural terms rather than as a source of foreign exchange or an economic development mechanism. However, both inbound and outbound growth will be stymied unless potential infrastructural problems, particularly airport development and the country's transport network, can be remedied. Despite such problems, the future of Japanese outbound tourism looks extremely bright. The strength of the economy, the pattern of Japanese development assistance and investment, and the desire of the Japanese to travel overseas will mean that Japan will continue as the

Table 2.8: Forecast Japanese overseas travel, 2001 ('000)

Region	2001	1990	% increase
Europe	5 000	3 000	67
Africa	400	140	186
South East Asia	14 000	7 000	100
Oceania	2 000	610	228
South Pacific Islands	2 000	1 000	100
South America	250	130	92
Hawaii	2 500	1 440	74
North America	4 000	2 000	100
Total*	30 150	15 320	97

*Total number of travellers on a regional basis exceeds the actual number.

Source: Japan Travel Bureau Foundation in Japan Travel Bureau 1991: 67

Asia–Pacific region's major source of tourists and as a dominant force in tourism development throughout the Pacific Rim. Although the relationship of host regions to Japan has not been without its negative effects, it would appear that Japanese investment patterns and tourist flows are assisting regional integration rather than providing for regional domination. Japan serves as the economic model for many of the countries of East Asia. Indeed, the pattern of Japanese tourism also appears to be followed by other Asian countries such as Korea and Taiwan (see Chapter 4). Therefore, an understanding of Japanese tourism patterns and Japan's economic and political role in the Pacific Rim is critical to identifying the trends, patterns and issues surrounding tourism in the Pacific and Japan's relationship with the countries of the Asia–Pacific region.

Suggestions for further reading

The growth of the Japanese economy and the development of tourist trade with various nations in the Pacific region are concisely discussed in Wevers (1988) *Japan, its Future, and New Zealand*; Bollard (*et al.*) (1989) *Meeting the East Asia Challenge: Trends, Prospects and Policies*, and Garnaut (1990) *Australia and the Northeast Asian Ascendency*. The economic behaviour of Japanese transnationals and Japanese investment strategies receives an excellent analysis in Edgington (1990) *Japanese Business Down Under: Patterns of Japanese Investment in Australia.*

Detailed accounts of the Japanese tourism industry are to be found in the Economist Intelligence Unit (1990b) 'The travel and tourism industry in Japan', *EIU Travel and Tourism Analyst*, and Ministry of Transport, Japan National Tourist Organization (1991) *Tourism in Japan 1991*. The annual report of the Japan Travel Bureau (1991) *JTB Report '91: All About Japanese Overseas Travellers*, provides a wealth of information on the growth of Japanese outbound travel, market segments, expenditure patterns, preferred destinations, and future growth predictions. The interrelationship of the Japanese tourism industry with the Pacific Rim, and with East Asia in particular, is comprehensively discussed in a special 1991 edition of AMPO, *Japan–Asia Quarterly Review: Special Issue on Resort Development* and in Mackie (1992) 'Japan and South East Asia: the international division of labour and leisure', in *Tourism and the Less Developed Countries*.

Discussion and review

Key concepts

'Ten Million Programme', trade surplus, travel-related expenditure, 1987 Law for Development of Comprehensive Resort Areas, 'Tourism Action in the 90s', 'Two-way Tourism 21', package tours, independent travel, outbound travel market segments, Japanese overseas tourism investment and development assistance, political economy of golf, 'economic co-operation', quality of life indicators, available leisure time, level of disposable income.

Questions for review and discussion

1 How correct is it to say that Japan is the superpower of the Pacific?
2 What was the 'Ten Million Programme' and what was its significance for Japanese trade and tourism?
3 How significant is domestic travel for the Japanese tourism industry?
4 What are the different goals of the Japan National Tourist Organization (JNTO) in relation to inbound and outbound travel?
5 How has the value of the yen influenced outbound tourism growth?
6 What are the characteristics of Japanese investment strategies in the Pacific region?
7 Why are the aims of the twelfth five-year plan of the Economic Planning Agency significant for tourism growth in the Pacific?

3 The newly industrialised economies of North East Asia: Korea, Taiwan and Hong Kong

> Growth has proceeded faster for longer in Northeast Asia over the past four decades than had previously been known in human history (Garnaut 1990: 8).

The emergence of the NIEs

The Newly Industrialised Economies (NIEs) of North East Asia (see Figure 3.1) have been the focus of a massive shift in the centre of gravity of world production. Although world attention has primarily been on the Japanese 'economic miracle', other Asian economies, particularly those of Korea, Taiwan, Hong Kong, and China, are increasingly asserting themselves in the global market-place. Measured in terms of current national accounts data and exchange rates, the share of Japan, the People's Republic of China, the Republic of Korea, Taiwan and Hong Kong in world production had risen from 8 per cent in 1960 to 20 per cent in 1987 (Garnaut 1990).

The economic development of the region has led to dramatic improvements in per capita disposable income and to marked changes in spending patterns. For example, the per capita income of Taiwan rose from US$144 in 1960 to US$5862 in 1988, of Hong Kong from US$348 to US$9597 and of the Republic of Korea from US$156 to US$4081 (Garnaut 1990).

Rapid economic growth has had substantial implications for tourism. The improvement of transport services and associated infrastructure as part of the countries' industrialisation programmes, increased interest in the outside world, lessening in restrictions on overseas travel, increased disposable income, and greater leisure time has meant that North East Asia is emerging not only as the fastest growing tourist generating region in the Pacific Rim, but in the world.

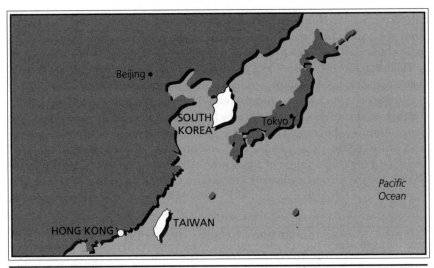

Figure 3.1: North East Asia

This chapter examines tourism in Korea, Taiwan and Hong Kong in terms of inbound and outbound market growth and the difficulties experienced in tourism development. The People's Republic of China will be examined in Chapter 5. The three countries discussed in this chapter share commonalities in terms of their geographical location and their rapid economic growth. There are also substantial differences in terms of the role of government in tourism, development strategies, restrictions on nationals travelling overseas, and significance attached to tourism as a source of foreign exchange. However, all three countries are paying increased attention to the value of inbound tourism, although, as we shall see, with varying degrees of success.

Korea

Last summer's Olympic Games in Seoul meant more to Korea than merely basking in the prestige of hosting the world's premier sporting event. The massive media coverage accorded the Games also provided the Hermit Kingdom with a marvellous opportunity to rejoin the mainstream of international society.

The world, until then familiar only with the television image of student riots, ruthless political infighting and stone-faced security forces, was to see a different Korea on its television screens and its newspapers. It saw, for the first time, that Seoul had become an international city (Asia Travel Trade 1989c: 15).

The Republic of Korea, otherwise known as South Korea, has become both a major tourist-generating region and a destination in the north east Pacific in the last decade. 'The Hermit Kingdom' has broken into the international travel industry on the basis of its significant number of attractions for inbound tourists and the increased interests and opportunities for its nationals to travel overseas.

In much the same way as Japan arrived on the international tourist scene with the 1964 Olympics in Tokyo, for many people around the globe the arrival of South Korea into the world tourist market was marked by the hosting of the 1988 Olympic Games in Seoul. South Korea used the 1988 Seoul Summer Olympic Games to indicate its new found economic position in the world (Jeong 1988) and, in conjunction with the Asian Games of 1986 to develop a range of tourist infrastructure that would lay the foundation for the nation's tourism industry in the 1990s (Chon & Shin 1990; Economist Intelligence Unit 1990c). The Olympics were perceived as a

Table 3.1: Korean tourist trade balance, 1970–1991 (US$000's)

Year	Tourist Receipts	Travel Expenditure	Balance
1970	46 772	12 424	34 348
1971	52 383	14 808	37 575
1972	83 011	12 570	70 441
1973	269 434	16 984	252 450
1974	158 571	27 618	130 953
1975	140 627	30 709	109 918
1976	275 011	46 234	228 777
1977	370 030	102 714	267 316
1978	408 106	208 019	200 087
1979	326 006	405 284	-79 278
1980	369 265	349 557	19 708
1981	447 640	439 029	8 611
1982	502 318	632 177	-129 859
1983	596 245	555 401	40 844
1984	673 355	576 250	97 105
1985	784 312	605 973	178 339
1986	1 547 502	612 969	934 533
1987	2 299 156	704 201	1 594 955
1988	3 265 232	1 353 891	1 911 341
1989	3 556 279	2 601 532	954 747
1990	3 558 666	3 165 623	393 043
1991	3 426 416	3 784 304	-357 888

Source: The Bank of Korea in Ministry of Transportation 1992: 85

means to overcome the poor image of Korea in the international tourism market, particularly the USA, because of such factors as *M.A.S.H.* (the highly popular television series based on the fictionalised exploits of a USA field hospital during the Korean War), the devastation of the Korean War, the shooting down of Korean Airlines Flight 007 in the early 1980s, student riots, and the ongoing political instability between North and South Korea (Hall 1992b).

Undoubtedly, the Korean War has had a dramatic impact on inbound travel into the nation and has been a factor in the slow development of the country as a destination. The country received only 6700 foreign travellers in 1958, 680 000 in 1973, and 976 400 in 1980. In the Olympic year of 1988, Korea had a 24.9 per cent increase over the previous year and received 2 340 500 visitors, only to increase the following year by a further 16.6 per cent to record 2 728 100 visitor arrivals (Chon & Shin 1990; Economist Intelligence Unit 1990c).

In contrast to South Korea, the North had only 25 000 foreign visitors in both 1988 and 1989. Visitors to the North have to be guided, 'locals are fearful of foreigners, tours are cancelled, schedules are changed for no reason whatsoever and hotel rooms are bugged' (*Asia Travel Trade* 1990h: 50). Nevertheless, North Korea is starting to promote itself overseas in the hope of attracting foreign tourists and their exchange, with the possibility of joint tourism projects being undertaken between North Korea and South Korea. However, according to Breen (1991a: 62): 'Although the two Koreas are currently engaged in prime ministerial talks on reconciliation, they remain implacably hostile, with little chance of any joint tourism projects coming off in the short term'.

Although North Korea still retains strict control over the domestic and international travel of its residents, the South progressively lifted its restrictions during the 1980s. South Korea had two main reasons for imposing travel restrictions. First, for security during a period of superpower tension and continuing poor North–South Korean relations. Second, in order to retain foreign exchange for its economic development. Until 1983 Korean citizens were not allowed to travel overseas unless for business, employment, study or some other activity that was deemed to benefit the national interest. In 1983 overseas leisure travel was permitted for those aged fifty and older but only for spouses travelling together. Furthermore, people over the age of fifty could only holiday overseas if they deposited two million won (currency) with the Korea foreign exchange bank for one year. The effect of these restrictions is evidenced in that only 500 000 South Koreans travelled overseas annually between 1981 and 1987. In September 1987 the deposit was waived, and the age limit dropped from fifty to forty in January 1988. In April 1988 the Foreign Minister announced that the age restriction on overseas travel would be removed as of 1 January 1989, and as an intermediate step the age limit was lowered from forty to thirty as of 1 July 1988. According to the Assistant Foreign Minister, Hong Soon-Young, 'The liberalisation of overseas travel is designed to meet the growing trend of internationalisation of people's lifestyles, at the same time a new government is inaugurated' (cited in Crean 1988: 30). With the lifting of travel restrictions for certain groups in 1988, the number of outbound Korean travellers grew to 725 000. In 1989, the first full year without restrictions 1.2 million South Koreans travelled overseas. The figure is expected to rise further as the Korean economy continues to grow, with a prediction of 3.6 million travellers in 1996 and 5.4 million by the year 2000 (Hamdi 1991).

Tourism has played a significant role in the Korean Government's search for foreign exchange with which to fund economic development. Between 1981 and 1990 receipts from tourism grew from US$448 million to US$3559 million and have contributed significantly to Korea's balance of payments (Table 3.1). For example, there was a positive tourism trade balance of US$393 million in 1990, although it should be noted that this was considerably lower than the peak of US$1911 million in 1988, the year of the Seoul Olympics (McGahey 1991: 47). However, the explosion in overseas travel by Koreans following the ending of travel restrictions has impacted on the balance of tourism receipts, with the nation recording its first deficit in tourist trade of US$380 million in 1991.

The tourist trade deficit has brought warnings against 'excessive consumption' by government officials, while the government's austerity campaign 'includes provisions to punish travel agencies which the government concludes "abet or induce overseas travellers to indulge in excessive spending"' (Do-sun 1992a: 57). Nevertheless, while the government will undoubtedly use a range of measures to keep outbound travel within reasonable limits, it will be impossible for them to reimpose travel restrictions while the economy and the ensuing consumer expectations continues to grow.

The outbound market

As noted above, the removal of travel restrictions has had a profound effect on Korean outbound travel (Table 3.2). In 1987, 510 538 Koreans travelled overseas. The year 1989 saw a 67.3 per cent jump in outbound travellers from 725 200 to 1 213 100, while 1 560 900 travelled overseas in 1990 (Ministry of Justice in McGahey 1991: 46). In 1991 the growth rate remained high with 1 856 018 Koreans travelling overseas, an increase of 18.9 per cent. For the first ten months of 1992 outbound travel had increased by 10.6 per cent over the corresponding period in 1991 (Korea National Tourism Corporation 1992). In 1991 pleasure trips accounted for 35.1 per cent of all Korean outbound travel, followed by business trips (26.3 per cent), visiting friends and relatives (17.2 per cent) and training (5.1 per cent) (Ministry of Transportation 1992).

Preferred destinations are close, inexpensive and culturally similar (Table 3.3). Japan was the destination for 49.9 per cent of all outbound travel in 1989, with the USA attracting 15.2 per cent. In 1991, 79.9 per cent of outbound tourists travelled to Asia (the majority to Japan, Taiwan, Hong Kong and Thailand), 16.8 per cent to the Americas (mainly the USA) and

6.1 per cent to Europe (Ministry of Transportation 1992). Because of its geographic proximity and because many Koreans speak Japanese it is apparent that Japan will continue to be the primary Korean outward bound destination. However, Yarmy (1992: 90) predicts that 'the United States will soon begin taking market share at Japan's expense as more younger and prosperous Koreans get bitten by the travel bug'. The ASEAN market is also becoming increasingly significant, particularly Thailand and Indonesia, and interest in Pacific destinations, such as Australia, New Zealand and Tahiti, is also growing (Yoo 1989).

Safety is an important factor for Korean travellers. Outbound travel to the Philippines and Thailand dropped even before the Gulf crisis due to the kidnapping of a Korean tourist in the Philippines and the deaths of four Koreans in a boating accident in Thailand (Breen 1991a). In addition, the purchasing patterns of Koreans are changing as they become more used to the idea of overseas travel. Koreans are increasingly opting for shorter, more frequent, holidays. However, in absolute terms, long-haul markets such as North America and Europe will continue to grow. The Korean per capita GNP has now passed US$5000 thereby giving a greater percentage of the population disposable income with which to travel overseas. By 1995 it is expected that more than three million Koreans will travel overseas (Yarmy 1992).

Unlike the Japanese, the Korean Government 'has no targets for out-

Table 3.2: Departures of Koreans, 1982–1991

Year	Number (000's)	Year	Number (000's)
1982	500	1987	511
1983	493	1988	725
1984	493	1989	1 213
1985	484	1990	1 561
1986	455	1991	1 856

Source: Ministry of Transportation 1992: 61

Table 3.3: Departures of Koreans by region, 1990–1991

Region	1990	1991	% Growth
Americas	254 339	312 346	22.8
Europe	94 661	113 180	19.6
Africa	11 913	8 369	30.7
Asia	1 177 191	1 389 200	18.0
Oceania	22 820	32 923	44.3
Total	**1 560 923**	**1 856 018**	**18.9**

Source: Ministry of Transportation 1992: 63

bound travellers, except to generally try and discourage them from taking too many trips overseas' (*Asia Travel Trade* 1990h: 50). Due to the disparity between the amount that visitors were spending in Korea and the amount that Koreans were spending overseas (US$1203 to US$42 028 in 1990), the Korean Government has attempted to encourage Koreans to be more frugal in their overseas spending in the interests of national solidarity by not high-lighting the gap between rich and poor (Breen 1990). According to the Bank of Korea, Korea earned US$3.426 million in tourism receipts in 1991, a fall of 3.7 per cent from the 1990 figure of US$3.559 million (see Table 3.1). The average per capita expenditure of visitors was US$1203, a decrease of US$131 from 1990. The total expenditure of Koreans travelling abroad in 1991 was US$3.784 million, an increase of 19.5 per cent over 1990. The average capital expenditure of Korean outbound travellers was US$2039, an increase of US$11 from 1990 (Ministry of Transportation 1992).

Given the predicted increase of 30 per cent to 40 per cent in Korean outbound travel, the Korean Government has introduced credit card checks on those who travel overseas as a way of discouraging 'unpatriotic' behaviour (Do-sun 1992b). Rather than engaging in overseas travel as a form of conspicuous consumption, the Korean Government would prefer to avoid losing foreign exchange and is encouraging Koreans to take their holidays at domestic resorts. According to Sho Jaepil, publisher of the Korean monthly Travel Press, 'The austerity campaign was really a question of government suggestion rather than actual regulations. Now that travel has been liberalized there is no way it can be reversed' (cited in Breen 1991a: 57).

However, the growth in outbound travel in Korea is not all negative in terms of contribution to the Korean economy. The explosion in outbound travel has meant the rapid growth of travel agencies from 200 domestic agents in 1987 to 750 in 1990. Furthermore, approximately half of all out-bound passengers travel on the national airline KAL, with significant growth also expected on the second national carrier Asiana. The propor-tion of Koreans who travel on Korean airlines would seem unlikely to fall significantly over the next few years as Koreans are quite patriotic in their transport choices and will travel Korean wherever possible.

The rationale for much of the government's negativity towards outbound travel is the loss of 'foreign exchange earnings'. However, tourism earns the country more than its much higher profile automobile industry (McGahey 1991). Therefore, the real issue at the heart of the balance of the tourism trade question, may well be lack of government support and recognition for the tourism industry (Breen 1991b), particularly given the substantial growth that has occurred in the inbound market over the past decade.

The inbound market

Visitor arrivals to Korea have had an average annual increase of 11.5 per cent for the past decade (Table 3.4). In 1990 Korea had 2.96 million visi-tors and revenues of US$3.5 billion. In 1991 the target was 3.2 million visitors and associated tourist earnings of US$3.7 billion. However, while this figure was not reached, the 2 882 886 foreign visitors in 1991 represented an increase of 9.4 per cent on the 1990 figure. In 1991 the number of Korean residents overseas totalled 313 454, a decrease of 3.0 per cent. As in other areas of Asia the importance of group travel is declining, although the group travel market remains significant and accounts for 33.3 per cent of all arrivals in 1991 (1 063 676 visitors)—a drop in market share of 5.7 per cent. The primary purpose of visiting in 1991 was pleasure, accounting for 58.1 per cent of all inbound trips, followed by business (11.2 per cent), visiting friends and relatives (10.8 per cent), official visits (0.7 per cent), and conventions (0.1 per cent). The 1991 figures were broadly comparable with those of the previous year (Ministry of Transportation 1992).

Inbound arrivals grew by 8 per cent in 1991. For the first ten months of 1992 visitor arrivals had increased by 3.9 per cent (Korea National Tourism Corporation 1992). Arrivals from Europe and Africa both registered a relatively high growth rate of 28.4 per cent in 1991. Asia enjoyed the next highest growth rate of 9.9 per cent, arrivals from Oceania grew by 2.1 per cent, while arrivals from the Americas decreased by 3.1 per cent. Japan is by far the largest inbound market (Table 3.5). In 1991 visitors from Japan accounted for 1 445 090 arrivals (45.5 per cent of total arrivals) a decrease of 0.4 per cent in the number of Japanese visitors from the previous year. The USA generated 315 828 arrivals (9.9 per cent of total arrivals) representing a decrease of 2.9 per cent of 1990 arrivals. However, the growth of the Asian economies was reflected in the growth of Taiwanese visitors to 281 349 an increase of 33.3 per cent, while Thai visitors grew by 30.4 per

Table 3.4: Visitor arrivals to Korea, 1969–1991

Year	Visitors (000's)	Growth Rate (%)	Year	Visitors (000's)	Growth Rate (%)
1969	126.7	23.3	1981	1 093.2	12.0
1970	173.3	36.8	1982	1 145.0	4.7
1971	232.8	34.3	1983	1 194.5	4.3
1972	370.7	59.2	1984	1 297.3	8.6
1973	679.2	83.2	1985	1 426.0	9.9
1974	517.6	-23.8	1986	1 660.0	16.4
1975	632.8	22.3	1987	1 871.5	12.9
1976	834.2	31.8	1988	2 340.5	24.9
1977	949.7	13.8	1989	2 728.1	16.6
1978	1 079.4	13.7	1990	2 958.8	8.5
1979	1 126.1	4.3	1991	3 196.3	8.0
1980	976.4	-13.3			

Source: Ministry of Transportation 1992: 27

Table 3.5: Visitor arrivals to Korea by major markets, 1982–1991 (000's)

Nationality	1982 Visitors	%	1984 Visitors	%	1986 Visitors	%	1988 Visitors	%	1990 Visitors	%	1991 Visitors	%
Japan	518.0	45.2	576.4	44.4	791.0	47.7	1 124.1	48.0	1 460.3	49.4	1 455.1	45.5
Taiwan	91.3	8.0	93.5	7.2	94.8	5.7	124.2	5.3	211.1	7.1	281.3	8.8
Hong Kong	51.0	4.4	46.6	3.6	55.3	3.3	62.3	2.7	70.6	2.4	72.7	2.3
Thailand	8.0	0.7	10.1	0.8	11.3	0.7	13.8	0.6	29.4	1.0	38.3	1.2
Malaysia	19.8	1.7	25.6	2.0	16.7	1.0	15.9	0.7	24.8	0.8	23.1	0.7
The Philippines	13.7	1.2	8.0	0.6	14.8	0.9	51.1	2.2	86.6	2.9	143.9	4.5
Indonesia	7.0	0.6	9.3	0.7	10.0	0.6	9.9	0.4	21.0	0.7	23.6	0.7
Singapore	8.4	0.7	12.7	1.0	11.0	0.7	18.0	0.8	26.3	0.9	30.2	0.9
USA	151.2	13.2	213.0	16.4	284.6	17.1	347.3	14.8	325.4	11.0	315.8	9.9
Canada	10.4	0.9	13.2	1.0	19.9	1.2	24.5	1.0	25.4	0.9	23.7	0.7
UK	16.1	1.4	19.2	1.5	20.9	1.3	33.3	1.4	36.1	1.2	35.8	1.1
Germany	14.0	1.2	16.8	1.3	20.9	1.3	30.6	1.3	31.3	1.1	35.3	1.1
France	8.2	0.7	9.2	0.7	12.2	0.7	18.1	0.8	18.2	0.6	19.0	0.6
Switzerland	3.5	0.3	4.2	0.3	5.3	0.3	6.9	0.3	6.3	0.2	6.8	0.2
Netherlands	3.9	0.3	4.3	0.3	6.8	0.4	9.9	0.4	10.2	0.3	11.3	0.4
Australia	6.6	0.6	9.6	0.7	9.5	0.6	14.4	0.6	15.6	0.5	16.1	0.5
Sub-Total	931.3	81.3	1 071.9	82.6	1 387.5	83.6	1 904.3	81.4	2 398.4	81.1	2 531.5	79.2
Others	39.1	3.4	52.2	4.0	70.2	4.2	147.5	6.3	237.2	8.0	351.4	11.0
Total	970.4	84.7	1 124.1	86.6	1 457.7	87.8	2 051.8	87.7	2 635.6	89.1	2 882.9	90.2
Overseas Koreans	174.6	15.3	173.2	13.4	202.3	12.2	288.7	12.3	323.2	10.9	313.5	9.8
Grand Total	1 145.0	100.0	1 297.3	100.0	1 660.0	100.0	2 340.5	100.0	2 958.8	100.0	3 196.3	100.0

Source: Ministry of Transportation 1992: 50–1

cent to 38 289 and the Philippines to 143 932—increase of 66.2 per cent (Ministry of Transportation 1992).

The majority of visitors to Korea, approximately 95 per cent, arrive by air, with the remaining 4.5 per cent arriving by sea (Ministry of Justice in Economist Intelligence Unit 1990c). Despite the land border, there are no transport links between North and South Korea because of the continuing tensions between the two countries. However, sea arrivals will start to increase as a number of jetfoil and car ferry routes open up between Korea, and Japan and China. Although heavily dependent on air travel, South Korea suffered less from the impacts of the Gulf crisis at the end of 1990 and beginning of 1991 than many other Asian destinations because of its lower reliance on North American and European markets.

In 1991 and 1992 the main regions for South Korea's marketing activities were South East Asia and Japan. These regions were selected in part by geographical proximity and a growing awareness of Korea's year-round tourist attractions in South East Asia. However, they were also selected because of the shifts in Asian travellers' focus from long-haul to short-haul intraregional destinations for safety reasons at the time of the Gulf crisis. For example, skiing and winter tours were being promoted in Taiwan, Singapore, Hong Kong and Thailand while the Australian and New Zealand travel markets were being targeted as direct air-routes became available for the first time (Breen 1991a).

The 1988 Seoul Summer Olympic Games were critical in developing tourist infrastructure, creating a positive image of Korea and attracting tourists to the country. In terms of the immediate period surrounding the Games, the Olympics may be judged a success, attracting 241 000 tourists and participants. The eighty-six hotels in Seoul reported 100 per cent occupancy during the three-week Games. However, some officials have still been disappointed that the Games did not lead to a more substantial increase in tourism (Breen 1991b). Nevertheless, as with the latter half of the 1980s, great emphasis has been placed on events to anchor inbound tourism in the 1990s. The Taejon Expo held from August to October 1993, is predicted to attract ten million people including one million from overseas (Do-sun 1992a). Following the success of similar programmes in the ASEAN region, 1994 has been designated as Visit Korea Year (VKY) and marketing programmes for the year have been focused on Japan, South East Asia, the USA and Western Europe. In addition, 1994 is also the 600th anniversary of Seoul. The Taejon Expo and VKY will serve as catalysts for the development of further tourism infrastructure, in much the same way as the Seoul Olympics. Furthermore, Korea is aspiring to host a Winter Olympics in order to raise the profile of its winter tourist season. Nevertheless, as the next section indicates, the attractiveness of Korea to inbound tourists is expanding as tourist development begins to encompass the country's natural attractions and cultural heritage.

Tourism development

Korea maintains a mixed public–private approach to tourism development. Three key bodies come under the supervision of the Minister of Transportation: the Bureau of Tourism which is concerned with setting and administering government policy on tourism; the Korea National Tourist Corporation (KNTC) which serves as the national promotion board; and the Korea Tourism Association which co-ordinates and represents the interests of the private sector (Chon & Shin 1990).

Overseas tourism promotion and publicity are the most vital aspect of the KNTC's mission particularly given the importance of positive imaging following the aftermath of the Korean War and KAL 007. The KNTC operates twenty-one offices in fifteen countries. However, the KNTC also undertakes a number of other significant functions including:

- domestic tourism promotion
- tourism development through the provision of tourist facilities, accommodation, national park and natural area planning, and the development of Korean War battlefield sites
- tourism research
- education and training.

The government has provided substantial financial assistance to the tourism and hospitality industry, particularly for hotel construction and repair and for general tourism infrastructure, through the provision of special government funds, accelerated depreciation allowances and tax incentives. However, recognition of the sector by government is not as great as that received by the country's manufacturing industries. Indeed, the introduction of anti-inflationary measures such as an increased entertainment tax or a hotel tax may impact hotel and tourism development (Chon & Shin 1990). Nevertheless, Korea would appear to be well placed to take advantage of the growth in Pacific Rim tourism.

Accommodation

The increased interest in Korea from foreign tourists and greater leisure time and disposable income for Koreans has been matched by a corresponding growth in accommodation (Table 3.6). In 1965 there were only 37 tourist hotels with 1338 rooms in the whole of Korea. However, given the need to boost foreign exchange earnings, the figure had grown to 129 hotels with 19 702 rooms by 1981. At the time of the Olympics 265 tourist hotels were available with a total of 33 189 rooms. The impact of the Olympics on infrastructure development was dramatic. The 1988 figure represented an increase of 35 per cent in room availability over 1986. By 1989 a further 52 hotels representing an 8 per cent increase in rooms had been developed (Korea National Tourism Corporation in Economist Intelligence Unit 1990c). In 1991, 424 hotels (42 489 rooms) were registered with the Korean Government (Ministry of Transportation 1992). While the tourist hotels are primarily targeted at overseas travellers, the increasing affluence of Koreans and their growing acceptance with Western-style hotel accommodation, has meant that domestic tourists make up a substantial proportion of visitors.

In addition to the tourist hotels, development of alternative accommodation such as youth hostels and camping grounds is increasing. Traditional Korean traveller's inns called *yogwan*, similar to the Japanese *ryokan*, are also available for international tourists. Although not having the facilities of the tourist hotels, the experience of sleeping on a small mattress (*Yo*) with a quilt (*Ibul*) and a buckwheat filled pillow, and on a heated floor (*Ondol*) in cold weather, is becoming popular for those wishing to experience more authentic Korean hospitality.

Attractions

Seoul, the capital of South Korea, with the main international airport and nearly half of all the tourist hotel rooms, is undoubtedly the main focal point for overseas visitor activities. Seoul is the gateway to South Korea but many foreign tourists do not venture far beyond its museums, shopping districts and sports complexes. Therefore, substantial attention is now being paid to develop other areas of the country for tourism in order to encourage regional development.

Despite Western perceptions of a cold and bleak landscape reinforced by Korean War footage and the *M.A.S.H.* television series, Korea has a wealth of natural attractions ranging from its fifteen spa resorts to twenty national parks and nineteen provincial parks, containing historical temples and hiking trails. The country also has a wealth of beaches. For

Table 3.6: Tourist hotels and rooms in Korea, 1981–1991

Year	Hotels*	Growth Rate (%)	Rooms*	Growth Rate (%)
1981	129	4.9	19 702	6.2
1982	144	11.6	21 459	8.9
1983	154	6.9	22 800	6.2
1984	157	1.9	23 013	0.9
1985	165	5.1	23 771	3.3
1986	184	11.5	25 321	6.5
1987	222	20.7	28 043	10.8
1988	276	24.3	33 869	20.8
1989	321	16.3	36 211	6.9
1990	395	23.1	40 386	11.5
1991	424	7.3	42 489	5.2

*Until 1988, figures included youth hostels

Source: Ministry of Transportation 1992: 97

example, Haeundae beach resort near Pusan in the south attracts as many as 500 000 people a day in the height of summer (Breen 1991b).

Heritage tourism is a substantial special interest market being developed by the Korean Government. For example, attractions in Kyongju, the ancient capital of the Shilla dynasty, such as the Bulguk Temple, the Chomsongdae Observatory and the ancient burial mounds are becoming substantial attractions for overseas visitors as well as domestic tourists who are interested in Korean culture. In addition, the historic theme park experience is also becoming available to tourists with the opening in 1993 of Shillachon, a folk village which will reconstruct Shilla culture and history (Breen 1991b).

A significant growth area in tourist development is that of skiing and winter tourist experiences for visitors from South East Asia. Korea had seven ski resorts as of 1991 with more planned. However, skiing has only really taken off in Korea in the last decade. The first ski resort was not developed until the mid-1970s. The ski resorts are promoted primarily to the Japanese and the South East Asian market (PATA Travel News 1991), they offer cheaper skiing than Japan or Europe, and would appear to have excellent potential for future growth, especially if Korea hosts a Winter Olympic Games. In addition to the expansion of ski resorts, two other tourist attraction developments are worthy of mention. First, the development of the island of Cheju. Second, sites associated with the Korean War.

The southern island of Cheju received over three million tourists in 1990 with 200 000 of those from overseas. The island, long promoted as a honeymooner's destination, is now expanding to become a year-round activity-based domestic and international tourist destination. Indeed, Chungmun, on the southern coast of the island, is the site of a US$700 million integrated resort development, which 'aims to be the centerpiece of a "fantasy island" which the brochures will plug as the new Hawaii and, significantly after the 1997 Chinese takeover of Hong Kong, as the new shoppers' and funseekers' paradise in Asia' (Breen 1991b: 51).

The Korean War proffers mixed blessings for the Korean tourism industry. Although it has established a range of negative images which Korea needs to change, particularly in Western nations such as the USA, Canada, Australia and New Zealand, it also provides an opportunity for tourism development. Interest in war sites (such as the UN cemetery in Pusan and the demilitarised zone along the border) is increasing, and these sites are among the country's top ranking tourist attractions. Furthermore, many veterans and their families are now expressing interest in returning to former battlefield sites. Given the reduction in superpower conflict, it would seem likely that the legacies of the Korean War could yet be turned into historical attractions for international tourists.

The future

The tourism industry can expect to reap substantial rewards from Korea's rapid economic development. Currently, 43 million South Koreans have an average per capita income of won 3.9 million ($US5500). By the end of the decade, this figure is expected to double. In the same period, spending on leisure activities is expected to quadruple to won 1.3 million a year. In expectation of the leisure boom, the Kumho group (owners of Asiana, South Korea's second airline after KAL) is investing in hotel and condominium developments, amusement parks, marinas and golf complexes (Clifford 1991). However, environmental concerns are now starting to be raised about the country's industrial development practices which may damage its image overseas. There has also been protest over the construction of golf courses and the use of too much pesticide and fertiliser.

The growth of both inbound and outbound tourism in Korea over the last decade has been extremely rapid. The end of restrictions has led to a thriving outbound tourism industry, while the attractiveness of Korea as a destination for overseas travellers will continue to grow. In terms of both inbound and outbound travellers, the Korean tourism industry is very much tied to Japan. Japan will continue to be both the major destination and the major tourist generating region, but as other markets develop, particularly in South East Asia and the Pacific, their proportion of market share will decrease.

Given continued economic growth the Korean tourism industry can expect to remain strong. Although, like other Asian and Pacific countries, long-term tourism growth will be dependent on political stability both within the country and within the region. Korea has the potential to become another gateway to China and to act as the transport hub of the region. Should China undergo further unrest, however, the repercussions will be dramatic. Internally, tourism has gone hand-in-hand with the process of democratisation. However, the greatest factor in determining the future of tourism in the country will be the relationship between North and South Korea. The continued antagonism towards the wealthier South by the North casts a shadow over political, social and economic stability of the country. Political instability is one of the great threats of the tourism industry. Therefore, the future development of tourism in South Korea may well be more dependent on politics than the country's growing economy or its wealth of attractions.

Taiwan

Taiwan, otherwise known as the Republic of China, is one of the fastest growing economies in the world. However, it presents something of a paradox. Taiwan has substantial economic strength (in 1991 it was the thirteenth largest trading nation in the world and twelfth in the world for exports) but it lacks international standing due to its estranged relationship with mainland China. Nevertheless, the current real growth rate of around 7 per cent, substantial balance of trade surplus, and investment throughout the Pacific Rim has meant that Taiwan is emerging from its political isolation of the last twenty years. In particular, countries such as Australia, Canada and the USA are ignoring diplomatic pressure from the People's Republic of China and are attempting to attract Taiwanese investment.

As this discussion will illustrate, Taiwan has not been a substantial player in Pacific Rim tourism until very recently. Taiwanese economic development strategies since 1949 have been focused on manufacturing rather than service industries such as tourism. As Wieman (1990: 40) reported 'the government has devoted most of its energy and attention to industry and trade and, while a great deal of lip service has been paid tourism as a vital means of developing people-to-people ties in the absence of formal diplomatic relations with most of the world's countries, the words were never followed by much action'. Therefore, inbound tourism has remained limited while outbound has been restricted due to security and military requirements. Nevertheless, the increased wealth and leisure time of the Taiwanese and a lessening of Cold War tensions resulting in a lifting of travel restrictions, has meant that Taiwan is an increasingly important market in Pacific Rim tourism.

The outbound market

The traditional objectives of international tourism policy, to earn foreign exchange, has diminished in importance due to the ROC's own massive accumulation of foreign exchange reserves. Emphasis has now shifted toward outbound tourism that promotes international understanding, improves the image of the ROC, and strengthens substantive international relations (Republic of China Tourist Bureau 1992a: 7).

As in the case of Korea, Taiwan has only recently reduced the restrictions on its nationals travelling overseas. As of July 1988, the number of allowable overseas trips per person for tourism purposes increased from two to three per year; the age range during which males were prohibited to travel was shortened from 16–30 to 16–26 years; and the fee for tourist exit and entry permit was halved from NT$4000 to NT$2000 (New Taiwan dollar) (Wieman 1989b).

The lessening of travel restrictions combined with their increased spending power has made the Taiwanese one of the most sought after markets in the Asia–Pacific region (*Asia Travel Trade* 1990d). Table 3.7 indicates the numbers of Taiwanese travelling overseas and their destinations for the period 1980 to 1991. Outbound departures for 1991 represented a 14.4 per cent increase over the previous year. These figures follow on from the extremely high growth rates which have existed since 1987. Moreover, the proportion of departures to national population, 16 per cent, is the highest in Asia and more than double that of Japan (Republic of China Tourist Bureau 1992a).

Outbound travellers tend to stay abroad for an average of 11.06 nights.

Table 3.7: Destinations and numbers of Taiwanese outbound travel, 1980–1991

Main or First Destination	1980	1982	1984	1986	1988	1989	1990	1991
Hong Kong	63 812	81 558	109 975	121 427	621 864	810 977	1 245 764	1 368 295
Japan	173 581	260 414	292 127	253 524	340 488	474 245	591 495	653 242
South Korea	76 995	67 002	73 008	81 644	100 569	133 867	221 454	284 902
Singapore	19 563	24 124	29 648	30 831	45 989	70 924	96 607	153 811
Malaysia	4 418	8 996	12 974	30 841	42 251	59 938	57 074	79 820
Thailand	14 956	21 726	22 619	63 271	154 853	258 668	355 962	346 310
The Philippines	35 718	42 274	36 549	32 510	44 309	80 678	65 250	69 527
Indonesia	4 507	6 985	8 221	7 058	18 994	23 301	32 397	80 386
India	87	125	74	111	94	18	126	178
Middle East	8 438	8 870	9 447	4 182	2 862	1 334	1 038	1 088
Other Asia	169	360	930	1 735	2 721	1 945	2 378	1 531
Total Asia	**402 244**	**522 434**	**584 752**	**627 134**	**1 374 976**	**1 915 893**	**2 669 545**	**3 039 090**
USA	69 448	98 995	132 692	153 462	183 402	157 565	239 325	267 584
Other Americas	4 306	5 140	6 412	8 675	9 902	1 843	2 194	16 478
Total Americas	**73 754**	**104 135**	**139 104**	**162 137**	**193 304**	**159 408**	**241 519**	**284 062**
Europe	4 830	7 786	11 498	16 772	22 279	18 549	17 869	20,281
Oceania	1 300	1 444	1 741	3 475	4 781	1 134	428	7 894
Africa	2 773	4 870	3 309	3 410	6 652	12 829	12 955	14 749
Total	**484 901**	**640 669**	**750 404**	**812 928**	**1 601 992**	**2 107 813**	**2 942 316**	**3 366 076**

Source: Republic of China Tour st Bureau 1992b: 47; Wieman 1989b: 43

However, the average nights of stay depends markedly on the nature of the destination. For example, travel to the USA and Canada is for 18.81 and 19.86 nights respectively, while for Korea the average nights of stay is 6.76 (Republic of China Tourist Bureau 1992b). The primary purpose for 85 per cent of all Taiwanese outbound travel is pleasure. Given the continuing health of the Taiwanese economy and the desire of Taiwanese to travel overseas the average age of outbound tourists will drop as will the trip length. The initial wave of travel from Taiwan was marked by the majority of people taking package tours. However, as international travel experience grows, emphasis will shift towards quality travel experiences often undertaken by independent travellers, particularly in South East Asia.

Unlike many other nations in the Asia–Pacific region, Taiwan is not using tourism as a source of foreign exchange. Instead, as in Japan which launched an overseas tourism incentive plan to reach 10 million departures a year, Taiwan has utilised overseas tourism to ease pressure on its own domestic recreational resources and to achieve diplomatic and economic objectives, particularly in relation to its major trading partners. As the Republic of China Tourist Bureau (1992a: 7) has stated: 'Although the ROC government has not introduced any special incentive packages encouraging travel abroad, the high annual growth rate for overseas travel from the ROC has achieved some of the results sought by Japan's tourism policy'.

Relationship with the People's Republic of China

One of the most interesting aspects of Taiwanese tourism is the relationship of Taiwan (the Republic of China) to mainland China (the People's Republic of China). The lifting of travel restrictions for travel to mainland China to visit relatives in October 1987, meant that many Taiwanese can now visit the mainland both to see relatives and to experience the greater China of which Taiwan is still culturally a part. However, the diplomatic impasse between China and Taiwan has meant that no direct air or sea services between the two countries exists. The official statistics of Taiwan do not even recognise the existence of the People's Republic, yet many Taiwanese travellers who are recorded as visiting Hong Kong and Japan will only be using those countries as a stopover to the mainland. As Wieman (1989b: 43) noted, 'The necessity of travelling through a third area... adds to the inconvenience of the trip; so does the legal prohibition against direct contact between the two sides of the Taiwan Straits, which means that Taiwan agents have to hand off their groups to agents in Hong Kong'.

Officially, only residents with close relatives on the mainland are allowed to travel there and then only for the purpose of visiting those relatives, not for pleasure or business activities. However, the restriction is universally ignored, by government and tourists alike. 'Travel agents take care of all formalities, including the provision of names of relatives, and many tourists in the mainland today are native Taiwanese whose ancestors migrated to the island centuries ago' (Wieman 1989b: 43).

The inbound market

Taiwan is one of the few destinations in the Asia–Pacific to experience difficulties in maintaining inbound tourism growth. International arrivals in Taiwan declined by 3.5 per cent to 1.93 million in 1990, and a further 4.1 per cent to 1.85 million in 1991. (Visitor arrivals to Taiwan for 1977–1991 are indicated in Table 3.8.) Furthermore, the composition of international visitors has been slowly changing. Those who come for business and other non-pleasure purposes are gradually growing; while those who have pleasure as their major purpose has been declining (Wieman 1989a).

A number of reasons can be put forward for the falling number of inbound travellers (*Asia Travel Trade* 1989a, 1990d; Wieman 1989a, 1990; Republic of China Tourist Bureau 1992a). First, the rapid appreciation of the New Taiwan dollar, while a bounty for outbound travellers, has meant that Taiwan is a relatively expensive destination. Second, the annual promotion budget of only US$8 million is low compared to other Asian destinations and means that Taiwan does not have a strong presence in the competitive international tourism market. Third, unlike Korea, Hong Kong and Singapore, and despite being a manufacturer of many consumer goods, Taiwan has a lack of shopping opportunities for international travellers. Fourth, there is a lack of tourism attractions, particularly because some scenic areas have been restricted for tourism because of military activities. Fifth, deteriorating law and order is of some concern.

A number of other problems have also been identified. According to Wieman (1989c) and *Asia Travel Trade* (1990g), Taiwan also has high room prices because of a shortage of international hotels, with the shortfall increasing from 5089 rooms in 1989 to 7811 in 1991. There is 'little relief in sight: new construction is deterred by an extreme dearth of available land and astronomically high land prices in Taipei; by a severe shortage of construction workers; by a shrinking hotel labour pool; and by a decline in the overall investment climate' (*Asia Travel Trade* 1990g: 48). Nevertheless, the official hotel occupancy rates of the Tourist Bureau would appear to be at odds with the shortage argument, at least at the upper end of the hotel market. According to the Bureau, 46 hotels with 14 538 rooms are licensed as 'International Tourist Hotels' and 48 hotels with 5248 rooms as 'Tourist Hotels', which makes a total of 94 hotels with 19 786 rooms. The room occupancy rates reported to the Bureau in 1991 averaged 56.39 per cent for international tourist hotels and 45.13 per cent for tourist hotels (Republic of China Tourist Bureau 1992b). However, as with a number of Asian destinations, there is a lack of budget accommodation.

There is also a substantial lack of airline capacity to and from Taiwan (*Asia Travel Trade* 1990f). The rapid growth in outbound travel has taken seats away from inbound travellers. In response, China Airlines has expanded its fleet and there has been an increase in capacity on other airlines (Cathay Pacific, Singapore Airlines, Thai Airways, Malaysia Airlines,

Table 3.8: Taiwan visitor arrivals, 1977-1991

Year	Total		Foreign Visitors			Overseas Chinese		
	No. of Visitors	Growth Rate %	No. of Visitors	Growth Rate %	% of Total	No. of Visitors	Growth Rate %	% of Total
1977	1 110 182	10.1	933 936	9.4	84.1	176 246	14.3	15.9
1978	1 270 977	14.5	1 045 916	12.0	82.3	225 061	27.7	17.7
1979	1 340 382	5.5	1 096 735	4.9	81.8	243 647	8.3	18.2
1980	1 393 254	3.9	1 111 130	1.3	79.8	282 124	15.8	20.2
1981	1 409 465	1.2	1 116 008	0.4	79.2	293 457	4.0	20.9
1982	1 419 178	0.7	1 111 406	-0.4	78.3	307 772	4.9	21.7
1983	1 457 404	2.7	1 116 791	5.0	80.1	290 613	-5.6	19.9
1984	1 516 138	4.0	1 227 450	5.2	81.0	288 688	-0.7	19.0
1985	1 451 659	-4.3	1 195 443	-2.6	82.4	256 216	-11.3	17.6
1986	1 610 385	10.9	1 333 315	11.5	82.8	277 070	8.1	17.2
1987	1 760 948	9.3	1 510 972	13.3	85.8	249 976	-9.8	14.2
1988	1 935 134	9.9	1 696 677	12.3	87.7	238 457	-4.6	12.3
1989	2 004 126	3.6	1 768 541	4.2	88.2	235 585	-1.2	11.8
1990	1 934 084	-3.5	1 712 680	-3.2	88.6	221 404	-6.0	11.4
1991	1 854 506	-4.1	1 629 448	-4.9	87.9	225 058	1.7	12.1

Source: Republic of China Tourist Bureau 1992b: 11

Philippine Airlines, Korean Airlines). A number of bilateral agreements have also been signed to develop new air routes.

A number of environmental concerns also affects the attractiveness of the island to tourists. Taipei suffers major traffic congestion and insufficient funds have been invested in physical and social infrastructure development. Air and water pollution and damage to the environment represent a major problem in terms of tourism development. According to Wieman (1990: 40, 42):

some of the island's scenic resources have been ravaged by heedless entrepreneurs. Irreplaceable stone formations on the northeast coast have been destroyed by aquaculture farmers digging illegal abalone ponds, and Kaohsiung's Love River and Taipei's Tamsui are so polluted that just being near them requires an insensitive nose or a strong stomach. Where tourism-oriented development has occurred, the result has typically been an unsightly and disorderly hodge-podge of vendors' stalls, third rate hotels, and none-too-sanitary local restaurants.

However, in a somewhat contradictory fashion, Wieman goes on to note that the establishment of national parks 'impede development, since the park administration is heavily biased toward preservation rather than utilisation' (1990: 42).

The most substantial inbound market is the Japanese which at 825 985 made up 44.95 per cent of visitors in 1991. However, it should be noted that this represented a substantial drop from the 914 484 Japanese who visited in 1990. Japanese visitors have one of the shortest average length of stay of all visitors (4.81 nights) but by far the highest average daily expenditure per visitor (US$245.05) (Republic of China Tourist Bureau 1992b). According to *Asia Travel Trade* (1989a: 41), 'the Japanese keep coming partly because of Taiwan's reputation as a sex haven, but largely because they can still afford the island's increasingly outrageous prices'. In 1991, 78.61 per cent of all Japanese visitors to Taiwan were male (Republic of China Tourist Bureau 1992b). However, Japanese arrivals are shifting towards more travel by families, students, and younger age groups. As Lin (1990: 97) noted, 'Taiwan is a comfortable destination for the Japanese, because of the common points in the two nations' cultures and history. Many first-time Japanese travellers choose Taiwan for a destination because they can find a similar lifestyle and virtually no communication problems'. However, the Japanese are one of the few, if not the only, markets that can absorb the appreciation of the New Taiwan dollar, although perhaps the 1991 figures indicate that they do retain a degree of price-sensitivity. Therefore, in an attempt to overcome the relative cost of Taiwan as a destination, the Tourist Bureau and inbound operators are switching to less price sensitive areas such as conventions, incentives, business travel, the luxury Free Independent Traveller (FIT) market and special-interest tours (such as tea tours and handicrafts) and away from leisure travel (*Asia Travel Trade* 1990g).

Despite the poor inbound performance, the Tourist Bureau has only a small international promotion budget of NT$200 million (US$8 million) for the 1992–1993 financial year (Wieman 1992). Tied by lack of government interest in promoting inbound tourism, the Bureau has set a growth target of 5 per cent per annum over the coming years, and is primarily targeting mature travellers in Japan, the USA and Korea. However, like a number of other destinations in the region, it is also attempting to diversify into special interest tourism opportunities, particularly culture, adventure (including hiking, fishing, yachting, white-water rafting and rock-climbing) and nature-based tours.

A further positive step in encouraging greater inbound visitation is the introduction of visas on arrival thereby providing access to the 1.3 million people who transit Taiwan every year without entering the country (Wieman 1992). The benefits of easier provision of visas for visitors to Taiwan will be considerable, and should help to combat the loss of tourists who are visiting the mainland rather than Taiwan. As *Asia Travel Trade* (1989a: 41) observed: 'The mainland is not only cheaper and has far more scenic and cultural attractions than Taiwan, but its visas are also easier to obtain. Taiwan has diplomatic relations with few countries; in others, visas or letters of recommendation exchangeable for visas on arrival are issued by agencies that go by a variety of names [e.g. Sun Yat-sen Centers]'. In the light of several markets' unease with mainland China, the Republic of China Tourist Bureau (1992a) is promoting Taiwan as an alternative destination and is emphasising Taiwan's Chinese heritage through promotion of Bureau sponsored events such as a Chinese Food festival in August and a tourism festival to coincide with the Lunar New Year celebrations around January/February.

Tourism development

Tourism development in Taiwan is very much tied up with the government Tourist Bureau. The Tourist Bureau was formally established by the Ministry of Transportation and Communications in December 1972 in order to develop and effectively manage the nation's tourism industry. At the local and regional level, responsibility for tourism is divided among the Taiwan Tourism Administration of the Taiwan Provincial Government's Department of Communications, the Tourism Section of the Taipei City Government's Department of Transportation, the Tourism Section of the Kaohsiung City Government's Department of Reconstruction, and the tourism sections of the departments of reconstruction under the county and city governments in Taiwan province (Republic of China Tourist Bureau 1992a).

The Republic of China Tourist Bureau, like its Japanese counterpart, has responsibilities for both inbound and outbound tourism. In 1989, Dr Mao Chi-kuo, the Taiwan Tourist Bureau's Director General, defined the priorities for the Bureau as improving domestic travel opportunities, especially weekend travel; and competing effectively in the international market, particularly given the opening up of mainland China and the increase of those in search of a cultural tourism experience (*Asia Travel Trade* 1989b). In 1992 the priorities of the Bureau remain essentially the same, develop domestic tourism opportunities while simultaneously attracting a greater number of inbound tourists (Republic of China Tourist Bureau 1992a).

As noted above, one of the major problems in attracting international tourists is the lack of developed tourist attractions and associated infrastructure. Indeed, 60 per cent of overseas tourists do not get out of Taipei (*Asia Travel Trade* 1989b). Nevertheless, there is a slow, but growing recognition, that Taiwan does have a number of natural and cultural attractions that can enable it to compete effectively in the international market-place. These attractions are being developed by the Bureau and local government in a number of ways. First, the development and management of national scenic areas which act as focal points for domestic and international tourism. Second, the undertaking of tourism development plans for major highways. For example, in conjunction with the Taiwan Tourism Administration, an agency of the Taiwan provincial government, the Bureau has provided 50 per cent of the funds for infrastructure development for a number of major development projects, with the private sector providing the capital for the associated commercial operations (*Asia Travel Trade* 1989b; Republic of China Tourist Bureau 1992a). The projects include:

• development of four tourist areas: the North shore of Taiwan; Mt Kuanyin, a Buddhist site across the Tamsui River from Taipei; Mt Pakua, a commercialised Buddhist sanctuary at Changhua in central Taiwan; and Maolin, a primitive Bunun aborigine village in the south
• development of twenty-seven sites on Highway One (west coast), with an emphasis on coastal recreation and beaches
• development of eighteen sites on Highway Three, which provides access to the central mountain range
• further development of hot springs
• rural renewal schemes and the development of 'native based' tourism in order to attract cultural tourists.

The development of attractions is one thing, the availability of accommodation and transportation services is another. As noted above, despite assertions to the contrary, inbound tourists would appear to be well served at the international tourist hotel level. Indeed, a further twenty-three international tourist hotels having 6387 rooms developed with the assistance of the Bureau are scheduled to open between 1992 and 1995 (Republic of China Tourist Bureau 1992a: 19).

The lack of airline capacity is due not only to the rapid growth in outbound travel but also to the diplomatic problem of two Chinas. Interairline agreements are one mechanism used by the Taiwanese Government to overcome the lack of formal recognition with countries that recognise

China but not Taiwan. In order to sidestep the problem of one airline flying to both China and Taiwan, foreign flag carriers may establish subsidiaries to serve Taipei. For example, Japanese Airlines established Japan
Asia Airways while Qantas set up Australia Asia Airlines (Westlake 1991). In
addition, the development of new direct air routes is also expected to assist
in improving airline capacity, particularly with respect to Australia and
New Zealand. Therefore, with an improvement in the accessibility of
attractions, more frequent air services and the availability of accommodation, the Taiwanese inbound tourism sector is now in a better position to
take advantage of the growing Pacific tourism market.

Conclusion

*The government—the Legislative Yuan—will have to change its attitude before
anybody in the industry will be able to do anything about the inbound business. The
government doesn't think that tourism is important, especially when it has so much
foreign exchange reserves and the country is in a critical situation ['because of the
communist threat']. Members of the government don't know the importance of
tourists to this country; they should establish a ministry of tourism, provide more
funds, and strengthen international promotion. Foreigners, especially in Europe,
are confused about Taiwan. You say the Republic of China, they think PRC; you
say Taiwan, they think Thailand. We have to spend more on promotion (Benjamin
Chang, Managing Director of Foundation Tours, cited in Wieman 1990: 42).*

Taiwan is set to become one of the major tourist generating regions of Asia
in the 1990s. With a population of 20.5 million people, an annual average
growth of 25 per cent in outbound travel between 1985 and 1991, the
world's largest foreign exchange reserves and a growing economy, outbound travel should continue to grow albeit at a slower rate than the
1980s. The negotiation of direct airline agreements, for example, between
Australia and Taiwan will have substantial implications for tourism as well
as other trade and business contacts. According to Korporaal (1991), 70
per cent to 80 per cent of traffic on the route will originate in Taiwan and
most will be tourists. However, as the Taiwan economy continues to
expand and mature, other significant changes can be expected, in particular, attention will probably be paid by government to develop tourist and
recreation opportunities for both domestic and international travellers.

Despite official statements regarding the role of outbound travel to balance trading accounts and to promote goodwill, inbound tourism still generates substantial income for Taiwan (Table 3.9). In 1991 visitor expenditure totalled US$2.018 billion, almost double the 1981 figure, although
not as high as the peak of 2.698 billion in 1989. Undoubtedly, continued
appreciation of the New Taiwan dollar will have a significant impact on the
value of inbound travel. However, the growing importance of Taiwan as an
economic centre and as a potential bridgehead into mainland China will
mean that business travel will continue to be strong, while the development of special interest attractions will also contribute to moderate

Table 3.9: Visitor expenditures in Taiwan, 1982–1991

Year	No. of Visitors	Visitor Expenditure	% Change	Spending Per Person (US$)	Spending Per Person Per Day (US$)	Average Length of Stay (Night)
1982	1 419 178	953 000 000	-11.8	671.54	109.55	6.13
1983	1 457 404	990 000 000	3.9	679.53	105.19	6.46
1984	1 516 138	1 066 000 000	7.7	702.82	110.68	6.35
1985	1 451 659	963 000 000	-9.7	663.56	101.93	6.51
1986	1 610 385	1 333 000 000	38.4	827.49	120.45	6.87
1987	1 760 948	1 619 000 000	21.5	919.53	132.88	6.92
1988	1 935 134	2 289 000 000	41.4	1 182.93	168.99	7.00
1989	2 004 126	2 698 000 000	17.9	1 346.40	187.00	7.20
1990	1 934 084	1 740 000 000	-35.5	899.90	130.42	6.90
1991	1 854 506	2 018 000 000	16.0	1 088.39	148.89	7.31

Source: Republic of China Tourist Bureau 1992b: 33

increases in pleasure travel. Nevertheless, the greatest impact on both inbound and outbound travel in Taiwan will be the island's relations with the mainland and the ongoing democratisation process. Given political stability, Taiwan's economic future and consequent tourism development looks secure. Without such stability, inbound travel will be severely damaged and outbound growth will be seriously impeded.

Hong Kong: from colony to 1997

Hong Kong is one of the major travel destinations and tourist generating regions in North East Asia. Hong Kong is the gateway to China for many travellers, a major tourist stopover and an aviation hub for North East Asia. In 1991 Hong Kong had over 6 million visitors, a 1.7 per cent increase over the previous year. Over 2 million residents travelled overseas, while tourism receipts grew marginally by 0.9 per cent to HK$39.6 billion. Tourism is a substantial contributor to the colony's economy and accounted for about 7.5 per cent of the GDP in 1989.

The relationship with China plays a major role in the current and future fortunes of the colony. The political unrest in China in 1989 had a dramatic effect on the Hong Kong economy and on the tourism trade in particular. Tourist arrivals fell by 4 per cent to 5.460 million in 1989 compared with 5.693 million in 1988 (13 per cent higher). The inbound travel situation in Hong Kong only improved as political unrest in China died down. In the first half of 1990 total tourist spending rose 5.1 per cent to HK$18.7 billion. However, within the increase the impacts of the events at Tiananmen Square could still be seen. For example, spending by Japanese inbound tourists, the highest spending market in 1989, fell 3.4 per cent to HK$4.9 billion, with the spending of visitors from Australasia, North America, and Western Europe also reduced. In contrast, visitor numbers from Taiwan and South East Asia increased and spending by these markets was substantially higher. Total Taiwanese inbound tourist spending increased to HK$3.34 billion, accounting for nearly 18 per cent of all tourist spending, while South East Asian tourist spending rose by 20 per cent (Malik 1991: 114).

The improvement in inbound tourism in Hong Kong in 1990 and 1991 was assisted by improved inbound travel to China (see Chapter 5) and heavy discounting on the part of hotels, tour operators and airlines (Brevetti 1992). However, in the longer term, the critical factor in the level of inbound visitation will be the relationship of China to Hong Kong and the outside world.

Outbound travel

With a population of 5.9 million, solid economic growth, and increased personal disposable income, Hong Kong has become a sought after outbound travel market. Table 3.10 illustrates the 10.4 per cent average annual growth in Hong Kong outbound travel experienced from 1985 to 1991. The marginal rise in outbound travel in 1991 is associated with the

Table 3.10: Hong Kong outbound travel, 1985–1991

Year	Number (000's)
1985	1 133
1986	1 207
1987	1 386
1988	1 570
1989	1 814
1990	2 043
1991	2 046

Source: Hong Kong Tourist Association in New Zealand Tourism Board 1992e: 36

impacts of the political unrest in China on Hong Kong travel behaviour, although much of Hong Kong's outbound travel in 1991 was to nearby destinations such as China, Taiwan, Japan, and Macao. Increased interest is being shown by Hong Kong residents in destinations further afield, such as Singapore, Canada, Australia and New Zealand, particularly as the Chinese takeover of the colony comes closer.

Inbound travel: 'Hong Kong—Stay an extra day'

The majority of visitors to Hong Kong are from Asia with Taiwan (21.2 per cent of total arrivals), Japan (20.9 per cent) and South East Asia (16.7 per cent) the major markets. Arrivals from Western Europe increased by 7.0 per cent to 790 000 visitors and visitation from Canada and the USA increased by 1.8 per cent to 780 000. The depressed economies of Australia and New Zealand resulted in a decrease in arrivals from those countries of 7.8 per cent to 277 000 visitors. Arrivals from South Korea fell marginally by 0.1 per cent but their expenditure increased by 8.8 per cent to HK$1.1 billion. Taiwanese expenditure increased by 18.4 per cent to HK$7.0 billion, while the Japanese accounted for 24.0 per cent of total visitor spending at HK$9.2 billion (Hong Kong Tourist Association 1992). Table 3.11 outlines the growth in visitor arrivals by area of residence for the period 1982–1991.

The primary purpose of travel for visitors to Hong Kong in 1991, was a vacation (59.4 per cent). However, 10.8 per cent of visitors were travelling *en route* to another destination, thereby giving an example of the role that Hong Kong plays as a transport hub in the north east Pacific (Table 3.12). Just over half of the visitor dollar was spent on shopping in 1991, indicating the importance of shopping as an attraction of Hong Kong. The conference, meetings and incentive travel market is also of increasing significance. In 1991 there was a 12.6 per cent increase in the number of people attending conferences (137 000) and an 11.0 per cent increase in the number of events. The healthy state of business in the region was also indicated in the growth of the corporate events (corporate meetings and incentive travel) by 8.9 per cent from 764 to 832, while the number of visitors attending corporate meetings grew from 7960 to 12 910, an increase of 62.2 per cent (Hong Kong Tourist Association 1992).

In 1991, six new hotels were opened. At the end of the year, there were 82 hotels offering 31 163 rooms, an increase of 10.7 per cent over rooms available at the end of the previous year. Hotels achieved an average room occupancy of 75 per cent during 1991 (Hong Kong Tourist Association 1992). Given the continuing increase in hotel rooms and the current capacity problems at Kai Tak, Hong Kong's international airport, the Tourist Association has developed a 'Hong Kong—Stay an extra day' theme in order to promote an increase in the average length of stay. Some benefits have already been reaped from the campaign with the average length of stay of visitors growing from 3.33 nights in 1990 to 3.43 nights in 1991, which translates into an extra 900 000 visitor-nights for Hong Kong (Hong Kong Tourist Association 1992).

Tourism development

The over-riding factor in tourism development in Hong Kong is the Sino-British joint declaration on the future of Hong Kong signed in Peking on 19 December 1984, stating that Hong Kong would be restored to China on 1 July 1997. The return of the colony colours all business activity and deeply influences tourism investment and infrastructure development, most significant of which is the construction of a new airport.

The 4 July 1991 memorandum of understanding between Britain and China over the building of a new airport for Hong Kong had far deeper ramifications for the colony than the immediate economic necessity of the new airport. The agreement which was almost as significant as the 1984 Sino-British agreement on Hong Kong which provided the conditions for the return of Hong Kong to China, provided the Peking Government with the opportunity for direct involvement in the Territory's affairs before the handover of sovereignty. The editorial of the *Far Eastern Economic Review* made plain the fears of many Hong Kong residents: 'the agreement effectively makes all major fiscal decisions in Hong Kong subject to China's veto... In place of an administration by technically competent bureaucrats under an executive with a "high degree of autonomy" will be a government beholden to power-obsessed or corrupt cadres sent from Peking, or sleazy officials from Guangdong with links to Hong Kong businessmen' (18 July 1991: 11).

Nevertheless, the new airport development is essential. As the Chairman of the Hong Kong Tourist Association, Martin Barrow, stated:

We consider the earliest-possible completion of the new airport vital for Hong Kong's continuing to be the airline hub of Asia and for continuing success and future growth of the territory's tourism industry; Hong Kong could be welcoming 10 million visitors and earning HK$130 billion to HK$140 billion in tourism receipts annually by the year 2000—but only if there are no constraints on air traffic into Hong Kong (Hong Kong Tourist Association 1992: 2).

The present international airport at Kai Tak is almost at capacity. The

Table 3.11: Hong Kong visitor arrivals by area of residence, 1982–1991 (000's)

Region	1982	1983	1984	1985	1986	1987	1988	1989	1990	1991
Asia	1 410	1 459	1594	1 709	1 901	2 438	3 470	3 450	3 993	4 041
Australia and Pacific	245	257	311	302	307	298	307	311	312	285
Americas	465	546	682	781	861	981	952	813	808	822
Europe	390	404	437	502	575	690	782	715	742	795
Middle East and Africa	75	77	73	64	70	67	72	68	74	85
Not identified	8	11	10	12	20	27	6	5	5	4
Total	2 592	2 754	3 108	3 370	3 733	4 502	5 589	5 361	5 933	6 032

Source: Hong Kong Tourist Association 1992: 6

Table 3.12: Purpose of visit to Hong Kong, 1990–1991

Purpose	1990(%)	1991(%)
Vacation	55.0	59.4
Business/Meetings	24.6	23.2
En route	15.2	10.8
Visiting friends/relatives	3.0	4.2
Other	2.2	2.4

Source: Hong Kong Tourist Association 1992: 19

new development at Chek Lap Kok which is under construction is due to open in 1997 and is designed to handle 35 million passengers, 11 million more than Kai Tak's saturation point. However, the cost of the project is enormous, a projection of HK$38.2 billion (US$5 billion) in 1991 had grown to projection of HK$46.3 billion (US$6 billion) in April 1992 with the overall project predicted to cost HK$112.5 billion (US$14.5 billion) (Brevetti 1992).

The future of tourism in Hong Kong

When interviewed on departure, 78 per cent of visitors said they would definitely return to the territory, indicating a very high degree of satisfaction with Hong Kong as a travel destination (Hong Kong Tourist Association 1992: 28).

More than any other state in the North East Asian region, Hong Kong and its tourism industry is at the mercy of another nation. Until 1997 China determines the industry's fate through its pronouncements on investment, development, and political participation in the colony and, of course, its attitude towards the desire for democratisation within China. After 1997 the future of Hong Kong remains somewhat uncertain and the degree to which China can incorporate the rampant capitalism of Hong Kong within the centrist Chinese economy is unknown. However, it would appear likely that Hong Kong will retain its hub status until 1997 and probably well into the next century. Nevertheless, the flight of capital and the brain-drain that is affecting the colony prior to the return to Chinese rule may have short-term benefits for the outbound travel market, but will probably have serious long-term consequences for the colony.

The future of tourism in North East Asia

Rising incomes and increased interest in the outside world has generated demand in Northeast Asia for visiting and living for a while in foreign countries. In the higher income countries—Japan and Hong Kong—the trend is entrenched and deepening. It is a more recent but powerful tendency in Taiwan and the Republic of Korea. It is now even present in China (Garnaut 1990: 245).

The countries of North East Asia are set to become the major tourist generating regions of the Pacific Rim by the turn of the century. The three countries examined in this chapter, along with Japan which we discussed in Chapter 2, have all experienced substantial economic growth over the past three decades. The high rate of economic growth has seen traditional Asian societies transformed into consumer societies which, combined with policy changes by government to allow overseas travel in the cases of Korea, Japan and Taiwan, has meant the emergence of a high rate of outbound travel. The three North East Asian nations discussed in this chapter would appear set to have a continuing high rate of outbound travel over the next five years given:

- that their economies will continue to expand, though at lower growth rates than was experienced in the 1980s
- personal disposable income will continue to increase
- leisure and holiday time will increase as employers and governments pass on the benefits of economic growth
- outbound travel is unregulated.

The last factor will be very important for Hong Kong as the handover of the colony to the Chinese in 1997 comes closer.

In terms of inbound travel, the key factors will be cost; the development of infrastructure, especially transport and accommodation; the accessibility of attractions; and the degree of political stability. Again, this last factor will be critical for Hong Kong. However, given the geographical proximity of Korea and Taiwan, the stability of China and its attitude towards its neighbours will also affect these two countries. A further dimension to the political stability of China, Korea and Taiwan is the degree to which government can accommodate the rising expectations of a growing, educated, middle-class which is seeking greater democratic reform and, in the cases of Taiwan and Korea, a less authoritarian style of government.

The North East Asian economies have not, as yet, established a formal trading relationship as in the case of ASEAN or NAFTA. Nevertheless, considerable interest has been given to the development of a Pacific Region trading zone, particularly given the increasing economic integration of the Pacific Rim. However, a stumbling block for Taiwan remains in the form of its relationship to mainland China, while the relative independence of post-1997 Hong Kong is an unknown factor.

In conclusion, the North East Asian economies discussed in this chapter will continue to grow with considerable benefits for inbound and outbound travel. Significantly, much of the outbound travel will remain in the Pacific Rim with considerable benefits for economic and political relations between the generating and receiving nations. Indeed, Taiwan has a deliberate policy of using its outbound travel for diplomatic benefits and for improving trade balances. In Chapter 2 we noted how the Japanese increasingly invested overseas as outbound tourism grew. In the case of Taiwan, Hong Kong and, to a lesser extent, Korea, a similar pattern is emerging. The first wave of outbound travel from North East Asia is breaking on tourist destinations around the Pacific. The next wave, which is beginning to develop, will also include substantial investment in those same tourism destinations.

Suggestions for further reading

One of the most comprehensive accounts of the economic development of the North East Asian region is to be found in Garnaut (1990) *Australia and the Northeast Asian Ascendency*. Ariff (1991) *The Pacific Economy: Growth and External Stability* also provides a useful overview of the economic significance of North East Asia in Pacific trade.

Apart from regular reviews of tourism developments in trade journals, such as *Asia Travel Trade*, discussion of tourism in countries of North East Asia tends to be limited to government reports. Students interested in Korean tourism are recommended to examine the annual *Travel Manual* put out by the Korea National Tourism Corporation (1991) and the monthly and annual statistical reports. The Economist Intelligence Unit (1990c) and McGahey (1991) provide valuable overviews of the inbound and outbound market segments; while Chon and Shin (1990) discuss the various issues facing the accommodation sector in Korea.

For information on tourism in Taiwan, students are directed to the annual report of the Republic of China Tourist Bureau (1992a) and their annual *Report on Tourism Statistics* (1992b). Wieman (1989, 1992) has produced several reports on the Taiwan tourism industry which are worthy of examination.

The Hong Kong Tourist Association (1992) produces a series of annual reports and monthly statistics which provide the most up-to-date accounts of tourism in the colony. Students interested in the ramifications of the Chinese takeover in 1997 should regularly consult the *Far Eastern Economic Review* which is based in Hong Kong.

Discussion and review

Key concepts
North East Asia, Newly Industrialised Economies (NIEs), rapid economic growth, role of government in tourism, development strategies, restrictions on nationals travelling overseas, significance attached to tourism as a source of foreign exchange, Seoul Olympic Games, national image, tourist trade deficit, heritage tourism, spending power, rapid growth in outbound travel, price-sensitivity, transport hub, 'Hong Kong—Stay an extra day', Sino-British joint declaration.

Questions for review and discussion
1 What are the implications of rapid economic growth in North East Asia for tourism?
2 Why was the hosting of the 1988 Summer Olympic Games in Seoul significant for tourism in Korea?
3 How has tourism played a role in attracting foreign exchange to Korea?
4 What were the main reasons for imposing outbound travel restrictions in South Korea and Taiwan?
5 What is the relationship of Taiwan to the People's Republic of China and why is this important for tourism?
6 How has tourism growth in Hong Kong been affected by its relationship with the People's Republic of China?

4 ASEAN: 6-in-1 tropical paradise?

> The world's only 6-in-1 tropical paradise!
> (promotional campaign slogan for Visit
> ASEAN Year 1992).

ASEAN: regional co-operation and economic development

Founded in 1967 as a non-communist bloc of East Asian countries, the Association of South East Asian Nations (ASEAN) plays a major role in the region's economic, social and political development (see Figure 4.1). The six members of ASEAN—Brunei, Indonesia, Malaysia, The Philippines, Singapore and Thailand—are moving steadily towards greater economic co-operation in light of difficulties in the General Agreement on Trade and Tariffs (GATT) talks, the strengthening of other regional trading blocs such as the European Community, and the signing of the North American Free Trade Agreement (NAFTA) among Canada, Mexico and the USA. For example, in a speech to the United Nations General Assembly on 24 September 1991, Malaysian Prime Minister Datuk Seri Mahathir Mohamed called for the formation of an East Asian Economic grouping (Awanohara 1991). More concrete progress towards regional economic co-operation was forged at a meeting in Manila on 22–23 October 1992 when the economic ministers of the ASEAN nations agreed on a schedule of tariff cuts that will commence on 1 January 1993 and continue for the next fifteen years (Tiglao 1992: 50).

The development of greater economic co-operation within the region has substantial implications for tourism, the most obvious being joint marketing campaigns such as Visit ASEAN Year. Joint economic development strategies are emerging which also have substantial implications for tourism, the most apparent of which involves the establishment of a 'growth triangle' between the Malaysian State of Johore, Singapore, and the Indonesian Province of Riau. In addition, the improvement of rail services between Singapore, Malaysia and Thailand will further integrate the tourism economies of the region.

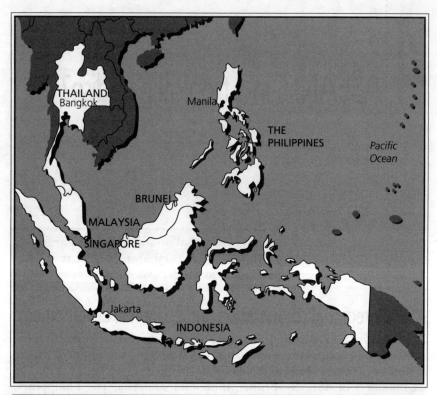

Figure 4.1: ASEAN countries

Supported by a series of 'visitor years', tourism in the ASEAN countries has grown rapidly over the past two decades and has become a vital source of foreign exchange and an essential element in government economic strategies for all except oil rich Brunei. However, tourism development has not been without its negative aspects. With attention focused on economic growth, little concern was initially shown for the environmental and social effects of tourism. However, coastal pollution, damage to community values, and the spread of AIDS have all highlighted the need for countries to address the planning dimensions of tourism if the growth of the past ten years is to be maintained.

This chapter examines tourism in five of the six ASEAN nations. Brunei is not discussed as tourism plays an extremely small role in the country's economy which is dominated by oil and gas exports. Each country is analysed in terms of its inbound and outbound markets, the condition of its tourism infrastructure, the impacts of tourism, and the key factors which have determined the course of tourism development, particularly the role of government. The factors of political stability and management of the environmental and social impacts of tourism are two particularly important factors in the maintenance of inbound tourist growth, while the economic development of the region has seen the emergence of a potentially strong outbound market.

Indonesia

Indonesia is in the process of converting from a manufacturing economy to a service economy, which makes the delivery of the product rather than the creation of the product the most important thing—M. Soeparno, President of Garuda (cited in Teh & Wong 1989: 37).

Indonesia, and Bali in particular, has long been one of the focal points for tourism development in South East Asia. Tourism has a significant role in the Indonesian Government's development priorities for Indonesia but it is geographically focused on certain centres such as Bali (Denpasar, Nusa Dua), western and central Java (Jakarta, Yogyakarta, Bogor, Bandung, Surabaya), northern Sumatra (Banda Aceh, Medan, Danau Toba), and Sulawesi (Toraja land) (Lee 1989, Teh 1989b; Economist Intelligence Unit 1991). Bali is undoubtedly the focal point for leisure-oriented travel, although the demand for the destination is so great that substantial room shortages have appeared during the peak season (Teh 1989e).

Indonesia has a planned economy that provides the central government with substantial opportunities to utilise tourism as a mechanism for regional development. The focal point for Indonesian economic development is a series of five-year development plans (Repelita). The current plan, Repelita V, began in April 1989 and continues until March 1994.

During Repelita IV, inbound visitation hit the one million mark for the first time at the end of 1987. During the period 1984–1988, US$918.6 million in foreign money and Rs2.15 billion from local interests funded a total of 264 investments, including 182 hotels, 40 recreational facilities, 21 travel bureaus, 10 marine resorts and 11 restaurants (Teh & Wong 1989). In 1989 tourism represented 5.8 per cent of export earnings compared to 2.8 per cent in 1985 (Economist Intelligence Unit 1991). Joop Ave, the Directorate General of Tourism Chief, has argued that the results of the fourth five-year plan helped establish tourism as a mechanism for economic development in the eyes of the Indonesian Government. The government is aiming for tourism to become the second largest foreign exchange earner by 1994 (after oil and gas) and to provide employment for the rapidly increasing population. In order to achieve this goal, the Directorate General has set a target of at least 2.5 million arrivals and US$2.25–3.15 billion in foreign exchange earnings by the end of the Repelita V period: 'The Indonesian Government is now pretty convinced of the tourism potential... We hope to retain both the minimum length of stays at 12 days and per diem at US$75. If we achieve those targets, we will have made US$2 billion in foreign exchange revenue by the end of Repelita Five' (*Asia Travel Trade* 1989d: 20). Out of the 2.5 million target, Europe is to contribute

725 000, ASEAN 550 000, Japan 425 000, Australia 375 000, North America 225 000 and others 200 000 (Teh 1989e). 'However, industry observers are quick to point out that while the country can achieve its... target arrivals, it may not readily achieve an even distribution of tourists throughout its 17 tourist-designated provinces' (Teh 1990: 27).

Government has been actively involved in creating an awareness of the benefits of tourism. However, as the following discussion indicates, the emphasis on tourism development and promotion in Indonesia is oriented towards the role of tourism as a foreign exchange earner rather than on the development of outbound or domestic leisure travel.

The outbound market

Outbound travel is considered a luxury in Indonesia with approximately half a million passengers per year travelling overseas. A high departure tax is also a significant barrier to outbound pleasure travel. The average length of holiday for outbound Indonesians is between two and three weeks with 'a good portion of the growing FIT traffic' being 'parents who combine a holiday with visits to their children studying abroad' (Teh 1989f: 49). Group travel is the preferred package for travellers especially for families. 'FIT traffic tends to consist of business people who combine work with add-on packages' (Teh 1989f: 49), while the most popular destinations are the USA (often via Japan and/or Hong Kong), Europe and Asia. However, the growth of the Indonesian middle class may mean greater emphasis on short-break holidays to Singapore, Malaysia, and Thailand. Nevertheless, the large population (181.4 million) and a rate of economic growth of over 5 per cent, means that the nation would appear to have potential as a sizable tourist-generating region by the end of the century.

The inbound market

Indonesia has had substantial growth in inbound visitor arrivals in the last five years with an average growth rate of approximately 20 per cent (Table 4.1). In 1991 Indonesia attracted 2 569 870 visitors, over three times the 1986 figure of 825 035 visitors. Of the long-haul markets, the major

Table 4.1: International arrivals to Indonesia 1986–1991

Year	Total	% Change
1986	825 035	-
1987	1 060 347	28.52
1988	1 301 249	22.70
1989	1 625 965	24.95
1990	2 177 566	33.92
1991	2 569 870	18.02

Source: Teh 1989d; Directorate General of Tourism 1992

inbound markets are Japan (11.32 per cent), Australia (8.53 per cent), Taiwan (6.4 per cent), the USA (3.94 per cent), the UK (3.93 per cent) and Germany (3.68 per cent) (Table 4.2). However, it should be noted that the United States and European market share for 1991 was substantially affected by the Gulf crisis and a significant increase in inbound travel from those markets can be expected in 1993 and 1994. The ASEAN market is also significant for short-haul travel, particularly weekend breaks with Singapore holding 27.66 per cent of the market and Malaysia 12.39 per cent. Given the growing economic wealth, increased leisure time and the development of consumer expectations, the contribution of ASEAN countries to inbound numbers in Indonesia will continue to grow rapidly throughout the remainder of the decade.

Indonesia has set a target of between 2.5 million and 3.5 million arrivals by 1993. However, the figure lags considerably behind those of its ASEAN neighbours—Singapore (almost five million), Thailand (four million), and Malaysia (three million) (Teh 1989d). Nevertheless, the receipts from inbound tourism in Indonesia exceed that of its ASEAN partners:

As Indonesia's tourist destinations are so spread out, its industry goes beyond looking at the total number of tourists... Malaysia with about three million arrivals in 1987 earned US$657 million in tourism receipts but Indonesia with about one million visitors earned US$954 million the same year... The reason? The average length of stay for visitors in Indonesia is between 12 and 14 days, the highest in ASEAN (Teh 1989b: 10).

The three most popular Indonesian destinations are Bali, Jakarta and Yogyakarta. The Korean and Taiwanese markets prefer the Jakarta–Yogyakarta–Bali route with a seven day average stay. In comparison, the Japanese spend four to five days in Bali and take day trips to Yogyakarta to see Borobudur. Europeans stay for between twelve and fourteen days, while recently the US market has started to venture out to newer destinations such as Toraja, Kalimantan, and Irian Jaya. Australians and New Zealanders tend to focus their activities on Bali.

Attracting the overseas visitor

Like other countries in South East Asia, Indonesia has used a combination of events, such as cultural festivals, and Visitor Years to raise its profile in overseas tourism markets. In April 1989, the PATA Travel Mart, a major tourism exchange, was held in Bali to promote Indonesia's 45th year of independence (1990), while an Indonesian festivals programme was launched in the USA in September 1990. However, the key promotional event was Visit Indonesia Year (VIY) which used the campaign slogan of 'Let's go Archipelago'. A total of 125 events, many of them festivals and cultural celebrations (primarily focused on Java and Sumatra) were included as part of the VIY calendar. Examples of festivals include the Jakarta Festival, the Arts Festival in Bali, and the Kraton (Sultan's Palace) Festival in Yogyakarta. Visitor years provide a valuable focal point for a

Table 4.2: Visitor arrivals to Indonesia by country of residence, 1990 vs. 199

| Country of | 1991 | | | 1990 | |
Residence	Number	% Share	% Change	Number	% Share
TOTAL ASEAN	1 082 149	42.11	27.49	848	38.98
Brunei Darussalam	7 531	0.29	99.71	3 771	0.17
Malaysia	318 475	12.39	68.11	189 446	8.70
The Philippines	23 440	0.91	35.45	17 305	0.79
Singapore	710 709	27.66	14.43	621 069	28.52
Thailand	21 994	0.86	27.68	17 226	0.79
TOTAL ASIA	626 294	24.37	21.84	514 030	23.61
Bahrain	75	0.00	-63.77	207	0.01
Bangladesh	1 012	0.04	5.31	961	0.04
Hong Kong	60 009	2.34	20.11	49 961	2.29
India	11 633	0.45	24.44	9 348	0.43
Japan	290 907	11.32	10.44	263 398	12.10
Korea, South	61 405	2.39	39.20	44 113	2.03
Pakistan	1 934	0.08	13.83	1 699	0.08
Saudi Arabia	12 442	0.48	0.78	12 346	0.57
Sri Lanka	1 745	0.07	20.68	1 446	0.07
Taiwan	164 556	6.40	37.89	119 339	5.48
Other Asia	20 576	0.80	83.52	11 212	0.51
TOTAL EUROPE	481 684	18.74	-0.56	484 383	22.24
Austria	12 918	0.50	-6.17	13 768	0.63
Belgium	8 938	0.35	-17.55	10 840	0.50
Denmark	7 724	0.30	7.56	7 181	0.3
Finland	4 605	0.18	-9.42	5 084	0.23
France	54 227	2.11	-1.02	54 786	2.52
Germany	94 596	3.68	8.17	87 455	4.02
Italy	44 846	1.75	6.69	42 034	1.93
Netherlands	85 882	3.34	-20.19	107 609	4.94
Norway	3 920	0.15	16.98	3 351	0.15
Spain and Portugal	11,898	0.46	-2.74	12 233	0.56
Sweden	11 806	0.46	-12.69	13 522	0.62
Switzerland	28 679	1.12	6.04	27 045	1.24
UK	101 062	3.93	9.97	91 897	4.22
Other Western Europe	4 247	0.17	-18.28	5 197	0.24
USSR (former)	2 897	0.11	402.95	576	0.03
Other Eastern Europe	3 439	0.13	90.53	1 805	0.08

| Country of | | 1991 | | 1990 | |
Residence	Number	% Share	% Change	Number	% Share
TOTAL AMERICAS	129 335	5.03	1.62	127 278	5.84
Canada	20 957	0.82	3.51	20 246	0.93
Central America	2 462	0.10	259.42	685	0.03
South America	4 572	0.18	-7.60	4 948	0.23
USA	101 344	3.94	-0.05	101 399	4.66
TOTAL OCEANIA	247 061	9.61	23.11	200 678	9.22
Australia	219 306	8.53	22.19	179 483	8.24
New Zealand	25 493	0.99	24.43	20 488	0.94
Other Oceania	2 262	0.09	219.94	707	0.03
TOTAL AFRICA	3 347	0.13	40.63	2 380	0.11
Egypt	252	0.01	-38.08	407	0.02
Other Africa	3 095	0.12	56.87	1 973	0.09
GRAND TOTAL	2 569 870	100.00	18.02	2 177 566	100.00

Source: Center Research and Development Tourpostel in Directorate General of Tourism 1992

country's tourist activities. For example, many Jakarta hotels were refurbished for VIY although there was a fear that a price hike by Jakarta hoteliers may deter some potential tourists (Teh 1989d). Nevertheless, although the growth rate of inbound tourism in Indonesia was not as great as in previous years, VIY was able to provide a valuable counter-balance to the effects of the Gulf War in European and United States markets.

In order to cater for the rapid growth in inbound tourists, Garuda, the national airline, has expanded its flights to Australia (Melbourne and Sydney), Japan (Nagoya and Tokyo), Europe, the USA, New Zealand and Korea. Garuda is also expanding its connections with the domestic network in order to meet the demand for travel to destinations outside Bali and Java (*Asia Travel Trade* 1989f). However, comments by Jeffrey (1990a: 59) indicated that substantial problems exist with the domestic air services outside the major tourist destinations: 'Woe betide "Let's Go Archipelago!"... if the country's domestic airline, Merpati Nusantara, continues to run as it now does... if travellers really want to "go archipelago", they must do it on government-ordained group packages, which severely limit the choice of islands, or they must be prepared for patience-testing sessions doled out by Merpati employees'.

Difficulties with air transport, as with other tourism infrastructure raises the question of whether Indonesia is trying to do too much too soon (Teh 1989b, c; Teh & Wong 1989). In order to provide the infrastructure required to support the rapid inbound growth rates, the Indonesian Government has actively sought foreign investment. In 1988, overall foreign investment in Indonesia totalled US$4.4 billion, compared with US$1.5 billion in 1987. But of the US$4.4 billion only about US$856 million in joint ventures and Rs1.5 trillion went directly into tourism-related projects (Teh & Wong 1989). Indonesian marketing campaigns have been well supported by the domestic private sector, although substantial concerns have been raised about the long-term availability of funds beyond VIY 1991 and Visit ASEAN Year (Teh 1989c). According to Teh and Wong (1989: 35):

Indonesia is busily courting foreign investors in tourism development to help provide the necessary infrastructure for its burgeoning inbound industry, projected to grow at 15 per cent per annum. But despite the emergence of investment management bodies [and] new banks... Indonesia's blueprint for expansion may be a case of too much too soon.

Although certain sectors, most notably hotels and resorts, have enjoyed an unprecedented wave of investment interest, that phenomena must be weighed against the sobering fact that a resort built in the middle of nowhere with no access roads is useless, as is a hotel in a region lacking air service because there is no airport... Indonesia's biggest handicap in the tourism stakes is its lack of basic infrastructure. An infusion of foreign capital—on its own—is just not enough... (Teh & Wong 1989: 35, 36).

In 1989 Indonesia had 391 classified hotels with 29 253 rooms, out of which 9000 rooms were supplied by the 18 four-star hotels and 11 five-star hotels (Teh 1989b). According to *Asia Travel Trade* (1989d: 21), the international tourists preference in Indonesia 'is for hotels above the three-star category. Out of the 9000 rooms available in Jakarta, only 29% are supplied by the four- to five-star hotels'. Desire for more hotels has led the Government to remove bureaucratic obstructions, relax its foreign investment regulations, expand its joint-venture programmes, ease restrictions of foreign ownership, and actively encourage further domestic and foreign investment, particularly in the light of political turmoil in other South East Asian countries. The major sources of investment in the tourism industry are Japan, Hong Kong, Germany, the USA, the UK, Singapore and South Korea (Teh & Wong 1989). In addition, an education and training programme is being conducted to meet the manpower needs of the industry. For instance, it has been estimated that the hotel sector alone will require at least one million more workers to meet the target of 3.5 million arrivals set for the end of Repelita V in March 1994 (Teh 1990: 31).

Another dimension in the development of the Indonesian tourism industry was the creation in May 1990, of the Indonesia Tourist Promotion Board (ITPB). The ITPB is private sector oriented and features some of the main stakeholders in Indonesia's tourism and hospitality industry plus representatives from other sectors indirectly involved with tourism such as banks and brewing. The ITPB was seen by many in the Indonesian tourism industry as a source of extra funds for the VIY and for longer-term marketing and promotion. In the 1990–1991 financial year (April to March) the Directorate General of Tourism (DGT) had a budget of Rs7.36 billion (US$4 million) of which Rs44.6 million was set aside for Visit Indonesia Year (VIY) events and activities. In addition, the DGT entered into joint VIY marketing and promotional campaigns with Garuda in the USA, Europe, Australia, Japan, ASEAN (mainly Singapore and Malaysia), and new markets such as the Middle East (Teh 1990). The DGT have placed substantial emphasis in their promotional strategies on the development of long-haul markets. In particular, they have focused on three main regions: first, the USA with a Discover Indonesia programme (launched January 1988) and with a festivals promotion programme; second, North East Asia (Korea and Japan), where a special emphasis given to the development of further airlinks and promotion to both the leisure and the business market (the need for language training is regarded as a weak spot in this market); third, Australia and New Zealand, where Garuda has increased flights to Sydney and Melbourne and has developed a link with Auckland.

On a regional basis, the DGT has been promoting the opportunities available for short-term breaks in Indonesia to Singapore and Malaysia. In addition, Bali and Jakarta are increasingly being promoted as convention centres for the Australian and Asian meetings market. However, one of the main features of the campaigns to both the long- and short-haul markets has been the emphasis on Indonesia's culture and environment, and in particular marine and heritage tourism.

Marine and heritage tourism

The image of Indonesia as a tourist destination has traditionally been associated with the 'exotic' tropical island of Bali and 'sun, sand, surf and sea'. However, in recent years, with a more experienced and sophisticated tourism market, Indonesia has been adding value to their existing tourism product by diversifying into 'environmental' and 'heritage' tourism, and into marine-based tourism activities such as yachting, boardsailing and scuba-diving, in particular. One of the main values of marine-based tourism is that it builds on the readily available resources of the Indonesian archipelago and can therefore be developed to take pressure off Bali (Teh 1989e).

Several projects are being developed as part of the emphasis on marine tourism. In the Riau Archipelago (which is a major component of a 'growth triangle' involving Malaysia's Johore state, Indonesia's Riau province and Singapore), the islands of Batam and Bintan are being developed to attract the ASEAN market and international visitors to Singapore. The Tanjun Bintan resort on the north coast of Bintan island, is to comprise five hotels and a number of bungalows providing a total of 2500 rooms when complete. The other facilities in this resort complex include a marina with 100 berths, an amenity centre with shops, restaurants, discotheques, bars and sports facilities, and a jetty for cruise ships. In North Sulawesi, the Manado Bay area is being developed to attract the North American and Japanese markets with 1250 rooms being constructed over the 1989–1994 period and provision for a further 1000 rooms by 1999. Marine features will include a diving centre, sports and recreational facilities, and boats for cruising (Teh 1989a). The Maluku region is being developed to cater for the Australian market with a marine tourism resort being located at the island of Neira in Banda, while a smaller scale project is being constructed in the Riau Archipelago. The impact of these projects on inbound tourist flows will be substantial. According to Teh (1989a: 22): 'Arrivals to the marine project areas are expected to reach a total of 255 000 foreign and 85 500 domestic tourists by 1993, the end of the short-term planning period. It is anticipated that the international tourist flow to the project areas will increase by 10 per cent to 411 000 and domestic arrivals by 5 per cent by the end of the medium-term planning period in 1998/99'.

The Japanese International Co-operation Agency (JICA) has also identified a number of marine tourism related projects to be implemented in the Anyer-Banten region of western Java up to 2010. For example, the Old Banten Site project is concentrated on developing the historic, cultural and religious aspects of Banten Lama, 80 km from Jakarta. The area already attracts more than one million visitors per year, mainly pilgrims, to the Great Mosque and the Chinese Temple. As part of the development, a Heritage Garden is to be constructed which will be designed to introduce visitors to the local history and culture (Teh 1989a).

Banten is seen by some commentators to be an alternative to Bali. According to Wuryastuti Sunario, the Singapore-based regional director of the Indonesia Tourist Promotion Office for ASEAN and Hong Kong: 'We are trying to offer alternatives to Bali which is becoming overcrowded and expensive. Bali's beaches are the island's main attractions. We hope to convince tourists that there are beaches in Indonesia other than in Bali—beaches in an unspoilt area that is not overrun with people. Anyer is such a place' (in Lee 1989: 20). Anyer also has a number of 'heritage' attractions including the Krakatoa Museum and the Ujong Kulong wildlife reserve, home of the rare Java rhinoceros and other indigenous fauna. According to Lee (1989: 20): 'Banten's tourist potential has not been sufficiently exploited; yet the region is rich in natural attractions. Chief of these is Krakatoa...'. The Anyer-Banten area has been attracting backpackers and domestic tourists since the late 1970s but has not been easily accessible to the international market, even though it is relatively close to Jakarta. For example, the Mambruk Beach Resort at Anyer was first built to provide accommodation for expatriates working in a nearby industrial estate but gradually developed into a resort hotel as the project grew, with the lack of a sandy beach being solved by the construction of a lagoon and an adjacent marina. Anyer-Banten region's target markets will be Europe, Australia, and South East Asia, particularly Singapore and Malaysia, and the Jakarta weekend market. However, a key element in the project's success will be the region's ability to take tourists away from Bali (Lee 1989).

Role of Bali—Bali plus?

Bali represents a major problem for Indonesian tourism planners. Bali grew rapidly through the late 1980s. January to October 1988, 'saw an increase of 19.3% in the number of airport arrivals over the same period for 1987, with a total of 290 847. Average occupancy figures for all the deluxe hotels ranged from 80+%–90+% for the second half of 1988' (*Asia Travel Trade* 1989e: 32). Tourism, including craft industries, now contributes approximately 20 per cent of the gross provincial product of Bali (Wall 1993). The enormous growth in demand for rooms on Bali led to large scale construction of new hotels and the extension of existing properties. For instance, in 1991 the number of star rated rooms on the island grew to 4500 from 1745 in late 1988. To many tourists, especially those from Australia and New Zealand, Bali *is* Indonesia. However, inbound tourism to Bali cannot continue to grow at such a rapid rate without placing enormous stress on the physical infrastructure and social fabric of the island. As Wall (1993: 39) reported, 'Problems of coastal erosion, water supply, waste disposal and uneven development are now evident and are likely to increase if tourist arrivals grow as projected and measures are put in place to relieve the pressures'. In order to distribute inbound tourism and its economic benefits more evenly within the country, the Indonesian Government is trying to create a situation in which visitors travel to Bali and then go on to visit other points of Indonesia. One mechanism to achieve this has been to designate tourism regions which are to have priority in the development of their resources. As of 1991, 17 such regions have been designated: Aceh, Bali, Central Java, East Java, Jakarta, Riau, South Sumatra, East Kalimantan, Maluku, East and West Nusa Tenggara, North and South Sulawesi, North Sumatra, West Sumatra, West Java and Yogyakarta. In addition, the government has designated a number of tourism development corporations (TDCs) to plan and co-ordinate tourism development at select locations. The first corporation at Nusa Dua in Bali serves as the model for the seven other TDCs (Lombok, Lampung, Biak, Batam, Belitung, Bintang in the Riau Archipelago and Baturaden in Central Java. However, while the Bali TDC is a state corporation funded from the central government, the new TDCs are partnerships between the private sector and the provincial governments (Economist Intelligence Unit 1991). Given the current pattern of tourism development in Indonesia, it is therefore likely that by the late 1990s, Bali will still be a destination in its own right but will also serve as the distribution point to tourist destinations in other parts of the country and South East Asia.

The impacts of tourism

The Indonesian Government's plan to control tourism development in Bali is indicative of the realisation that unless natural resources are protected, the industry will not be sustainable. For example, the Minister for Population and Environment, Emil Salim, has warned the people of Lake Tobar in northern Sumatra that they must stop burning the nearby forests and polluting the lake with household wastes or the tourists will stop coming. However, the problem facing the protection of the Indonesian environment is not really lack of awareness or ability to prevent pollution, it is enforcement. As the 1988 United Nations Development Programme report on marine tourism in Indonesia warned: 'If garbage, foul odours and damaged nature are not prevented, tourists will leave and the investments in the resorts will be wasted' (in Gelston 1989: 57). Tourism developers are already required to conduct an environmental assessment of their project which must demonstrate that the project is economically and technically feasible and that it will have minimal negative impacts. In addition, the establishment of an environmental protection agency is also expected to have a substantial effect on the environmental quality of tourism destinations. However, in the longer-term, as with many other countries in the region, it will be the implementation of laws and regulations that will be critical in determining the environmental well-being of tourism regions.

The future

We must take into consideration the impact that any tourism development will have on our people and culture. An investment which is not supported and supportive of society becomes counter-productive. It is always in the back of our minds, for example, when we set out to develop Bali—we want tourism but we don't want to destroy the cultural fabric. So in development, socio-cultural factors come first, not economic. If the locals don't want tourists, we don't develop. It's as simple as that.

The question now is, how many tourists can Bali carry before it is destroyed? We have to look at the strength and culture of the society. Therefore, the development plan has to be such that it does not jar with the values of the society where development is taking place.

Tourist development must also take into consideration the environment, be it nature or culture because these are tourist assets and they have to be treated as such.

Therefore, we are looking for planned growth rather than a boost in growth which can get out of hand. Growth may be slow, too slow for us marketing people but it prolongs the life cycle and supports the progress and development of the community for which it serves (Wuryastuti Sunario in Teh & Wong 1989: 39).

Indonesia has experienced very large inbound growth rates in recent years. Growth has been centred on Bali and parts of Java. However, the Indonesian Government is now attempting to diversify both the tourism products that it offers and the resort destinations that overseas tourists visit. As the country's oil, gas and timber supplies dwindle, increasing emphasis will be placed on inbound tourism. Nevertheless, despite tourism's economic significance, the sustainability of tourism development in the country will depend on two factors: first, protection of the environment; second, political stability.

As noted above, Indonesia is attaching great importance on the preservation of its environment for tourism. While there has been criticism of the logging of Indonesian rainforest by conservation groups such as Greenpeace, the government has been more receptive to establishing conservation measures in tourist areas. Marine and heritage tourism rely on sound environmental management practices. Cultural practices also need to be sustained as overseas travellers seek authenticity in their tourist experiences. However, the problem for Indonesia will be not enacting the required legislation, but in implementing it on the ground. Therefore, in the environmental arena the greatest challenge for the government will be in ensuring that adequate environmental standards are developed and then policed.

As with many countries in the region, political stability plays a great part in determining the attractiveness of a country for tourists and for investors. As Teh and Wong observed (1989: 37), 'the growth of tourism is largely contingent on the country's stability, the factor which most affects its investment prospects. The relative calm characterised by President Suharto's five terms may be diluted as opposition to a sixth term mounts... Suharto's term expires in 1993, which might also explain Indonesia's eagerness to lure foreign investors'. At the time of writing, President Suharto has made it clear that he will stand for another term. Nevertheless, questions are increasingly being asked about the nature of post-Suharto Indonesia. Will Islamic fundamentalism increase? Will the military take an even stronger role in the running of the country? How will independence movements in East Timor, Irian Jaya and Aceh react to the end of the Suharto era? All these questions will have a bearing on tourism development at the turn of the century. Nevertheless, one thing is certain, tourism investment in much needed infrastructure and the consequent attraction of the country as a destination will disappear without stable government.

Indonesia is at the crossroads in its tourism development. Continued economic growth will see the emergence of a substantial outbound travel market by the end of the century. The economic significance of inbound travel will probably increase as oil and gas exports decline and as tourist flows become more dispersed throughout the archipelago. Bali will continue its present role as the major tourist destination but will also gradually become one of the major air transport hubs in the region. Given the maintenance of political stability and the preservation of its environment and culture, Indonesia appears set to become a major force in South East Asian tourism.

Malaysia

Tourism is emerging as a major industry in Malaysia. The hosting of Visit Malaysia Year in 1990 signalled the seriousness with which the government viewed tourism as a mechanism for regional economic development and a source of foreign exchange. Malaysia has experienced a strong rate of growth in GDP in the early 1990s of between 5 per cent and 8 per cent, with an estimate of 8.8 per cent for 1992. Given the desire of the government to maintain high rates of growth in order to boost economic development prospects towards the turn of the century, increased attention has been paid to inbound tourism development, particularly as the prospect of declining oil reserves and 'fluctuating prices of major export products like rubber and palm oil [give] added urgency to tourism development' (*Asia Travel Trade* 1990n: 32).

In Malaysia official response towards tourism has been substantially influenced by the perceived conflicts that occur between secular tourism and Islamic values (Din 1988, 1989). Nevertheless, tourism is seen in a generally positive light, particularly in terms of its potential economic and employment contributions, although there was recognition that a community's character could be disrupted (Ap *et al.* 1991).

The potential of tourism to contribute to economic development is illustrated in Table 4.3 which presents the tourist receipts for Peninsula Malaysia for 1985–1990. In 1985 tourism contributed 1543.1 million ringgit to Peninsula Malaysia. In Visit Malaysia Year (1990), tourist receipts for Peninsula Malaysia had increased almost three-fold to 4473.3 million ringgit (approximately US$1658 million) from 7 079 107 tourist arrivals. The 1990 figure is even more significant when the tourism earnings for East Malaysia (Sabah and Sarawak) are added. In 1990 tourism receipts for Sabah increased to Rgt 129.1 million from Rgt 94.4 million, while Sarawak's tourism receipts increased from Rgt 140.6 million in 1989 to Rgt 201.2 million in 1990 (Tourist Development Corporation Malaysia 1991:

Table 4.3: Tourist receipts for Peninsula Malaysia, 1985–1990

Year	Tourist Receipts (Ringgit millions)
1985	1 543.1
1986	1 669.2
1987	1 795.1
1988	2 011.7
1989	2 802.7
1990	4 473.3

Ringgit M$2.698=US$1 as at 21 November 1990

Source: Tourist Development Corporation Malaysia 1991: 11

15). In 1992 Malaysia was targeting eight million arrivals and receipts of US$3 billion, while for 1994 a target of 13 million arrivals and receipts of US$4.5 billion has been set (Astbury 1992).

Since 1990 Malaysia has had a surplus on its travel account and is keen to ensure that inbound tourism continues to contribute to the country's development. Prime Minister Mahathir Mohamad has set a target of 20 million tourist arrivals by the year 2000, representing an annual growth in arrivals of close to 14 per cent (Astbury 1992). However, as the following discussion will indicate, such high growth rates will not be easy to sustain, requiring as they do substantial amounts of infrastructure development, particularly in terms of transport and accommodation, and an ongoing effort to ensure that environmental controls are implemented. The success of Visit Malaysia Year, while laying a firm basis for tourism development in the 1990s, will need to be carefully nurtured during the decade if growth is to be maintained.

The outbound market

Although government emphasis has been placed on inbound tourism, the rapid economic development of the country has meant that there is a growing outbound market (Table 4.4). The relative weakness of the Malaysian ringgit (M$) has meant that outbound travel is an extremely price sensitive market, with rising costs in other Asian markets leading to potential outbound tourists delaying overseas travel and/or visiting domestic tourist destinations. Indeed, with those who do travel, evidence suggests that there is a preference for multi-city itineraries because they believe that they are getting better value for money (*Asia Travel Trade* 1990n).

The majority of Malaysia's outbound travel is within the ASEAN region to Singapore, Thailand and Indonesia. Because of the multi-racial composition of Malaysian society, China and India are major long-haul destinations. In May 1989, following reductions in regional tensions, the Government relaxed travel restrictions for China-bound travellers which significantly expands the number of Malaysian Chinese who are now able to visit China on social and VFR excursions (*Asia Travel Trade* 1990n). The substantial number of Malaysian Indians also means that there is a strong

Table 4.4: Malaysian outbound travel, 1985–1990

Year	Total ('000s)
1985	1 837
1986	2 116
1987	2 439
1988	2 974
1989	2 828
1990	2 995

Source: Tourist Development Corporation of Malaysia in New Zealand Tourism Board 1992e: 42

interest in visiting India, especially Kashmir. However, ethnic and religious unrest in India has meant that growth in this market has been severely limited. Other destinations increasingly promoting themselves to Malaysian outbound travellers include Australia (especially Western Australia and the Northern Territory), New Zealand and Sri Lanka, particularly in the casino, business travel, and leisure markets. However, a major problem facing the development of outbound travel to these, and other, destinations is a shortage of air seats for group bookings because of the strength of the inbound market.

The inbound market

Malaysia has experienced substantial growth in inbound arrivals over the past decade. As discussed above, the Prime Minister has set a target of 14 per cent per annum growth in inbound arrivals until the year 2000. Table 4.5 illustrates Malaysia inbound tourist arrivals from 1985 to 1990. Visitor arrivals to Peninsula Malaysia in 1990 were 7.079 million compared to 4.5 million in 1989. These figures represent an increase of 55.5 per cent compared to 34.9 per cent in the previous year. In 1990 Sabah recorded 65 516 arrivals representing a 19.7 per cent increase over the previous year's figure of 54 731, while Sarawak recorded a 39.4 per cent increase from 238 197 in 1989 to 332 149 in 1990 (Tourist Development Corporation Malaysia 1991).

The Tourist Development Corporation of Malaysia (TDC) is responsible for all government tourism-related activities and is the agency charged with marketing Malaysia overseas. In terms of inbound tourism, target markets are broken down according to a variety of factors including (*Asia Travel Trade* 1990n):

- economy of generating region
- airline capacity between generating region and Malaysia
- strength of generating region's currency compared to that of Malaysia
- government policies on travel restrictions
- consumer response to TDC marketing activities.

Following its market research activities, the Corporation has identified

Table 4.5: Tourist arrivals in Malaysia 1985–1990	
Year	Total
1985	3 109 106
1986	3 217 462
1987	3 358 983
1988	3 623 636
1989	4 846 320
1990	7 476 722

Source: Tourist Development Corporation Malaysia 1991: 11

the following primary and secondary target markets for its promotional activities:

- Primary target markets: Singapore, Japan, Australia, UK, Germany, USA, Thailand, Hong Kong, Taiwan, South Korea.
- Secondary target markets: France, Italy, New Zealand, Canada, Scandinavia, Switzerland.

The breakdown of inbound tourists for 1990 for Peninsular Malaysia by country/market is presented in Table 4.6. ASEAN visitors contribute around 75 per cent of total arrivals to Malaysia and, given the economic growth of the region, will continue to be the mainstay of the Malaysian tourism industry. According to *Asia Travel Trade* (1990n) there are substantial differences between the behaviours of the Asian and non-Asian markets. Asians are sightseers who tend to stay two to three days, while Western visitors average around a week with relaxation, especially at beach resorts, as a major travel motivation. Group tours still dominate the Asian market although there is an increase in FIT travel and homestays. Furthermore, the markets are also spatially differentiated with the Genting Highlands being a primary area for the Asian market, especially Taiwan, Hong Kong, and Thailand; the Kuala Lumpur–Malacca region attracts the Japanese, United States and Australian markets; while Penang is a primary destination for Japanese honeymooners and the Australian market (*Asia Travel Trade* 1990n).

Although Visit Malaysia Year (VMY) was the catalyst for the very large increase in visitor numbers in 1990, expectations are that high rates of

Table 4.6: Tourist arrivals in Peninsula Malaysia by market, 1990

Origin	%
ASEAN	73.8
Japan	6.8
Taiwan	2.6
UK	2.6
Australia	2.0
USA	2.0
India	1.5
Hong Kong	1.4
Germany	1.0
Korea	0.8
France	0.5
Others	5.1

Note: percentages have been rounded; total tourist arrivals: 7 079 107

Source: Tourist Development Corporation Malaysia 1991: 12

growth will continue. Nevertheless, a number of issues are raised by Malaysia's inbound targets, particularly the attraction of tourists after Visitor Years are completed and the provision of adequate infrastructure to support tourism development.

Visit Malaysia Year 1990

I guess people will be drawn to a certain country during a particular year provided they know enough of it and early enough—Tunku Iskandar (in Teh 1989g: 55). Visit Malaysia Year 1990, another of the ASEAN clone 'Visit' years, has been well-received by the tourism and travel industry as a gimmick to sell Malaysia (Teh 1989g: 56).

Visitor years are a feature of ASEAN tourism. Fired by the success of the Visit Thailand year in 1987 (Rurakdee 1991) the Malaysian Tourist Development Corporation designated 1990 as Visit Malaysia Year. Visitor Years are an excellent means to raise the awareness of a destination in the international market-place provided not too many other countries in the region are attempting a similar strategy. According to Mokhti Abas, President of the Malaysian Association of Tours and Travel Agents (MATTA) (in Teh 1989g: 56), 'The VMY concept is good for boosting the country's image in view of the common norm of saying that Malaysia is not very well known. This well help to elevate the awareness of Malaysia in the tourist markets'.

Visitor Years provide an umbrella for a range of festivals and events. They present an opportunity to repackage existing events and to develop new ones. In the case of VMY, a total of 107 events ranging from festivals, sports tournaments and cultural shows were drawn up for the whole year. The national day celebration on 31 August was chosen as the anchor event, while individual Malaysian states also had their own programmes with local key events being the birthday celebrations of the states' respective rulers and governors (Teh 1989g: 60).

The promotion of VMY was well co-ordinated. The general promotion and publicity campaigns for VMY started with the launch of the VMY logo and publicity campaign in November 1988. However, the actual promotion by overseas operators and tour wholesalers did not commence until the calendar of events was released in April 1989 (Teh 1989g: 55). Profile for VMY in the ASEAN countries and in the broader international arena was also assisted by the hosting of the South East Asian Games in August and the Commonwealth Heads of Government (CHOGM) meeting in October 1989.

Despite fears that increases in hotel accommodation prices would detract visitors, VMY was an immediate success. The Tourist Development Corporation estimated 'that 2.3 million tourists arrived in Malaysia between January and June [1990], a 15 per cent increase over the nearly 2 million tourists recorded for the same period [in 1989]. Tourism revenue between January and May [1990] was estimated at M$1.9 billion, a 72.7 percent increase over the M$1.1 billion collected over the same period [in

1989]' (*Asia Travel Trade* 1990n: 27). As discussed above, the total arrivals and revenues for the year represented a substantial increase on the 1989 totals. However, inbound tourism and revenues late in the year were undoubtedly affected by the Gulf crisis.

After VMY?

Far-sighted planning is needed. We can ride on the VMY in 1991 and ride on the Visit ASEAN Year 1992 in 1993. The question is what will happen in 1994?—Ivo Nekvapil, Pan Pacific Kuala Lumpur General Manager (in Teh 1989g: 59).

VMY was an undoubted success. Nevertheless, substantial problems emerge in trying to maintain profile in the market-place while also developing the appropriate infrastructure. One short-term solution is to host another Visitor Year and this has been done in 1992 with Visit ASEAN Year. However, in the longer term destinations need to develop a tourist product that is sustainable in the market and which fits in with the existing resource base. The solution for Malaysia was to focus on the marketing of its cultural and natural attractions 'in keeping with current world interest in the Green movement and conservation' (*Asia Travel Trade* 1990n: 23).

Malaysia has adopted a strategy which focuses on its competitive advantages in the regional and world tourism markets. This approach has been noted by Datuk Ng, Deputy Culture and Tourism Minister, 'Malaysia should optimise what it has—its natural products, friendly people, a good portion of English-speaking population, and a variety of cultures and food' (in Teh 1989g: 64). As Badri Masri, Director-General of the Malaysian Tourist Development Corporation, states 'Our marketing strategy or gimmick is to focus on natural attractions. That does not mean all tourists come here solely for nature. We use natural attractions to draw their attention to come here, but I am sure that once they are here, they will also go for our cultural and shopping facilities' (in *Asia Travel Trade* 1990n: 23). However, as *Asia Travel Trade* has observed Malaysia's motives in highlighting its natural and cultural resources are grounded more in reality than in idealism and altruistic environmental concern. 'We cannot sell our night-life, which is not as strong as Hong Kong and Singapore. Thus we have to develop on something that we are strong at, and in this case [that's] Malaysia's natural heritage' (Azmun Harun, Malaysian Association of Hotels President, in *Asia Travel Trade* 1990n: 23).

The push for 'green tourism' by Malaysia would appear to be appropriate given the country's tourism resources. However, a number of issues emerge in the selection of such a marketing and development strategy, particularly the problem of achieving a balance between conservation and tourism. Is the infrastructure in parks and reserves adequate to allow greater visitation and to maintain heritage values? There has been an increase in lodging facilities at national parks, although the siting of such facilities may impinge on conservation goals. Therefore, as the next section discusses, the provision of appropriate infrastructure will be critical to the success of Malaysia's post-VMY strategy.

Tourism development

In order to encourage the development of tourism infrastructure, the Central and State Governments of Malaysia offer a number of generous financial incentives for investment in the accommodation and tourism sectors. The supply of hotel rooms has not kept up with the growth in inbound and domestic tourism, as indicated by the increase in average hotel occupancy rates (Table 4.7). In 1991 the number of international standard rooms had grown to approximately 47 500 (Teh & Masterton 1990). However, according to Astbury (1992) in order to host 20 million tourists in the year 2000, Malaysia will need 180 000 hotel rooms—over triple the present number. Furthermore, according to Badri Masri, TDC Director-General, 'Our marketing trend is for the mass tourists, by going through the travel trade especially for new markets and directly to consumers. We are also not catering for the upmarket tourists only, but we practise non-discriminatory tourism where even budget travellers and backpackers are welcome' (in Teh & Masterton 1990: 41). Therefore, there is a need to develop properties which cater to the budget and FIT travellers and, as Teh and Masterton observed, such a development would assist the growing self-drive market, particularly in the domestic sector.

Air accessibility is also a crucial issue in Malaysian tourism. The national carrier, Malaysian Airlines (MAS), expanded its capacity on international services to 102 515 seats per week in 1991, while domestic capacity increased to 128 056 seats. Nevertheless, substantial capacity problems remain which require the government to allow more foreign airlines to service Malaysia's air routes. Ground handling facilities at Kuala Lumpur are also generally inadequate to meet the growth in visitor arrivals and will require substantial upgrading as the decade progresses. There is a shortage

Table 4.7: Malaysian hotel supply and average occupancy rates, 1985–1990

Year	Hotel Room Supply	Average Hotel Occupancy Rates (%)
1985	35 720	50.1
1986	38 178	50.9
1987	39 455	55.8
1988	40 760	62.2
1989	43 149	66.9
1990	45 032	72.9

Source: Tourist Development Corporation Malaysia 1991: 10

in connecting services on the feeder routes to Thailand and Singapore. In the case of Singapore, many Malaysian visitors use Singapore as either their entry or departure point, and the growth of Singapore as the main air transport hub in South East Asia will ensure that this role continues. One aspect of the relationship between Singapore and Malaysia is the increasing integration of the Johore state economy with that of Singapore. Transport connections between the two are being substantially upgraded in order to cater for the expanding flow of tourists and business between the two countries. For example, Desaru in the south east corner of Johore is being developed as one of the largest single resort destinations in South East Asia. A M$1.3 billion project has Japanese, United States, and Malaysian finance with the Japanese International Co-operation Agency (JICA) identifying the region as having the potential to become Malaysia's premier tourist resort (Teh 1989h).

Environmental concerns

The rapidly-growing tourism industry and the marketing focus on heritage has meant that the Malaysian Government is paying increasing attention to environmental protection, particularly in coastal areas where pollution and environmental degradation has been most visible to tourists. For example, facilities or hotels with more than 80 rooms and the development of recreational facilities on islands in waters which are gazetted as national marine parks are regulated under the Environmental Quality (Environmental Impact Assessment) Order 1987 under the Environmental Quality Act of 1974. In addition, developers have to submit environmental impact assessments to the Department of Environment who must give their approval before the project can go ahead (Teh 1989h). The Environmental Orders are a response to faecal coliform contamination of coastal waters near resort developments. 'Traditionally, developers have built hotels along beaches, then installed a big septic tank which emptied sewage into the seas' (*Asia Travel Trade* 1990n). Penang, in particular, has been severely criticised for its sewage problems, but a new centralised sewage plant in the Batu Ferringhi area will undoubtedly assist in improving the image of the region as a tourist destination. In addition, the Malaysian Government has established over twenty-five marine parks and protected areas since 1985 in order to restrict the illegal collection of coral and coral shells (Teh 1989h).

Despite the positive steps the government has taken towards environmental protection, the country's federal system of government has meant that environmental responsibilities are dispersed between the various levels of government. There is no single environmental authority in Malaysia empowered to make decisions regarding the environmental dimensions of tourism development. 'Authority for various natural resources is haphazardly divided under different government umbrellas and respective state authorities. Forest parks, for example, fall under the jurisdiction of the national Wildlife Department. Land matters come under the state authorities while marine life and fisheries is overseen by the Fisheries Department' (*Asia Travel Trade* 1990n: 30)

The future

For Malaysia, where tourism is an emerging industry and natural assets are plentiful, the prospects for sustained tourism development are good. This is provided adequate attention is paid towards planning and management of tourism—Peter Ho Yueh Chuen, Assistant Director-General, Department of the Environment (in Asia Travel Trade 1990n: 29).

Malaysia has set itself an ambitious growth target in inbound tourism. The rapid economic development of the ASEAN region and the Pacific Rim does mean that such an objective is obtainable. However, the major obstacle to continued high growth rates will be the provision of infrastructure, particularly accommodation and transport, and the maintenance of environmental quality. The latter issue is especially problematic. Prime Minister Mahathir Mohamad's target of 20 million tourist arrivals by the year 2000 will place enormous strain on the heritage tourism resources of Malaysia. Undoubtedly, the tourism potential of Sabah and Sarawak will be developed, relieving some strain from Peninsula Malaysia, but the Peninsula will still be the main destination for inbound travellers. Malaysia's domestic tourism industry will also have grown substantially, placing even further stress on infrastructure and resources. At such high rates of inbound travel growth, the present favourable attitudes towards tourism in some communities may be eroded. Therefore, Malaysia will have to carefully manage its tourism development, continue to encourage investment, and evaluate the cost and benefits of growth in tourism numbers.

The Philippines

From being regarded as one of the wealthiest Asian countries during the 1950s, the Philippines has shuddered in economic, social, environmental and political crises over the past two decades. Natural disasters, rampant political corruption, and poor economic growth has meant that the country has slumped substantially in economic and social indices. Since the early 1970s international tourism has been seen as both a contributor to the country's ills, through sex tourism, corruption and the provision of tacit support for authoritiarian rule; and as a solution, because of tourism's ability to generate foreign exchange. As the Philippines negotiates the 1990s, tourism has become a prominent component in the country's planned economic revival. However, the task is substantial. When President Corazon Aquino came to power in 1986, she 'inherited a bankrupt nation with a negative growth rate, a $26 billion foreign debt, 70 per cent of the population at or below the poverty line, and a country that lost between 10 and 20 billion dollars to the systematic plundering of the Marcos government' (Richter 1989: 51). Five years on, the level of foreign debt has hardly changed. Now, under the presidency of Fidel Ramos, the Philippines is launching an ambitious 20 year master plan for tourism which has led to a renewed optimism about the direction of the industry and its potential for growth (Jaleco 1992). However, as the following discussion will demonstrate the success of the plan will greatly depend on the degree to which the country can overcome the unwanted legacies of the Marcos years.

Tourism under Marcos

No regime has more blatantly used tourism policy for political leverage than that of ex-President Marcos of the Philippines. Although tourism contributed to many of the regime's political and economic objectives, it achieved those gains at enormous cost to the Filipino economy. As time went on, the insensitive development of tourism in the midst of deteriorating economic and social conditions spawned a counter use of tourism—opposition violence against the tourist industry. Thus one finds in the case of the Philippines a microcosm of the political uses and abuses of tourism (Richter 1989: 52).

Ferdinand Marcos was elected President in November 1965. He won a second term in office four years later. On 21 September 1972, he imposed martial law declaring that the country was faced with a serious communist insurgency. Until the declaration of martial law, tourism had been a low priority of the government. However, 'within eight months of the declaration of martial law, tourism was a priority industry eligible for a variety of tax incentives and customs concessions. The regime had set up its first Department of Tourism [DoT] by May 11, 1973' (Richter 1989: 54-5). Several reasons can be provided for the Marcos Government's new found interest in tourism. First, tourism could be utilised by the regime to create a favourable image of the country and the Marcos Government for international tourists and for foreign governments. Second, international tourist visitation could be held up by the regime to be an endorsement of its activities and of martial law in particular, thereby providing legitimacy for its undemocratic activities. Third, tourism was a means by which Marcos could provide rewards to his supporters by giving them favourable considerations in development projects and by providing government finance. Finally, the President's wife, Imelda Marcos, had her own ambitions regarding the development of the Philippines as an international tourist destination.

In an effort to maintain the legitimacy of the Marcos regime with overseas governments and investors, the government launched into tourism development with unbridled enthusiasm. For example, the regime used such events as the Miss Universe contest and the 'Thriller in Manila' world heavyweight title fight between Mohammed Ali and Joe Frazier to improve the international image of the country. The hosting of the 1976 International Monetary Fund (IMF)–World Bank Conference led the regime to fast-track the construction of twelve luxury hotels, the Philippine

International Convention Center, and the Philippine Center for International Trade and Exhibitions, all for the conference and all at enormous cost to the government. As Richter (1989: 56) commented: 'The tantalizing prospect of hosting 5000 VIPs, even for just a week led to a rush to complete 12 luxury hotels within 18 months, though the tourism master plan had not expected such accommodation needs for at least a decade'. The size of the government commitment to the project was enormous (US\$410–US\$545 million) and was completely out of proportion to either the infrastructure requirements of the Filipino tourism industry or the economic and social needs of the country. The expenditure on hotel financing was between thirty and forty times the amount that the Marcos Government had spent on public housing. 'The relative size of this commitment ... was between one-seventh and one-fifth of the government's total proposed 1976 expenditure of \$3.05 billion. It was more than the nation's total 1976 borrowing from the World Bank of \$315 million' (Richter 1989: 57). Nevertheless, the conference was a political success for the Marcos Government and economic and military aid to the country was increased from both the USA and the IMF–World Bank.

The 1980 American Society of Travel Agents (ASTA) Conference in Manila which had over 6000 delegates in attendance was also seen as a means to enhance the profile of the Marcos Government in the domestic and international media. However, just minutes after Marcos had given the opening address, a bomb exploded, missing the President but injuring several delegates. The ASTA Conference caused irreparable damage to both the standing of the Marcos regime in the USA but also the attraction of the Philippines as a destination. Tourist arrivals dropped by 10 per cent immediately following the bombing protest and continued to decline for the remainder of the Marcos reign. This trend was exacerbated by the assassination of opposition leader Benigno 'Ninoy' Aquino in late 1983 at Manila International Airport in front of the world's media (Richter 1989).

Tourism policy post-Marcos

Whether the Philippines will be able to build a solid tourist record... is still open to question. The Aquino government has had to retrieve tourism policy from its disastrous and expensive excesses and recast it according to the needs and budget of the impoverished nation. This it has done with flair, taste, and imagination (Richter 1989: 81).

Upon assuming power in 1986, President Corazon Aquino also gave tourism a central role in the country's economic development. Aquino had two main political motives in promoting tourism. First, she needed to reassure countries such as the USA and Japan that there would be no major policy reversals in her government's economic planning which would damage overseas economic interests, thereby guaranteeing the continuing supply of aid and investment (Richter 1989). Second, the foreign exchange that tourism can supply was much needed for the country's economic development and in the repayment of foreign debt.

Under the Aquino Government, the Department of Tourism set about building on the country's existing natural and cultural resources and many empty hotels in order to attract foreign visitors. However, two of the most financially lucrative markets under Marcos were curtailed by Aquino. First, there was a major crackdown on sex tourism. Second, no new casinos were established under Aquino. The latter is especially notable as the country's eight casinos, operated by the Philippine Gaming and Amusement Corporation were the third leading revenue-generating agency of the Government (P2.5 billion in 1988) with 70 per cent of casino earnings from foreign players, mainly Japanese, Hong Kong and Taiwanese visitors (Blanco 1989).

In order to attract more foreign visitors, the Department of Tourism provided incentives to both existing and new hotels and established a five year tourism development programme from 1989 to 1993 (*Asia Travel Trade* 1989g: 30) with the goals of increasing

- tourist arrivals from 1.04 million in 1988 to 3.5 million in 1993
- tourism receipts from US$1.4 billion in 1988 to US$8.7 billion in 1993
- average tourism expenditure from US$115.65 per day in 1988 to US$186.26 in 1993.

Nevertheless, such predications were dependent on the perception of the political stability of the country.

In 1989 visitor arrivals topped 1.2 million, with visitor expenditure of US$1.7 billion. However, the coup attempt of December 1990 crippled the tentative recovery of the Philippines tourism industry which had already suffered the image problems associated with six coup attempts in the previous three years. Because of fighting, 1600 guests had to be evacuated from their hotels. The Philippines could not live up to the images of the Department of Tourism's 'Fiesta islands' promotional campaign. In addition, 'The national carrier, Philippine Airlines, estimates it lost 135 million pesos (US$6million) between 1 and 12 December, when Manila airport was closed and domestic commercial flights were grounded because of the fighting between government and rebel forces' (Robinson 1990: 19).

A new direction for tourism?

Even with its political problems, the Philippines has had approximately one million visitors a year since 1989. Tourism is a substantial contributor to the country's economy. In 1991 tourism generated gross revenues of US$1.4 billion, employed 2.47 per cent of the labour force and contributed 5 per cent to the country's Gross Domestic Product. Out of every tourist dollar spent in the country, 62 cents is retained. Nevertheless, there are major problems, including the need to upgrade Manila international airport, and a shortage of government funds for infrastructure development (Lim 1992).

Tourism development in the Philippines is now guided by a 20 year master plan completed in 1991. Funded by the UN Development Programme and executed by the WTO and the Department of Tourism, the plan has been given the support of President Fidel Ramos. As with many other governments in the Asia Pacific region, the Philippines is considering corporatising the Department of Tourism and focussing its activities on destination and product development, marketing and promotional activities. Funding for such a corporation is unclear given the poor state of government finances, but funding possibilities include profits from government duty free shops, a proportion of travel and hotel room taxes, and possibly through the selling off of state tourism assets. However, the significance of tourism to the Philippines is perhaps indicated by a proposal to attach the new corporation to the office of the president.

The key elements of the master plan are to improve the country's image overseas, and make better use of existing facilities and infrastructure within the framework of a deregulated civil aviation and generous incentives for overseas investors. A total of P52 billion (US$2 billion) is required to implement the plan, including P22.8 billion (US$912 million) on accommodation, P18 billion (US$720 million) on infrastructure, P5.6 billion (US$224 million) on transport, and P5.4 billion (US$216 million) on education and training, and other programmes (Lim 1992). The visitor arrival targets under the plan are far more realistic than the goals of the 1989 plan discussed above, and have been set at 1.5 million in 1993, 1.7 million in 1996 and 5.3 million in the year 2010.

The future

The future of tourism in the Philippines is tied up in its short- and long-term political stability. The country desperately needs stability in order to attract foreign investment with which to establish the required tourism infrastructure and also to improve the battered image of the country in the international market-place. Nature has been cruel to the Philippines in recent years in the form of typhoons, earthquakes and volcanic eruptions, all of which have further reduced the nation's tourism. Nevertheless the climate, culture and natural landscape does make it attractive to overseas leisure tourists. The days of the Philippines being regarded as a major sex tourism destination fortunately appear over. However, the fundamental inequalities that exist between classes and regions and which force people into prostitution need to be addressed before sex tourism can be extinguished. Therefore, if the present master tourism plan can be effectively implemented, tourism may become a major contributor to the reconstruction of the Filipino economy and to a stable, peaceful society.

Thailand: lotus blossom or wilted flower?

Thailand, a country bursting with rapid economic expansion, stands at a cross-roads as its policymakers come to grips with major economic and social changes. These changes are fundamental and in time will have profound effects not only on the tourism industry but the society as a whole.

Its transformation from an agricultural to an industrial society is already having a deep and widespread impact on its economic and social infrastructure. Thailand has become one of the newly industrialized countries (NIC) of Asia and it is now having to bear the price of economic success—congested city roads, increasing pollution and galloping property prices (Corben & Robinson 1990: 16).

Thailand, one of the fastest growing economies and tourist destinations of South East Asia in the 1980s, faces major problems in the 1990s. These include slowing growth and environmental and social problems that must be overcome if development is to be sustained. These concerns have only been exacerbated by the first ever annual decrease in foreign arrivals in 1991 (Hail 1992a). Therefore, fears exist that Thailand may be following a boom and bust pattern of development. According to Corben (1990e: 35), the two years of rapid growth with over 20 per cent growth rates in visitor arrivals which followed Visit Thailand Year 1987 may 'dissolve into a painful hangover of the 1990s'. The acute hotel shortage of 1988, the 25 per cent average increase in tariffs in 1989, and the massive hotel development which commenced in 1989, may lead to an oversupply in the early 1990s which although not necessarily leading to a slump will at least mean a period of lower growth and lower profitability (*Asia Travel Trade* 1990m; Corben 1990e; Corben & Robinson 1990). 'Underlying the "rates bonanza" is mounting unease, driven by the current wave of hotel construction in Bangkok and major resort areas of Thailand, that the high demand for tourist accommodation and facilities cannot climb much further' (Robinson 1989b). In 1989, it appeared that the Thai Board of Investment (BOI) was going to cut investment privileges in Bangkok and other locations. However, the BOI reversed its stance and in March 1990, approved twelve first-class hotel projects for Bangkok, compared to eleven major projects for the whole of 1989 (Corben & Robinson 1990: 18).

The issue of the supply of hotel accommodation is only one component of the difficulties inherent in providing appropriate levels of infrastructure in a rapidly growing economy. As a report by the United Nation's Economic and Social Commission for Asia and Pacific (ESCAP) pointed out, Thailand 'has paid a price for success, which has come too quickly and almost unexpectedly... As the "Land of Smiles" is beginning to learn, beside billions of baht in foreign exchange, tourists also leave a multitude of problems' (in Corben & Robinson 1990: 16), including prostitution, drug addiction, AIDS, erosion of traditional values, increases in the cost of living, unequal income distribution, rapid increases in land prices in some locations, pollution, and environmental degradation. The following section will examine the various issues which have emerged in Thai tourism in the last decade and will discuss the possibilities of the country avoiding boom and bust development and establishing a sustainable tourism industry.

The outbound market

An average GDP growth in Thailand of 9.95 per cent between 1985 and 1991 has created a new middle class with increased income and leisure time. The development of a consumer society has lead to substantial increases in the number of Thais travelling overseas and their frequency of travel. Between 1985 and 1991, Thai outbound travel grew at an average of 10 per cent per annum. In 1989, 800 658 Thais travelled overseas; by 1991, the figure had reached 967 640 (New Zealand Tourism Board 1992b). The Government's abandonment of a 1000 baht (US$40) exit fee may spur growth even further but the major determining factor will probably be the cost of airfares.

As in most Asian countries, older travellers (over 35) tend to travel in groups while younger travellers increasingly travel as individuals. For short-haul trips of three or four days, Thais travel to Hong Kong and Singapore, while for long-haul trips, Thais travel to Europe and the USA although Australia, Canada, and New Zealand are becoming increasingly popular (*Asia Travel Trade* 1990k: 45).

The inbound market

The tourist image of Thailand was transformed in the 1980s. In the 1970s and early 1980s, Thailand was perceived by outsiders as an exotic back-packers' paradise of padi fields, Buddhist temples, and cheap accommodation. At the beginning of the 1990s, Thailand appealed to substantially wealthier tourists, incentive travellers, and the convention market. The number of four- and five-star hotels has rapidly increased together with golf courses and resort development. For example, Pattaya is being developed as a mega-resort which caters for business people, budget groups, and the elderly as well as those visitors who normally travel 'to a destination traditionally associated with little more than broads, bars and beaches' (Teh *et al.* 1989: 39).

Table 4.8 shows the growth in tourist arrivals in Thailand between 1985 and 1990 along with tourist expenditure. Table 4.9 breaks down the figures for 1989 and 1990 by market share. Malaysia is Thailand's largest source of visitor arrivals, with many travelling by road to the Thai province of Songkhla. Of the non-ASEAN countries, Japan (11.99 per cent), Taiwan (9.08 per cent) and the UK (6.01 per cent) rank as the most important, with Australia, Germany, the USA and Hong Kong all having significant market shares.

The Tourism Authority of Thailand (TAT) is expecting to more than double the 1990 figure of 5.3 million visitor arrivals over the present decade. According to Corben (1990e: 39–40), 'In the year 2000, about 12

Table 4.8: Tourist arrivals and income in Thailand, 1985–1990

Year	Visitors (million)	% growth	Tourist Expenditure (million baht)
1985	2.438	3.9	31 768
1986	2.818	15.6	37 321
1987	3.483	23.6	50 024
1988	4.230	21.5	78 859
1989	4.809	13.7	96 386
1990	5.299	10.2	115 700

Baht 25.35=US$1.00

Source: Tourism Authority of Thailand in Rurakdee 1991: 182

Table 4.9: Tourist arrivals in Thailand by market, 1989–1990

Country	Visitors ('000) 1990	1989	% growth	% 1990
Total	5 298 860	4 809 508	+10.7	100.00
Americas	381 894	366 016	+4.34	7.21
Canada	74 550	68 450	+8.91	1.41
USA	291 635	282 924	+3.08	5.50
Europe	1 326 752	1 207 332	+9.56	24.96
France	194 618	189 282	+2.82	3.67
Germany	239 915	220 824	+8.65	4.53
UK	318 220	293 174	+8.54	6.01
Africa	31 943	27 484	+16.22	0.60
Middle East	76 924	112 865	-31.84	1.45
Saudi Arabia	6 489	42 976	-84.90	0.12
East Asia/Pacific	3 214 779	2 844 662	+13.01	60.67
ASEAN	1 195 011	1 120 461	+6.65	22.55
Malaysia	804 629	766 172	+5.02	15.18
The Philippines	48 121	52 324	-8.03	0.91
Singapore	289 411	258 404	+12.00	5.46
Australia	226 785	198 940	+14.00	4.28
Hong Kong	265 585	259 574	+2.32	5.01
Japan	635 555	546 967	+16.20	11.99
Korea	144 747	110 665	+30.80	2.73
Taiwan	480 896	396 184	+21.38	9.08

Source: Thailand Immigration Division in Rurakdee 1991: 184

million arrivals are expected to spend an average of nine days in Thailand, compared with the 1989 figure of 7.6 days. Long-term forecasts indicate that the industry will contribute about 800 billion baht (US$32 billion) to the country's earnings in the year 2000, compared with 91 billion baht (US$3.64 billion) in 1989'.

In order to achieve the 12 million goal, the TAT has identified four priority areas for the development of Thai tourism product: conventions and meetings; family-oriented leisure travel, which is possibly also an attempt to minimise the country's reputation for sex tourism; sports travel, particularly golf and marine tourism such as diving and yachting; and incentive travel, with the USA becoming a major source of incentive travellers for Thailand and more attention being placed on the European and Japanese markets (Corben 1990a). Co-operative marketing campaigns, such as Visit ASEAN Year, are being developed to promote South East Asia as the tourist centre of Asia and the Pacific Rim (Corben 1990e). Increasingly, the Thai Government is promoting the country and Bangkok in particular, as the gateway to Cambodia, Laos, Vietnam, Burma and even China. The Thai push to be perceived as the tourist hub of South East Asia is in direct response to the success of Singapore, and more particularly of Malaysia and its Visit Malaysia Year in 1990, in attracting non-ASEAN tourists. Indeed, Rurakdee (1991: 184) observed: 'it is possible that if Malaysia is able to retain high growth in the tourism industry, preserve and restore natural resorts, and increase hotel rooms to cope with the current shortage of accommodation, the Thai tourism industry will inevitably be in jeopardy'. Therefore, as the following section discusses, Thailand has major infrastructural, political, environmental and social problems which need to be addressed before it can claim the position as the tourist hub of South East Asia.

Tourism development

Tourism is the top earner in Thailand's rapidly-growing economy. Thailand's earnings from tourism in 1990 were expected to be approximately 100 billion baht (US$4 billion) on a projection of between 5.2 and 5.5 million overseas visitors (*Asia Travel Trade* 1989i). In 1991 the Tourism Authority of Thailand (TAT) had been aiming for foreign exchange earnings of 144 billion baht (US$5.76 billion) (Corben 1990e), although the decline in visitor numbers in 1991 meant that this figure was not reached.

Given the failure of tourism growth to live up to government expectations, it is not surprising that criticism has emerged of the reported benefits of tourism to the Thai economy. Dr Somchai Ratanakomut of Chulalongkorn University has argued that the notion that tourism is Thailand's greatest earner of foreign exchange is misleading because as much as 56 per cent of income generated by tourism goes directly on importing goods and materials to cater for foreign tourists. According to Ratanakomut, 'Of the 50 billion baht worth of foreign currency derived from tourism [in

1987], 28 billion baht was spent on importing luxury goods. As a result, only 44 per cent remained with those involved in the tourism industry' (in Robinson 1990: 9). Nevertheless, Ratanakomut does acknowledge that substantial indirect flow-ons to the Thai economy occur through the employment created by the tourism industry. However, most official considerations of the value of tourism to the Thai economy do not fully consider the costs of infrastructure and social and environmental problems.

A central issue in Thailand's economic development is the provision of physical and social infrastructure. Bangkok, the major gateway for tourists visiting Thailand, suffers from substantial urban planning problems, particularly the lack of an appropriate road and transport network. A report by the Japan International Co-operation Agency stated 'The direct and indirect traffic costs are almost equivalent to 60 per cent of Bangkok's gross regional product, commuting hours are prolonged, environments deteriorated and investments and tourism are discouraged' (in Corben 1990d: 9).

Investment is presently concentrated in the Bangkok region. The government policy to decentralise further development from Bangkok has only met with limited success, paradoxically, because of a lack of suitable infrastructure in the provinces (Corben & Robinson 1990). The government is being encouraged by industry to supply the required infrastructure but it does not wish to bear the costs completely and is seeking private sector investment in power generation plants, transport, telecommunications, and industrial estates, particularly from foreign investors including its present major sources of Japan, Hong Kong, the USA, Taiwan and Singapore. One mechanism for the input of private funds into infrastructure development and the reduction of government debt is the privatisation of state enterprises. However, the implementation of such measures is not without significant conflict within the Thai Government and technocracy. For instance, plans to privatise Thai Airways and thereby open up sources of non-government funds for fleet expansion met with considerable resistance and delay (*Asia Travel Trade* 1990i).

Thailand has been establishing strong links with neighbouring countries in order to develop regional tourism. Bangkok is being developed as the hub for other regional centres in Burma (Rangoon, Mandalay); Laos (Vientiane), Cambodia (Phnom Penh); and Vietnam (Hanoi, Ho Chi Minh City). Examples of the developing tourism relationship of Thailand to its neighbours include Thai Airways International's assistance to the Vietnamese to develop their state airline, and the commencement of direct flights by Bangkok Airways to Cambodia (Tasker & Handley 1991).

Sections of government and industry have been pushing for further rapid tourism development. However, Thailand's tourist image has become badly tarnished in recent years. Several prominent tourist industry figures including the Minister for Tourism, Mechai Viravaidhya, and the Vice-President of the hotels association, David Wiig, have questioned whether the country can sustain tourism at present levels without causing irreparable damage to the country's culture and environment (Kelly 1991). Three central problems can be identified: perceptions of political stability, the sex tourism industry and the threat of AIDS, and the impacts of tourism development on the environment.

Political stability

In Thailand, the military have long had a major role in determining the fates of governments. The military has been the major constant among the system of shifting allegiances within the political élite and has been a factor behind the short life spans of most Thai Governments since the Second World War. The military coup rather than the ballot box has been the most common method of achieving office. Fortunately, however, coups in Thailand have generally been bloodless and the omnipresent state bureaucracy has managed to maintain an image of stability which has continued to attract both tourists and investors (Elliot 1983; Richter 1989). The rapid economic growth of recent years and the consequent emergence of an educated middle class has also led to calls for greater public participation in political affairs, a reduced role for the military in politics and increased anti-corruption measures.

In May 1992, the disenchantment exploded when the army shot at and beat demonstrators as part of a clamp-down on political protest and anti-government marchers. It was only with the involvement of the monarchy that the situation became calm. The images of the violence in the streets of Bangkok were relayed around the world deeply harming the tourist trade and also damaging the perceptions of political stability that had been so crucial for the attraction of foreign investment. Many tourists cancelled their trips while the convention industry was also badly damaged. For example, the Australian Federation of Travel Agents decided to proceed with its annual convention in Bangkok in late July only after receiving assurances from the government, and with the Tourism Authority of Thailand underwriting the convention. Hotel occupancies during the time of the convention were low. The Thai Hotels Association estimated that the average occupancy rate among its member hotels in Bangkok, Phuket and Chiang Mai was between 30 per cent and 35 per cent, compared to the normal low-season level of 50 per cent to 55 per cent (*Asia Travel Trade* 1992).

The coup has had both short- and long-term impacts on the Thai tourism industry. In the short term, inbound tourist numbers slumped dramatically. Accommodation suffered from low occupancy rates of between 10 per cent to 30 per cent and the tourism industry as a whole suffered from heavy discounting, with overall loss estimates by Bangkok Bank and other tourist enterprises ranging between 10 billion baht and 30 billion baht (US$400 million to US$1.2 billion) (Hail 1992a). In the longer term, the marches and the subsequent violent response has led to altered tourist perceptions of the safety and stability of Thailand akin to traveller's responses to the massacre at Tiananmen Square in Beijing in 1989 (see

Chapter 5). The sustainability of Thai tourism growth will therefore be dependent on the government and TAT re-establishing a positive image of Thailand in the international market-place; an image that, as discussed below, has already been affected by sex tourism, AIDS, and the quality of the environment.

Tourism, prostitution and AIDS

In 1989 the Thai Public Health Ministry started campaigning against prostitution and the promotion of Thailand as a sex tour destination. The primary reason for the campaign was the recognition that sexually transmitted diseases such as AIDS could pose major problems for Thailand's rapidly growing tourism industry. A Ministry survey of AIDS and Thailand's prostitution industry indicated that about 3000 prostitutes in Thailand were carrying the AIDS virus and a World Health Organization report estimated that the number of infected people in Thailand was between 45 000 and 50 000 compared with the official figure of 14 000 (Corben 1990c: 7). In tourist centres such as Chiang Mai, tests have suggested that one of every two prostitutes in the region carries the virus (Robinson 1989a).

According to the Thai Deputy Public Health Minister, Suthas Ngernmuen (in Robinson 1989a: 11):

Thailand's profitable tourist industry has been an inhibiting factor in promoting AIDS awareness... More than two-thirds of the overseas visitors entering Thailand are single men, and medical officials avoided publicising the appalling AIDS statistics for fear of damaging the country's healthy tourist business... But it is long past time for the government to change Thailand's image as a sexual paradise.

We should promote tourism in more appropriate ways, and campaign more against AIDS.

The Thai Government has considered a number of options to curb the spread of AIDS including operating testing programmes for certain visitors, and distributing condoms in hotels or at the airport. Part of the AIDS programme includes 'rehabilitating' and skilling prostitutes, while the Defence Ministry is providing an AIDS education programme for service personnel. The Public Health Ministry has proposed the issuing of health cards to brothel workers which would indicate the holder's personal background and the results of tests conducted for sexually transmitted diseases, including AIDS (Corben 1990c). The issuance of three-monthly health cards is only an indirect measure of controlling AIDS and does relatively little to deter the sex tourist. Instead, health cards may only further attract visitors to certain brothels or locations and may also allow the possibility of corruption in order to obtain cards which give workers in the sex industry clean bills of health. If the Thai Government is to be serious about controlling AIDS, major emphasis has to be given to replacing Thailand's image as a sex tour destination and in providing alternative economic and social support mechanisms for those who use prostitution as a means of employment. However, as Corben (1990c: 9) reported, 'tourism authorities in

Thailand are extremely sensitive to reports about sex activities and the rising incidence of AIDS and other sexually-transmitted diseases in Thailand'. After a damning examination of the sex trade and the major role it plays in Thailand's tourism industry by the *Far Eastern Economic Review*, the Governor of the Tourism Authority of Thailand (TAT), Dharmnoon Prachuabmoh, attacked the journal and argued that 'Any effective measures adopted by the Thai Government to curb the spread of AIDS would be fine with us. It is the welfare of the Thais, not the tourist dollar, that must come first' (Corben 1990c: 9).

The AIDS scare has already impacted some Thai tourist destinations. Visitor arrivals by road from Malaysia were estimated to have dropped by over half for most of 1989 at the southern town of Hat Yai, renowned for its bars and massage parlours (*Asia Travel Trade* 1989i, 1990l). Similarly, AIDS has tarnished the image of Pattaya and this, associated with environmental problems, is believed to have contributed to a sharp decline in the number of visitors to the resort area. According to Pa-nga Wattanakul, the President of the Pattaya Hotels Association, 'although there had been a 13 per cent increase last year in the number of tourists coming to Thailand, there had been a decrease of 30 per cent in each of the past two years [in visitors to Pattaya]' (in *Asia Travel Trade* 1990l: 56).

In order to attract more female tourists and counteract Thailand's image of sex tourism and AIDS, the chairman of the Tourism Authority of Thailand and a leading anti-AIDS campaigner, Minister Mechai Viravaidya, planned a Women's Visit Thailand year campaign in 1992. According to the Minister

We want women to come particularly from countries where some of their men have come here on sex tours... We want them to see what their men get up to and how they have exploited uneducated women and children. We want their women to come and see the good Thai women and encourage Thai women to stand up to the brutality and disrespect they have suffered. More action must come from Thai women themselves, otherwise the country will still be seen as the brothel of the world (Kelly 1991: 44).

The Minister's stance has led him to be severely criticised by some members of the tourism industry and accused of a conflict of roles (Hail 1992b). It is readily apparent that some sections of Thailand's tourism industry are still keen to promote sex tourism because of its financial benefits. However, the long-term health implications, through the spread of AIDS and other STDs, and social impacts of sex tourism is enormous and represents a potential time-bomb for Thailand's development programme. In order to meet the challenge of AIDS to the Thai society and economy, the government must overcome official corruption and deep-rooted cultural attitudes towards sex and the role of women. Such a task will not be easy, but unless the government takes firm and decisive action not only will the broader tourism industry be damaged, particularly that geared towards the family market, but also the human base of Thai economic development.

Environmental impacts

From its wild mountain forests aflame with rhododendrons, to its dense tropical jungles and photogenic offshore islands, Thailand is a place of visual and sensory splendour...

With this natural abundance of beauty comes a vital responsibility for its care and preservation—advertisement (Thai Airways International 1992).

Given the growing international awareness of the environment as a tourist attraction, Thailand's natural heritage has increasingly been promoted overseas. For example, Thai Airways International launched a promotional campaign in 1992 which highlighted the country's national parks. 'To encourage awareness of Thailand's natural heritage, and the urgent need to preserve this unique environment, Thai Airways International invites you to explore the wonders of our national parks with our 'Discover Thailand's Natural Heritage' ticket' (Thai Airways International 1992). Despite the image of tropical rainforest, coral reefs and well-managed national park systems, environmental destruction and pollution has become one of the major issues facing the Thai tourist industry in the 1990s. The TAT has reported that 'major destinations... face physical deterioration caused by the destruction of the environment and a lack of regulation of land use and constructions and related service business' (*Asia Travel Trade* 1990j: 47). Some destinations have fared worse than others. 'Pattaya has reached the stage where it should focus on preserving its environment instead of aiming for promotion and future development...' (Robinson 1989c: 51). According to *Asia Travel Trade* (1989h: 48):

Raw sewage, including waste water and human excrement, is allegedly being dumped in the sea, in such quantities that the sea water is now a danger to the same people who generated the waste in the first place. It is a critical problem for Pattaya, a town whose existence depends on sun-seeking holiday makers and which, in terms of tourist dollars, is second to Bangkok as Thailand's biggest revenue spinner.

The first major hotel was not opened in Pattaya until 1961. However, with the use of the area for rest and recreation by United States soldiers during the Vietnam War, the city was transformed from a fishing village into a resort. 'The fun-seeking nature of Pattaya's original clientele quickly led to the establishment of numerous bars, restaurants and massage parlours' (*Asia Travel Trade* 1989h: 50). In 1977, 434 000 tourists visited Pattaya. In 1987 the number of visitors had increased five-fold to 1.85 million, and by 1989 the figure had reached approximately three million. According to Thailand's National Environment Board, during the ten years between 1977 and 1987 faecal contamination at Pattaya increased 87 per cent, and an average of 6 per cent per year from 1987 to 1989. The seriousness of Pattaya's environmental problems have had several effects. First, it has forced the Thai Government into improving the area's drainage and sewage facilities. Second, it has led to assistance from the hotels in supporting infrastructure development which will reduce pollution levels. Third, it has meant the growing environmental movement in Thailand has been able to use the case study of Pattaya to indicate what inappropriate tourism development can do to the environment. The third point will probably be the most significant in the long term. For instance, as a result of the potential environmental disaster at Pattaya, the Government decided in 1989 to suspend large scale tourist development proposals in nineteen of the country's national parks, particularly those with fragile marine environments such as coral reefs. Indeed, such is the damage presently being done to the nation's coral reefs that artificial reefs are being constructed around Surat Thanai in Southern Thailand because coral reefs are being destroyed by fisherman using explosives to catch fish, and tourists picking coral from the sea (Robinson 1989c).

The tourist resort area of Phuket is also suffering from major environmental problems. As in the case of Pattaya, resorts such as Koh Samui and Phuket are in danger of becoming overdeveloped without the appropriate infrastructure being put in place. Waste water and effluent is pumped directly into the sea lowering both water and amenity quality. According to a report produced by First Pacific Asia Securities (Thailand) Ltd. (in Corben 1990b: 21):

> Thailand faces the threat of losing some of its major attractions through mismanagement by the industry itself. Environmental preservation is required if the long-term value of Phuket tourism is to be maintained. The Thai government needs to increase its role in the long-term environmental management policy... top priority should be given to the conservation of beach front areas, including artificial measures where necessary to reinstate the natural environment.

Despite the undoubted seriousness of Phuket's pollution problems, action is slow in coming. As Corben (1990b: 21) commented, 'However grim the warnings, it still remains to be seen whether the government has the resources to restrain development since any effort to control Phuket's growth will immediately bring the government into conflict with investors, both local and foreign'.

Thailand's environmental problems are the result of a piecemeal approach to regulating tourist resort developments. 'Thailand's problem with uncoordinated resort development is partly due to the variety and number of government agencies involved in efforts to regulate resort areas more closely—leading to some confusion over responsibilities' (Robinson 1989c: 53). The Tourism Authority of Thailand sought in 1989, for the first time, tighter controls on the management of coastal tourism development and included 'support for conservation activities and development of tourism to maintain cultural heritage' as one of eight guidelines for the development of the Thai tourism industry (*Asia Travel Trade* 1989h).

'Overall, tourism industry members in Thailand acknowledge that environmentalism is much higher on their agendas than ever before. Despite the gloomy predictions of environmental campaigners, industry representatives say there is great hope for the future of Thailand's many resorts'

(Robinson 1989c: 53). The government has considered the establishment of a multi-agency taskforce to co-ordinate development of the tourism industry in Thailand. The national park system has grown to cover 34 503 square kilometres or 24 per cent of Thailand's forested area (Thai Airways International 1992). Improved legislation may also be one mechanism to assist in increasing consideration of environmental values in the tourism planning process, but legislation and regulations are useless unless they are implemented and enforced. As *Asia Travel Trade* (1990j: 47) reported, 'Moves to control development on the tourist island of Koh Samet and squelch bungalow construction that encroached on national park land didn't come until years after the first pleas to stem such development'.

Enactment of the National Environmental Act in Thailand on 4 June 1992 represents substantial improvements in environmental protection and rehabilitation. However, the new approach is so advanced that the manpower and associated skills are not yet in place to effectively implement the new programme (Handley 1992), although the government is starting to take action. For example, due to complaints about denial of access to local people at golf courses and sports facilities (Handley 1991) and the environmental impacts of golf courses through misuse of fertilizers and pesticides, the government closed down a golf course and Tourism Authority of Thailand lodgings on the Khao Yai National Park north west of Bangkok (Corben 1992).

Other social and environmental development considerations include giving tourism a much higher priority in the 1992–1996 Seventh Economic Plan which will include giving the TAT greater representation on co-ordination committees responsible for the implementation of economic and social policy. Under the Plan, the TAT is aiming for growth rate targets similar to those achieved in the late 1980s, but is paying more attention to social problems, such as drugs and crime, environmental problems, and infrastructure improvements. According to the Governor of the TAT, Dharmnoon Prachuabmoh, the aim of tourism policy under the five year plan will be the promotion of a balance between economic and social development in order to ensure the industry's future: 'If we find that tourism development has had a negative impact we might revise our plans' (in Corben & Robinson 1990: 18).

The future

The Thai tourist industry has reached the depths of the off season with business down 30% on last year, the result of several factors some of which may have a lasting effect. The industry is suffering from being caught at the centre of criticism over development which is seen as a threat to the environment and local culture, while the creation of a consumer society is increasingly questioned, not only by fringe groups but by a cross-section of society reaching into the government (Kelly 1991: 44).

Thai per capita GDP rose from US$775 in 1986 to US$1420 in 1990. However, economic growth is slowing down and substantial development problems are beginning to emerge. Growth is regionally uneven, while the lack of rural and urban planning has led to inadequate transport and communications infrastructure and major environmental problems. The issues for the Thai Government should be clear. Corben and Robinson (1990: 21) argue, 'The overall warning is that the "fast-track" approach to economic growth could ultimately be to the detriment of the environment, the tourism economy, and critically-needed basic infrastructure development'.

Tourism has been a great contributor to Thailand's economic development over the past two decades. However, as is now widely acknowledged, tourism is not without its negative effects. Undoubtedly, tourism has been responsible for the spread of disease, environmental degradation and unwanted social impacts. Therefore, if Thailand seeks to maintain tourism growth and economic growth over the remainder of the decade, it needs to integrate tourism development within the country's religious, political and social structures. In the case of Thailand less, or at least slower, development may be better.

Singapore

Singapore is probably the most 'Western' of all South East Asian nations. Since the development of the country's tourism industry in the late 1950s, Singapore has had consistent high growth to become one of the tourism, transport and business hubs of the region. An international trading centre, Singapore has a dynamic economy, the world's busiest port, and 'has become a gateway into the South East Asian region in terms of trade and capital flows' (Toh & Low 1990: 249) and is fast becoming a rival to Hong Kong as an international commercial centre (Economist Intelligence Unit 1990d).

Tourism is a substantial contributor to the country's economy. Tourism employs about 6 per cent of the workforce and ranks as the third most important industry, contributing about 16 per cent of total foreign currency earnings (Ministry of Trade and Industry 1986; Kee & Ghosh 1990). Singapore has had a surplus in the travel balance (travel export minus travel import) since 1960. This surplus has increased from 0.7 per cent of GDP in 1960 to a high of 10.2 per cent in 1981. In 1990 the balance of travel was 8.3 per cent (Table 4.10). The drop occurred because of the increasing number of Singapore residents travelling overseas (Singapore Tourist Promotion Board 1992). However, with a small population base of 2.8 million the travel balance is likely to remain in surplus for many years.

The outbound market

With a 6 per cent average rate of growth in GDP between 1985 and 1989 and slightly more in 1990 and 1991, the propensity of Singapore residents to travel overseas for holidays has been steadily increasing. Singapore had an average annual 10.4 per cent growth in outbound travel from 1985 to

Table 4.10: Contribution of tourism to Singapore's gross domestic product and balance of payments

Item	1960	1970	1980	1985	1990
Travel export (S$)	30.5	279.9	3 068.4	3 653.0	7 609.3
as % of service exports	4.7	16.4	20.4	20.3	20.3
as % of total exports of goods and services	0.8	4.6	5.7	5.6	5.9
Travel import (S$)	15.3	31.9	712.6	1 349.4	2 409.6
as % of service exports	4.8	3.9	7.8	11.9	10.3
as % of total exports of goods and services	0.4	0.4	1.2	2.1	1.9
Balance of travel (S$)	15.2	248.0	2 355.8	2 303.6	5 199.7
as % of GDP	0.7	4.3	9.4	5.9	8.3

Source: Singapore Tourist Promotion Board 1992: 15

Table 4.11: Outbound travel from Singapore, 1985–1991

Year	Number (000's)
1985	679
1986	725
1987	826
1988	879
1989	1 038
1990	1 237
1991	1 232

Source: Singapore Tourist Promotion Board in New Zealand Tourism Board 1992e: 15

Table 4.13 Visitor arrivals in Singapore by country of residence, 1991

Country of Residence	Total	%	% change from 1990
TOTAL	5 414 651	100.00	1.7
Americas	326 817	6.04	-3.1
Canada	58 544	1.08	-4.2
USA	253 761	4.69	-2.9
Other Americas	14 512	0.27	-0.1
Asia	3 693 072	68.21	7.8
ASEAN[1]	1 680 342	31.03	16.5
China	42 333	0.78	50.0
Hong Kong	213 053	3.93	9.7
India	209 654	3.87	-3.2
Japan	871 313	16.09	-10.3
Korea	133 435	2.46	22.5
Burma (Myanmar)	23 729	0.44	26.7
Pakistan	37 768	0.70	13.7
Sri Lanka	55 965	1.03	17.0
Taiwan	287 084	5.30	27.7
West Asia	84 289	1.56	-11.3
Other Asia	54 107	1.00	19.0
Europe	888 013	16.40	-5.9
Austria	17 962	0.33	-22.7
Belgium and Luxembourg	15 810	0.29	-11.9
France	69 599	1.29	-4.7
Germany[2]	142 367	2.63	1.0
Greece	14 108	0.26	-22.8
Italy	51 832	0.96	-7.9
The Netherlands	72 210	1.33	-2.2
Scandinavia	95 185	1.76	-5.3
(former) Soviet Union	25 050	0.46	26.0
Spain	15 481	0.29	-13.3
Switzerland	57 689	1.07	-4.5
UK	274 693	5.07	-7.4
Other Eastern Europe	21 440	0.40	NA
Other Western Europe	14 587	0.27	-4.9

Country of Residence	Total	%	% change from 1990
Oceania	449 908	8.31	-18.3
Australia	367 963	6.80	19.4
New Zealand	61 987	1.14	-14.8
Other Oceania	19 958	0.37	-6.8
Others	56 841	1.05	-11.4
Countries in Africa	55 729	1.03	-0.8
Not stated	1 112	0.02	-86.0

1 Excludes Malaysian citizens arriving by land
2 Total includes East Germany but percentage change applies only to West Germany as data for East Germany prior to July 1990 is not available.
Source: Singapore Tourist Promotion Board 1992: 27

Table 4.12: Visitor arrivals to Singapore, 1975–1991

Year	Visitor Arrivals*	% Change	Average Length of Stay (Days)
1975	1 324 312	7.3	3.4
1976	1 492 218	12.7	3.4
1977	1 681 985	12.7	3.5
1978	2 047 224	8.9	3.6
1979	2 247 091	9.8	3.7
1980	2 562 085	14.0	3.7
1981	2 828 622	10.4	3.7
1982	2 956 690	4.5	3.8
1983	2 853 577	-3.5	3.7
1984	2 991 430	4.8	3.6
1985	3 030 970	1.3	3.5
1986	3 191 058	5.3	3.5
1987	3 678 809	15.3	3.4
1988	4 186 091	13.8	3.4
1989	4 829 950	15.4	3.32
1990	5 322 854	10.2	3.30
1991	5 414 651	1.7	3.26

* Excludes Malaysian citizens arriving by land
Source: Singapore Tourist Promotion Board 1992

1991 (Table 4.11). Of the 1.23 million Singaporeans who travelled overseas in 1991, 23.8 per cent travelled to long-haul destinations and 76.2 per cent went to short-haul destinations, mainly Malaysia and Indonesia (New Zealand Tourism Board 1992b). Nevertheless, the continued growth of the Singapore economy and the increased affluence of its residents means that long-haul destinations such as Hong Kong, Japan, Australia, New Zealand, the Pacific Islands and mainland China are showing substantial interest in outbound travellers.

The inbound market

Singapore has had a more than four-fold increase in visitor arrivals since 1975 (Table 4.12). In 1975 Singapore had 1.324 million visitor arrivals. By 1985 the figure was just over the three million mark. In 1991 the figure reached 5.414 million. However, the number of arrivals in 1991 represented only a marginal increase (1.7 per cent) over the 1990 result (5.322 million). Undoubtedly, the Gulf War had a major effect on visitor numbers to Singapore, particularly given Singapore's role as a regional transport hub. Evidence of this is to be found in the higher than expected rate of visitor arrivals in Singapore in the first seven months of 1992. This lead to a revision of growth for the year up to between 7 and 9 per cent from 6 to 8 per cent growth. This revised forecast means that between 5.79 and 5.9 million visitors were expected compared with 5.41 million in 1991 (Cadiz 1992).

Of the 5.41 million visitors in 1991, 78.59 per cent came by air, 8.85 per cent by sea and 12.56 per cent by land. The number of arrivals by means other than air is significant as it indicates the extent to which the island is a hub of the South East Asian region and the degree to which its tourism industry is integrated with the surrounding countries of Malaysia, Indonesia and Thailand. Repeat visitors make up 56.43 per cent of inbound travellers, with a similar proportion (57.86 per cent) who describe 'holiday' as their main purpose of visit (Singapore Tourist Promotion Board 1992).

Table 4.13 (p. 108) illustrates the number of visitor arrivals by country of residence to Singapore for 1991. As may be expected, the ASEAN market is clearly the most important, followed by Japan (16.09 per cent), Australia (6.80 per cent), Taiwan (5.30 per cent) and the UK (5.07 per cent). Given the high level of Japanese investment in the country, it should not be surprising that they constitute the largest group of non-ASEAN visitors. Of major significance to Singapore is the perceived safety of the destination which has made the country extremely attractive to first time travellers, especially Japanese and other Asian women travelling alone or in groups (Economist Intelligence Unit 1990d). Markets with the most rapid growth rates include China (50.0 per cent), Burma (Myanmar) (26.7 per cent), Russia (Soviet Union) (26.0 per cent) and Korea (26.7 per cent). However, with the exception of Korea all of these markets are commencing their growth from a low base figure.

Tourism development

What Singapore needs to do as it heads towards the 21st century from now until that point of time is to stop product development. The country is too small and you cannot expand too fast. Instead, Singapore must start improving the older, existing attractions—P.R. Gopal, President of the National Association of Travel Agents Singapore (in Wong 1990: 35).

Government plays an active role in all aspects of economic and social development in Singapore. In the case of tourism, deliberate government measures to encourage tourism growth include the establishment of the Singapore Tourist Promotion Board (STPB) in 1964 and the development of the national carrier, Singapore Airlines. Given the small size of Singapore, the government has also formulated a highly regulatory urban planning scheme which determines, to a great extent, the availability of tourist accommodation and the recreation and leisure patterns of tourists. In addition, the government has made a direct investment of over S$1 billion in the development of tourist attractions and associated infrastructure in order to prolong the length of stay of visitors to the country.

Under the combined influence of regulatory planning measures and inaccurate forecasts of tourism growth, hotel development in Singapore has undergone a cyclical pattern of development (Hamdi 1990). The intense competition in price, service and promotion that followed the expansion of room supply in the mid-1980s still lingers and has led to a degree of uncertainty in the development of the accommodation sector (Kee & Ghosh 1990; Khan, Chou & Wong 1990). In early 1992 there were 69 gazetted hotels with a total of 24 821 rooms, and a total of 3926 rooms under construction for 1995 (Cadiz 1992). Table 4.14 illustrates the changes that have taken place in hotel supply and demand for the period 1986 to 1991.

One of the markets which has been targeted to fill the rooms presently under construction is the meetings, incentives, conventions, and exhibition trade (MICE) which currently produces S$300 million (US$ 187.5 million) worth of business a year for Singapore. According to the STPB, the convention delegates spend approximately double that of the average tourist (S$1400–S$1500 compared to S$800 for the average tourist) and stay four to five days compared to 3.3 days (Hwu 1992). In order to further attract the market, the STPB is planning a three-year S$13 million (US$8.1 million) promotion campaign to publicise Singapore's convention facilities, which include the development of the Singapore International Convention and Exhibition Centre to be fully completed by 1995 at a cost of S$500 million (US$313 million) (Hwu 1992).

One of the main issues in the development of Singapore as a tourist destination is the appropriate balance between retention of the old city landscape and the creation of a modern metropolis. Undoubtedly for many tourists, there is much attraction in the history and culture of Singapore, particularly the Malay, Chinese and colonial heritage in arts and architecture.

Table 4.14: Gazetted hotel indicators in Singapore, 1986–1991

Year	Total Visitor Arrivals		Rooms Available		Average Occupancy	Average Room Rate	
	No.	%	No.	%	Rate (%)	S$	%
1986	3 191 058	5.3	22 080	16.1	64.7	76.80	-19.0
1987	3 678 809	15.3	23 431	6.1	68.7	69.80	-9.1
1988	4 186 091	13.8	24 669	5.3	79.3	73.20	4.9
1989	4 829 950	15.4	22 457	-9.0	86.4	95.00	29.8
1990	5 322 854	10.2	23 453	4.4	84.0	140.60	48.1
1991	5 414 651	1.7	24 300	3.6	76.8	150.70	7.2

Source: Singapore Tourist Promotion Board 1992: 20

However, there are some fears that traditional skills and trades such as dance, arts and crafts are dying out and concern that much of the spontaneity of street markets and bazaars is being lost in townscape restoration and in the construction of modern shopping complexes (Wong & Gan 1988; Wong 1990). According to Kee and Ghosh (1990: 76), 'In its urgency to build a modern metropolis and transform the economy into that of a world-class industrial state, many aspects of the oriental mystique and charm that are best symbolized in old buildings, traditional activities, and bustling roadside enterprise have been removed'. However, Prithpal Singh, Vice President of leisure and tourism for Hotel Properties Ltd which owns Hilton International, Le Meridien Orchard and the Glass Hotel, disagrees and has argued that Singapore is distinctly different from the rest of ASEAN: 'Singapore is forging a new image and a new identity and we are going away from the theme of culture and tradition, and moving into more recreational and man-made attractions, which, while they may not be authentic, have an appeal of their own' (in Wong 1992. 35). An example of the recreational attractions referred to by Singh is the S$90 million (US$55.9 million) Tang Dynasty City. Asia's largest historical and cultural theme park, modelled after Xi'an in China, is targeting one million visitors in its first year of operation. When fully completed in 1993, the theme park will include an underground palace, an imperial palace, a working film studio and a seven story pagoda (Cadiz 1992). In addition, a S$900 million (US$562.5 million) urban conservation project is being undertaken at Bugis Junction in the city. The project will include the addition of a 383 room Inter-Continental hotel and will retain façades and incorporate traditional architectural style (Cadiz 1992).

An example of a more appropriate form of development which protects heritage and environmental values is the development of Sentosa Island, just to the south of Singapore, as a coastal tourist resort. The Sentosa Development Corporation is investing about S$577 million on improving the facilities and infrastructure of the island. However, unlike other South East Asian countries, the development has been subject to strict environmental guidelines covering such items as building height, sewage treatment and vegetation in order to maintain the aesthetics of the island (Wong 1989). A S$60 million (US$37.5 million) Asian Village on Sentosa was due to open in December 1992 and was designed as a showcase for Asian lifestyles and culture. It consists of three attractions: three regional themed villages; 'Festive Asia', a 1000 seat village amphitheatre, and 'Adventure Asia', a family entertainment centre (Cadiz 1992).

The future

Increasingly, as the neighbouring countries also develop their infrastructure and natural attractions, the comparative advantages enjoyed by Singapore in terms of accommodation, communications, shopping, and other facilities are challenged (Toh & Low 1990: 263).

Singapore was able to establish itself as the hub of the tourism industry of South East Asia on the basis of its competitive advantages. Those advantages are now being eroded. For example, countries such as Malaysia and Thailand are actively promoting their heritage and marine tourism opportunities. Singapore's competitive advantage will increasingly lie in areas such as conventions and meetings, and corporate travel. Nevertheless, this does not mean that Singapore should ignore heritage and culture tourism resources. For many travellers, Singapore is the gateway to Asia and interest in Asian cultures and the history of Singapore is therefore high. One of the main facets of future promotion of Singapore will most likely be greater co-operative marketing strategies with other ASEAN and Pacific Rim nations in which the destinations are regarded as complementary rather than competing. For example, given their geographic proximity and increasing degree of economic integration, joint promotional activities between Singapore and the Malaysian State of Johore would appear to be desirable. In addition, Toh and Low (1990: 267) have argued that Singapore's cost structure must be kept to a minimum in order for it to remain competitive, while built attractions will only remain competitive up to a point. 'More important is the continuous investment in human resources development and training to upgrade professionalism and efficiency of tourist and related services'.

In comparison with its South East Asian counterparts, Singapore has been blessed with a high degree of political stability. This stability, plus some of the more positive aspects of a centralised economy, has led to strong economic growth and a correspondingly high level of personal income by Asian standards. Tourism has played a substantive role in Singapore's economic development and can be expected to do so in the future. Nevertheless, if Singapore is to retain its premier role in South East Asian tourism, it is essential that the government take steps to retain its competitive advantage while at the same time meeting the aspirations of its people.

The future of tourism in South East Asia

Tourism is of major importance to the economies of the ASEAN countries. Tourism is a vital source of foreign exchange, it generates substantial employment opportunities and is a significant instrument for regional and national economic development. Over the past two decades, inbound tourism has shown continued high growth, punctuated only by the effects of oil crises, natural disasters, and political instability. However, it is the latter which probably presents itself as one of the greatest challenges to inbound growth. In a world made ever smaller by communications technology, pictures of riots and coups are immediately broadcast around the world to be seen in tourism-generating regions. In the case of the Philippines and, more recently, Thailand, the visible effects of political instability have done great damage to those countries' tourism industries. Nevertheless, political instability is not limited to Thailand and the Philippines. As the region develops and consumer expectations rise, governments are faced with the prospect of managing aspirations for greater political participation from the growing educated middle classes.

Several other problems also emerge in maintaining tourism growth in the region. The lack of infrastructure at some destinations has led to sewage disposal problems, particularly for coastal resorts, posing health risks for tourists and locals alike. Similarly, a shortage of appropriate transport and communication infrastructure will restrict the ability of some destinations to increase their visitor arrivals. The provision of accommodation is obviously important, but unless transport is available to get the tourists there, the construction of further hotels and resorts becomes redundant. Health problems are also a concern in terms of the spread of AIDS which has been associated with sex tourism in Thailand and the Philippines. Official corruption, a focus on economic gain rather than social loss, and acceptance of certain roles for women in some countries has meant that sex tourism has proven extremely difficult to control. Nevertheless, AIDS and associated STD health problems have the potential to undermine the human resource component of economic development and clearly pose a threat to the attraction of countries and regions in certain tourist markets. In addition, government will be required to take an active role in determining the appropriate level of tourism development in a number of destinations. Given the growing interest of tourists in the environment, government agencies will have to play an active role in setting visitor numbers and activities in national parks and environmentally sensitive areas if the physical drawcard is not to be lost.

It is perhaps ironic that the very factors that lead to degradation of the physical and social environment—that of rapid economic growth and regional development—are also the same factors which have led to increased outbound travel in ASEAN countries. Economic growth is leading to the development of consumer societies with greater disposable income and increased leisure time and therefore a greater propensity to travel. A market trend has already been picked up by countries outside the region, such as Australia and New Zealand. These are countries seeking to expand their own inbound tourism numbers, in addition to greater intraregional travel between the six ASEAN countries.

The ASEAN countries will continue to be one of the major destinations in the Asia Pacific region for the rest of the decade. Outbound numbers will also grow rapidly. The most significant factors in terms of the rate of growth of inbound travel will be the provision of infrastructure, the state of the environment and the level of political stability. However, as the end of the century approaches, ASEAN governments may well have to consider new planning and policy strategies in order to maintain the desired returns from tourism. Strategy will have to consider quality as well as quantity and provide a more accurate assessment of the short- and long-term costs and benefits of tourism development, in order to determine levels of tourism growth that are sustainable in terms of people, resources and destinations.

Suggestions for further reading

Comprehensive discussions of economic development within the ASEAN nations are to be found in Ariff (1991) *The Pacific Economy: Growth and External Stability;* Bollard *et al.* (1989) *Meeting the East Asia Challenge: Trends, Prospects and Policies;* and Drysdale (1988) *International Economic Pluralism: Economic Policy in East Asia and the Pacific.*

Useful overviews of tourism development and tourist flows in the region are to be found in the Economic Intelligence Unit (1990a) report *Far East and Pacific Travel in the 1990s,* and in the collection of papers in Hitchcock *et al.* (1992) *Tourism in South-East Asia.* More critical discussions of tourism in South East Asia are to be found in Hong (1985) *See the Third World While it Lasts;* Richter (1989) *The Politics of Tourism in Asia;* and Hall (1992a) in a discussion of sex tourism in South East Asia. The book by Richter, in particular, contains excellent chapters on tourism in the Philippines (Chapter 3, The Philippines: The Politicization of Tourism, pp. 51–81) and Thailand (Chapter 4, Thailand: Where Tourism and Politics Make Strange Bedfellows, pp. 82–101) as well as a broad account of issues in tourism development and tourism's unwanted impacts.

The above publications provide an invaluable guide to readings on tourism in individual countries in ASEAN. However, in addition to government reports (for example, Directorate General of Tourism 1992, *Statistics on Visitor Arrivals in Indonesia*) and articles in trade journals (especially *Asia Travel Trade*) students should also refer to national studies such as that undertaken by the Economic Intelligence Unit on Indonesia (1991) and Singapore (1990d). Numerous articles have been published in recent years on the problems that Singapore faces in promoting itself as a destination and in maximising the economic benefits of tourism to the country, students should examine the articles by Kee & Ghosh (1990), Khan *et al.* (1990), Toh & Low (1990) and Wong & Gan (1988).

A substantial body of academic literature is also available on various aspects of tourism in Thailand, especially in response to the environmental and social aspects of tourism such as sex tourism and the potential for the spread of AIDS and other sexually transmitted diseases. In addition, to the work of Hong (1985), Richter (1989), Hall (1992a), and Hitchcock *et al.* (1992) noted above, students should consult Elliot (1983) and the work of Cohen (1979, 1982a, 1982b, 1988, 1989).

Elements of Malaysian tourism have been discussed in Ap, Var and Din (1991) and Din (1988, 1989) the latter focusing on Islamic influences on tourism. The effects of tourism development on Malaysia are discussed in Hong (1985) and Ling (1991), while the recent work of Hitchcock *et al.* (1992) should also be examined. In addition, students should consult government publications and statistics such as those produced by the Tourist Development Corporation Malaysia (1991).

A development research project with substantial implications for tourism throughout the ASEAN region is the Bali Sustainable Development Project which is a collaborative programme between the University of Waterloo (Canada) and Gadjah Mada University (UGM) in Yogyakarta, Indonesia. The sustainable development strategy for Bali which the project is developing, may be seen as a potential model for both Indonesia and other South East Asian countries. For further details of the project and its tourism component see Wall (1993) and Wall & Dibnah (1992).

Discussion and review

Key concepts

Association of South East Asian Nations (ASEAN), regional trading blocs, Visitor Years, environmental and social impacts of tourism, cultural festivals, foreign investment, infrastructure requirements, marine tourism, heritage tourism, enforcement, Islam, target markets, mass tourist, budget travellers, backpackers, Free Independent Travellers (FIT), self-drive market, hotel supply, air accessibility, feeder routes, environmental concerns, coastal pollution, sex tourism, corruption, martial law, social concerns, co-operative marketing campaigns, political stability, AIDS, hub, travel balance, theme parks.

Questions for review and discussion

1 How have 'Visitor Years' brought benefits to the ASEAN countries?
2 Why does Indonesia, with substantially fewer travellers, receive greater income from tourism than Malaysia?
3 How is marine tourism being developed and promoted in the ASEAN countries?
4 Is Malaysia's target of 20 million visitor arrivals by the year 2000 feasible?
5 In what ways has tourism impacted on the physical environment in ASEAN countries and what has been done to ameliorate unwanted impacts?
6 How has politics influenced the growth and development of tourism in the Philippines?
7 How can sex tourism best be controlled in Thailand?
8 Will Singapore be able to maintain its position as the hub of South East Asia?

5 China: the sleeping tourism giant

> Now is a critical time for China's tourism develop-
> ment... China is facing serious challenges from
> home and abroad. China needs time and money
> to perfect facilities and services, to build a good
> image and win customers, but the financial diffi-
> culties will not be overcome quickly. China has to
> compete for the same market with counterparts
> in the Asia and Pacific region, most of which are
> well established and have a sophisticated tourism
> industry, eg Singapore, Hong Kong and Thai-
> land, with similar products, but better service and
> cheaper prices (Guangrui 1989: 62).
>   The increasing openness of the Chinese econ-
> omy in the last ten years has been nowhere more
> noticeable than in the development of its tourist
> industry. The scope for tourism in this vast coun-
> try is clearly enormous, and recent growth rates
> in tourist arrivals and receipts have indicated
> clearly the country's potential in the interna-
> tional tourism market. The massacre in Tianan-
> men Square and the repression which followed it
> threaten to bring this business to a grinding halt
> (Lavery 1989: 77).

Chinese tourism and the modernisation of China

Tourism has been one of the boom industries of post 'open door' China
and has come to play an extremely significant role in economic and
regional development, and international relations. However, the political
unrest of 1989, particularly the events of Tiananmen Square, has led to
considerable difficulties within the Chinese tourism industry for planning
and investment and poses substantial problems for improving the image of
China as a tourist destination. See Figure 5.1.

Although the first travel service handling overseas tourists was set up by
the People's Republic of China over thirty years ago, it is only since 1978
that there has been major expansion in inbound tourism. Until 1978
tourism was regarded almost solely as a diplomatic tool and focused on

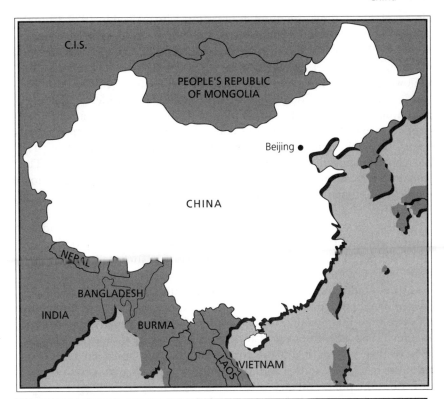

Figure 5.1: China

visitors from other communist countries and friendly third world or non-aligned nations. Since the shift by the Chinese Government in 1978 to an 'open door policy' in its relations with non-communist countries and the promotion of the doctrine of a 'socialist market economy', tourism has been regarded as a key element in the modernisation of China and a means to gaining important foreign exchange earnings (Choy & Gee 1983; Richter 1983, 1989; Guangrui 1985; Choy *et al.* 1986; Uysal *et al.* 1986; Hairui 1987). As Zhao Ziyang stated at the Thirteenth National Congress of the Communist Party of China in 1987:

> Our capacity to earn foreign exchange through export determines, to a great extent, the degree to which we can open to the outside world and affects the scale and pace of domestic economic development. For this reason, bearing in mind the demands of the world market and our own strong points, we should make vigorous efforts to develop export-oriented industries and products that are competitive and can bring quick and high economic returns (quoted in Tisdell and Wen 1991: 55).

The potential of tourism to net foreign exchange for the Chinese Government is substantial. For example in 1988, the year prior to the political unrest of Tiananmen Square, 3.17 million overseas tourists visited China, almost eighteen times the number of visitors who arrived in 1978. China's accumulated foreign exchange earnings from international tourism between 1978 and 1988 were estimated to be US$11.65 billion. At the end of 1988, there were 1496 hotels with 478 000 beds, and 1.57 million people owing their employment to tourism and 400 000 directly employed in tourism. In addition, domestic tourism is significant considering that over 300 million Chinese undertook domestic travel in 1988 with a combined expenditure of 18.7 million yuan (Tisdell & Wen 1990, 1991). 'In regional terms, the main concentrations of tourism employment are Peking (19 per cent), Guangzhou (17 per cent) and Shanghai (6.6 per cent). The remainder is distributed between 47 provincial cities (excluding those employed in tourism shops, other retail activities and the railways' (Lavery 1989: 80).

The significance of tourism for the economy has also meant a readjustment in government attitudes towards the role of tourism in a modernising Chinese state. For example, in 1986 tourism was included, for the first time, as part of the national social and economic development plan. However, the rapid growth of tourism has posed substantial planning and policy problems, particularly in terms of the determination of appropriate levels of foreign investment, and has not been without negative impacts. As Richter (1989: 23) observed: 'Chinese tourism policy is in a considerable state of flux, making it difficult for researchers and politically unnerving for those in Chinese tourism administration to say with great certainty what directions the policy will take'.

This chapter will emphasise the role that tourism has played in the modernisation of China and its impacts on the People's Republic's relationships with the outside world, and with Western nations in particular. It is divided into three main sections. First, a discussion of the growth in inbound, outbound and domestic tourism. Second, an account of tourism investment and infrastructure development. Third, an analysis of Chinese tourism following the events at Tiananmen Square and the associated political unrest of mid-1989, and possible patterns of future tourism development. The last section is important because of the relationship of China to neighbouring states such as Taiwan and Korea, and the takeover of Hong Kong in 1997.

Tourism growth since 1978

China can well be described as the sleeping tourist giant of the Pacific. China is the world's largest country in terms of population and is only now beginning to open itself up to substantial amounts of inbound, domestic and outbound travel. Unlike Japan, Taiwan and Korea, China still has a wide range of controls in place over nationals' ability to travel both within the country and overseas, as well as restrictions over the activities of foreign tourists in certain regions of the country. Nevertheless, substantial increases in inbound, outbound, and domestic tourism have occurred since 1978.

The inbound market

Overseas visitors to China can be broadly categorised into either 'visiting friends and relatives' (VFR) or organised tourists who are handled by travel services and organisations. The majority of foreign tourists fit into the organised category, while the overwhelming number of people from Hong Kong, Macao and Taiwan are either VFRs or daytrippers, often there for shopping. China does not regard 'compatriots' from Hong Kong, Macao and Taiwan as foreign visitors. Most of the compatriots visit China as independent travellers (Lavery 1989). 'The trend indicates that the percentage of organized tourists in the total arrivals had dropped from 42.3% in 1978 to 14.1% in 1987, while that of VFRs in the total from [Hong Kong, Macao and Taiwan] increased from 66.6% up to 92.2% during the same period' (Guangrui 1989: 51). Compatriots have accounted for approximately 90 per cent of total inbound travellers since 1978 and they have had a substantial impact on cross-border tourism although their effect on the broader national tourism economy is fairly limited because of their relatively low spending levels (Table 5.1).

Japan, the USA, the UK, Australia and the Philippines have been the major origin countries for foreign tourists in recent years, with Japan and the USA accounting for approximately half of all overseas visitors (Table 5.2). Following the lifting of many travel restrictions in the former Soviet Union, this country has shown substantial growth in outbound travel to China and given the long border between the two nations the Soviets may well surpass the United States market in several years time. Japan is by far the largest inbound market. However, the growth rate in Japanese inbound travel to China slowed substantially in 1988, perhaps because of a train accident near Shanghai in March of that year which claimed the lives of many Japanese travellers (Tisdell & Wen 1991). Similarly, the number of arrivals from the USA also fell in 1988, the first decline in this market since the commencement of the open door policy in 1978. Nevertheless, the instability that was experienced in the Chinese inbound travel market in 1988 was relatively minor when compared to the catastrophic effects that political unrest had on foreign visitation in 1989.

Table 5.3 illustrates the impacts of Tiananmen Square and the political unrest in China through the variation in visitor numbers from the top ten sources of foreign visitors between 1988 and 1989. With the exceptions of the (former) Soviet Union and the Philippines, every major source country had a double-digit percentage fall in outbound travel to China, with Japan experiencing almost a 40 per cent decline. The increased visitation from the (former) Soviet Union, is undoubtedly an indication of the reduction in tension between the two nations, a relaxation on travel restrictions and the experience of the Soviets with periods of martial law. Germany, Canada, Singapore and Thailand are also among the major new markets

Table 5.1: Chinese international visitor arrivals, 1978–1991

Year	Total		Foreign Visitors		Overseas Chinese		Compatriots		Taiwan	
	No. of Visitors	Growth Rate %	No. of Visitors	% Growth	No. of Visitors	% Growth	No. of Visitors	% Growth	No. of Visitors	% Growth
1978	1 809 221	-	229 646	-	18 092	-	1 561 483	-		
1979	4 203 901	132.4	362 389	57.8	20 910	15.6	3 820 602	144.7		
1980	5 702 536	35.6	529 124	46.0	34 413	64.6	5 138 999	34.5		
1981	7 767 096	36.2	675 153	27.6	38 853	12.9	7 053 087	37.2		
1982	7 924 261	2.0	764 497	13.2	42 745	10.0	7 117 019	1.0		
1983	9 477 005	19.6	872 511	14.1	40 352	-5.6	8 564 142	20.3		
1984	12 852 185	35.6	1 134 267	30.0	47 498	17.7	11 670 420	36.2		
1985	17 833 097	38.8	1 370 462	20.8	84 827	78.6	16 377 808	40.0		
1986	22 819 450	28.0	1 482 276	8.2	68 133	-19.7	21 269 041	29.9		
1987	26 902 267	17.9	1 727 821	16.6	87 031	27.7	25 087 415	18.0		
1988	31 694 804	17.8	1 842 206	6.6	79 348	-8.8	29 773 250	18.7	437 700	-
1989	24 501 394	-22.7	1 460.970	-20.7	68 556	-13.6	22 971 868	-22.8	541 000	23.6
1990	27 461 821	12.1	1 747 315	19.6	91 090	32.9	25 623 416	11.5	947 600	75.2
1991	33 349 761	21.4	2 710 103	55.1	133 427	46.5	30 506 231	19.8	946 632	-0.1

Overseas Chinese: refers to Chinese residing in foreign countries who hold a Chinese passport

Compatriots: Chinese national residing in Hong Kong, Macao and Taiwan (Taiwan became a separate category for statistical purposes in 1988).

Source: National Tourism Administration of the People's Republic of China 1992: 28

Table 5.2: Top five origin countries of foreign visitors to China, 1979-1991

Year	Country	%	Country	%	Country	%	Country	%	Country	%
1979	Japan	29.4	USA	18.7	The Philippines	4.8	UK	4.5	France	3.7
1980	Japan	32.0	USA	19.2	UK	5.4	Australia	5.4	The Philippines	4.3
1981	Japan	33.1	USA	19.3	UK	6.2	Australia	6.0	The Philippines	4.1
1982	Japan	32.1	USA	19.0	Italy	10.0	Australia	7.0	UK	5.5
1983	Japan	30.4	USA	19.3	Australia	6.2	UK	5.8	The Philippines	4.1
1984	Japan	32.5	USA	18.7	Australia	6.4	UK	5.5	The Philippines	3.8
1985	Japan	34.3	USA	17.5	Australia	5.7	UK	5.2	The Philippines	4.2
1986	Japan	32.6	USA	19.7	UK	5.4	Australia	4.9	The Philippines	3.6
1987	Japan	33.4	USA	18.3	UK	4.8	Singapore	3.7	Germany	3.5
1988	Japan	32.1	USA	16.3	UK	5.2	Germany	3.9	The Philippines	3.9
1989	Japan	24.6	USA	14.7	(former) Soviet Union	5.6	The Philippines	5.0	UK	4.9
1990	Japan	25.0	USA	13.3	(former) Soviet Union	6.3	UK	4.5	The Philippines	4.5
1991	Japan	23.6	USA	11.6	(former) Soviet Union	10.5	UK	4.2	The Philippines	3.9

Source: Guangrui 1989; National Tourism Administration of the People's Republic of China 1992: 26

Table 5.3: Top ten sources of foreign visitors to China in 1989 and variation in the number of visitors compared to 1988

Country	1989 Arrivals (No.)	% change from 1988
Japan	358 828	-39.4
USA	214 956	-28.6
(former) Soviet Union	81 347	+133.6
The Philippines	73 354	+2.7
UK	72 211	-25.2
Singapore	57 860	-11.5
Thailand	54 915	-16.6
France	51 905	-17.9
Australia	48 747	-20.2
Germany	52 799	-27.4

Source: National Tourism Administration of the People's Republic of China 1992: 26

that have developed in recent years (Lavery 1989; Yu 1992). However, while the number of foreigners visiting China fell by 20.7 per cent in 1989, the number of Chinese compatriots and overseas Chinese visiting China increased substantially. For example, despite the restrictions between the two Chinas, the number of Taiwanese visitors to the People's Republic increased by almost 25 per cent (Tisdell & Wen 1991).

The early 1990s has seen a substantial improvement in inbound tourism in China. The 4.7 million visitors in 1991 represented a 12 per cent increase on 1990 and a return to pre-Tiananmen Square figures, while tourism foreign exchange earnings increased 22 per cent in 1991 to US$2.8 billion. For 1992 it was expected that arrivals would pass five million with foreign exchange earnings over US$3 billion (Parker 1992a: 47).

China has developed extremely rapidly as an international tourist destination, although some expectations of the benefits of tourism for the Chinese economy and the ease at which China could sustain the initial high rate of inbound growth may have been dashed. For example, the national conference on tourism held at Beidaihe in September 1979 established a long-range plan targeted at receiving 3.5 million foreign tourists by 1985. Under the sixth five-year national economic plan (1981–1985), it was estimated that China would receive two million international tourists in 1985 and 3.5 million in 1990, 2.2 million being foreigners and 1.38 million being the 'four kinds of persons' (Chinese living abroad) (Dichen & Guangrui 1983: 84). However, in terms of ideology, organisation, resources, and personnel, many problems have emerged in the type, location, and supply of tourist facilities and attractions, the lack of trained staff, and poor management and administration, all of which have affected the rate of inbound growth and the development of new markets (Dichen & Guangrui 1983). For example, following Tiananmen Square, 'China's estimated

620 000 tourism workers underwent compulsory political indoctrination that aimed to cleanse their socialist minds, deepen their love of the Communist Party and, alarmingly, to cultivate their suspicions of foreigners, presumed by paranoid leaders to be bent on sundering communist rule' (Parker 1992a: 47). Therefore, the lack of stability in the growth rate is a direct reflection of the lack of political stability in terms of external relations with the outside world, shifting domestic attitudes and values, and a failure to understand the complex nature of the international tourism industry.

Domestic tourism

For many years under Communist rule, travel for leisure was considered as part of 'the lifestyle of the bourgeoisie which one should always guard against' (Guangrui 1989: 58). The implementation of the four modernisation policies has led to the development of a domestic tourism market where none existed before. According to the *Beijing Review* (1987: 31): 'More and more Chinese enterprises and government institutions have been using their welfare funds and monetary rewards to organize tours for their workers during the best seasons. Many leaders from different trades and professions try to organize meetings and business activities in tourist cities or scenic areas, taking the opportunity to enjoy the sights'. Furthermore, the annual average growth in national income of 8.7 per cent since 1978 (Lavery 1989) has flowed on into earnings and has meant that people now have more money to travel as well as greater freedom.

The growth of domestic travel opportunities has had a substantial impact on the establishment of domestic tourism operations. For example, in 1988 China had more than 600 travel businesses handling mainly domestic travel; before 1980 hardly any existed (Guangrui 1989). Approximately 90 per cent of domestic travellers are independents, although many are turning to agencies to assist in travel arrangements in order to secure accommodation and transport. About half of all domestic travel is paid for by government, although as government implements tighter control over spending and as personal disposable income grows, it is likely that the number of self-paid trips will increase quite dramatically. According to Guangrui (1989: 55):

Among the self-paid tourists, the bulk is composed of teachers and students, retired people, honeymooners, farmers and individual traders, who have more free time and disposable money... At the beginning domestic tourists used to accept sightseeing at historical sites and scenic spots as the main purpose of a tour but now more and more of them are seeking something special, creative and productive, eg tours for newlyweds, holidays and recuperation, enjoying cuisine, plum appreciation, language-learning and trips combining sightseeing with education, information collection and exchange, economic and technical investigation and business purposes.

Tourism administration

The China State Administration for Travel and Tourism (SATT) is the paramount government body responsible for tourism and which was created in 1978 at the time of the four modernisations. In 1981 SATT was separated from the Ministry of Foreign Affairs and established as an independent body. A Tourism Co-ordinating group was established in 1986 to co-ordinate policy at the ministerial level but was replaced in June 1988 by the National Tourism Committee. The Chinese Government's central aim is to expand the number of foreign visitors in order to increase foreign exchange income, improve the balance of payments situation, and to contribute to employment and national development.

In addition to the central government structure, each province, autonomous region, and city also has its own tourist bureau and/or administration. The bureaux or agencies 'are under the dual control of both local government and higher level tourist administration', with each agency operating relatively independently. As part of the economic reform occurring within China, many of the tourism industry activities controlled by government are being decentralised to allow for private investment and the establishment of joint ventures. However, despite the potential for duplication and inappropriate tourism planning, 'It is not deemed necessary to unify the industry, instead each government makes its own decisions under its own specific conditions' (Guangrui 1987: 57).

Within the hotel sector, the decentralised nature of tourism policy has led to substantial co-ordination problems. Tisdell and Wen (1991) reported that the 1300 hotels in China were owned by more than 350 different organisations, including the central government, local government, government departments, collectives, and individuals. Consequently, there is poor decision-making regarding the supply of hotels and political rather than economic or market considerations are seen to predominate official thinking.

Tourism infrastructure and investment

Because of the lack of exposure to the demands of mass domestic and international travel for over thirty years, the Chinese tourism infrastructure was very poorly developed when inbound and domestic tourism began to be encouraged again in 1978. Between 1979 and 1983 the dominant sources of tourism investment were SATT and various government departments and agencies. For example, in 1979 the State Council of China invested 360 million yuan in the construction of thirty hotels with a total of 17 000 beds (Uysal et al. 1986). Substantial levels of foreign investment did not occur until 1983 following the success of the first Sino-foreign joint venture hotel which was opened in 1982.

The introduction of foreign capital and management into the tourism industry has been a key factor in the modernisation of tourism and hospitality in China. Although the exact level of investment in tourism is extremely difficult to determine, the amount of foreign investment in 1984 alone was estimated to be US$1.828 billion, representing almost 70 per cent of all direct foreign investment into the country in this year (Table 5.4) (Tisdell & Wen 1990). Approximately one-third of the total direct foreign investment in China between 1979 and 1988 (US$7.3 billion) was used for hotel investment, with the main sources of overseas funds being Hong Kong, Japan, Macao, and the USA (Tisdell & Wen 1990).

Foreign investment has not only allowed for the construction of tourist facilities but has also led to the adoption of technological innovations, skill level improvement and the application of modern hospitality management skills (Yam 1987; Schrock, Adams & Lung 1989). Several problems have emerged in the growth of foreign involvement in the Chinese tourism industry. First, there has been a fear of foreign domination of the hotel sector with a resultant government reaction in the form of changes to the investment and joint venture approval process for tourism developments in some regions. Many of the concerns over foreign domination of the hospitality sector are derived from the substantial returns that overseas investors will be seeking from their ventures, both in terms of profits and in the form of interest on finance. Furthermore, given that the majority of investment is guaranteed by the central government, the government is faced with the prospect of having to meet some of the debt burden during a period of low occupancy rates. Second, there has been a negative reaction from government to some overseas owned or managed operations, because of the payment of management fees to these operations regardless of the profitability of ventures. For example, in 1986 at the China Hotel in Guangzhou 'the total wage for the 90 foreign management staff was 120 per cent to that of the 2800 Chinese employees' (Tisdell & Wen 1990: 18).

Table 5.4: Amount of foreign investment in tourism in China in 1984

Tourist sector	Number of projects	Amount of foreign investment ('000 US$)	Percentage of total foreign investment
Hotel and business centre	82	1 555 860	85.08
Amusement facility centres	10	29 955	1.64
Taxi and cruise company	29	31 000	1.71
Food	11	9 801	0.54
Other tourist services	16	201 980	11.04
Total	**148**	**1 828 596**	**100**

Source: *Almanac of Chinese Economy* in Tisdell & Wen 1990:36

Table 5.5: Tourism investment plans for 1985–1990 for the Chinese state and for the fifteen main tourist cities

Investment purpose	State-level investment plan $(1 \times 10^8$ Yuan)	15 main tourist centres $(1 \times 10^8$ Yuan)	Combined total	%
Scenic spots	10.82	22.13	32.95	12.04
Tourist hotels	74.04	151.94	225.98	82.60
(Foreign capital)	(41.98)	(79.70)	(121.68)	(44.48)
Tourism education	1.50	2.05	3.55	1.30
International conference and shopping centre	3.05	7.64	10.69	3.91
Total	**89.88**	**183.70**	**273.58**	**100**
Total foreign capital	**41.98**	**80.50**	**122.48**	**44.77**

Source: Adapted from Tisdell & Wen 1990: 39

Third, there is concern from some conservative government officials and Communist Party members over the role that business operations have in the spread of Western ideas in China. Tourism has also been blamed by some commentators for the introduction of unwelcome social practices. For example, in 1983 Dichen and Guangrui argued that tourism had brought

'unhealthy' and 'uncivilised' influences… into China. Some weak-willed Chinese, youngsters in particular, could not withstand such influences and blindly pursue the way of life of the foreigners. Also smuggling, contraband trafficking, divulging state secrets and other offences occurred. These have violated the decency and image of socialist China and should not be tolerated (1983: 78).

Some six years on, the negative social impacts of tourism had not declined in significance for Chinese authorities. In particular, the effects of tourism on Chinese socialist values remains a major concern.

Following a few years of tourism development many undesirable practices have arisen, eg asking for an exorbitant payment and unreasonable commission, accepting (or demanding) bribes, prostitution, and illegal selling and buying of foreign currencies. These hardly existed even during the cultural revolution but have emerged in most tourist areas. Accepting tips, contrary to socialist ethics, was rampant for a time among tourist guides and service people. The practice was so serious that in August 1987 the SATT, with the approval of the State Council, issued special regulations to stop the practice of tipping (Guangrui 1989: 61).

Finally, substantial problems exist in the quality of service, sanitation, and cleanliness at many of the hotels, restaurants, and tourist facilities visited by foreign tourists. Tourism education and training has been a priority for China's tourism authorities. However, investment in training has lagged substantially behind that placed into the development of physical infrastructure (Guangrui 1987). As Schrock *et al.* (1989) reported:

Once people are inside the open door, they have found difficulty in achieving international service standards... service workers are surprised that tourists demand more from them when the tourists are already enjoying the best the country has to offer. Even after ten years of being open to international tourists, such basics as confirmed reservations, property maintenance, quality control, sanitation, and staff training are large hurdles to overcome (1989: 68–9).

Probably the central problem which China faces, is the imbalanced investment in tourism infrastructure. Accommodation was overbuilt, while investment in transportation and attractions lagged behind during the 1980s. For example, an examination of the investment plans of the state and of the fifteen main tourist cities for the period 1985–1990 indicates that 85 per cent of funds were placed in hotel projects (Table 5.5). As the following sections indicate, removing the imbalances between accommodation, transport and attraction development will be one of the key issues facing Chinese tourism in the 1990s.

Accommodation

China witnessed the rapid development of hotels during the 1980s thanks to the establishment of Special Economic Zones (SEZs) in a number of cities and regions. Through the SEZs, government at both municipal and regional level was able to offer tourism developers inexpensive land, tax holidays of three to five years, a flat corporate income tax rate of 15 per cent, and an inexpensive labour force (Cook 1989). The success of the government incentives is demonstrated in the six-fold increase in the number of hotels and hotel rooms between 1980 and 1987. However, major problems still remain. There is a disproportionate provision of luxury hotels in comparison with budget and medium-grade accommodation. 'In China, hotels for foreigners, *Bin-guan*, are markedly differentiated from those for Chinese citizens, *Lü-guan*' with the latter being of 'a much lower standard' (Tisdell & Wen 1991: 59). Unfortunately, there is little flexibility for overseas visitors to utilise the *Lü-guan* even though, for example, 70 per cent of visitors to Beijing were seeking budget or mid-priced accommodation (Zhao 1989), although Parker (1992a) has noted greater domestic tourist use of five-star hotels. An additional problem is that hotels are not necessarily located in the areas where demand is concentrated. As Guangrui noted, 'In 1986... 13 cities listed as the 'hottest spots' received 85.1% of total tourist-days, with only 48.3% of the total hotel rooms available country wide'. Zhao Jian blamed the problems in the hotel sector on a 'lack of knowledge about the hotel industry, an unreasonable investment policy, and archaic finance and management systems' (1989: 63).

By the end of the 1980s, hotel supply was substantially exceeding overseas visitor demand. For example, 'the annual growth rate in the number of hotels in Beijing and Xi'an in the period 1984 to 1987 was 20.5% and 30.6% respectively, but the number of overseas arrivals increased by only 17.9% and 25.9%' (Tisdell & Wen 1990: 15). Such was the situation that, on 17 April 1988, the China National Tourist Administration (CNTA) announced that overseas joint-venture hotels would not be built until further notice in the major tourist destinations of Beijing, Shanghai, Guangzhou, Guilin, Xi'an and Hangzhou. It has also stated a desire to construct more medium- and low-class hotels (Economist Intelligence Unit 1989). Approval for any project that did not have a signed contract was rescinded. Such measures have undoubtedly slowed down the rate of accommodation development in China, although other major infrastructural problems still remain, especially in the provision of adequate transport services and attraction management and development.

Attractions

As of 1989, more than 480 cities and towns had been opened to overseas visitors. The key areas for tourism development are Beijing, Shanghai, Xi'an, Guilin, Hangzhou, Guangzhou, and Jiangsu and Hainan Provinces. Apart from the VFR market, culture is clearly the major attraction of China to foreign tourists (Lavery 1989). Substantial monies have been set aside to develop and restore internationally recognised historic sites and monuments, such as the Great Wall, the Palace Museum in Beijing, and the terracotta warriors in Xi'an. Discovered in 1974, the Terracotta warriors include 7500 life-size clay figures of warriors and horses buried around 200BC to guard the tomb of the first Qin Emperor. About 300 000 foreign tourists and one million domestic tourists visited Xi'an during 1987 with the Terracotta Warrior and Horse Museum being the most popular attraction. Overseas tourists stayed an average of 2.4 days and spent an amount equivalent to US$32 million (Mings & Liu 1989). The typical tourist travel pattern consists of touring Xi'an and its vicinity in buses, travelling from one historical site to another. One day is usually spent visiting the Qin tomb, the Terracotta Warrior and Horse Museum, the ancient village museum of Banpo (an archaeological site dating from 5000BC) and the imperial country estate of Huaqing Hot Springs, all to the north east of Xi'an. A second day is often spent visiting historical attractions within the city of Xi'an such as the Wild Goose Pagoda, a drum or bell tower, the great mosque and other sites, along with souvenir shopping (Zeppel & Hall 1992). Based on the tourist appeal of its cultural heritage, the city of Xi'an is undergoing a period of major hotel construction which will eventually increase the number of hotel rooms by 150 per cent (Mings & Liu 1989).

Historic trading routes which have been the subject of a number of documentaries, such as the Grand Canal, Yangtze River, and the Silk Road, have also attracted substantial numbers of foreign visitors as well as domestic tourists. A more recent tour is the 'Last Emperor tour' set in northern China, which follows many of the key points of interest from the Bertolucci film of the same name. A number of new tourist destinations have also become more accessible to foreign visitors. For instance, Lhasa in Tibet was strictly closed to tourists until 1984. In 1984 Lhasa had 1500 overseas visitors; in 1987, 43 000 tourists visited even though the tours were rather expensive (Guangrui 1989).

Despite the rapid growth in tourist numbers at many destinations, investment in tourism attraction development is still limited, leading to overcrowding at some sites during peak seasons and subsequent deterioration of site values and the tourist experience. For example, according to Tisdell and Wen (1990: 130), 'there are more than 260 spots with tourist value in Suzhou city, but only 20 have been renovated and opened. In the peak season about 200 thousand tourists visit these places daily, but the appropriate capacity is 20 to 60 thousand a day. Most of the gardens in Suzhou are deteriorating, due to lack of investment'. Similarly, Guangrui (1989: 56) observed: 'Accessibility, supporting facilities and services, and restoration and preservation of... attractions fall well short of the requirements and demands of the visitors due to the limited funds available and inadequate management'.

Special interest travel activities are also emerging as a significant component of the attractiveness of China as a tourist destination (Zeppel & Hall 1992). The cultural tourism aspects are particularly important (Oudiette 1990), especially the ethnic minorities of the south and west of the country. Gourmet tourism, such as tea sampling and genuine Chinese food is also attracting considerable interest. Finally, nature-based travel such as bird-watching, and visiting the Giant Panda habitat in Wolong Nature Reserve in Sichuan Province are also significant. Given the world-wide growth of interest in eco-tourism, it is likely that China's natural heritage will increasingly come to complement the role that its culture plays in attracting tourists (Singh 1992). As of 1987, China had 316 nature reserves occupying 1.8 per cent of its total land area. By the year 2000, Chinese authorities plan to have declared about 500 nature reserves including some 330 flora reserves, 130 fauna reserves and 35 reserves for conserving geological and other features, including hot springs (Xiyang 1987).

Transport

The development of a modern transport network has been a major priority in the revitalisation of the Chinese economy and is a key component of the current Eighth Five-Year plan. Tourism has greatly benefited from the increased provision of tour buses, taxi cabs, trains, and air networks. However, transport development has still tended to lag behind hotel construction with substantial problems occurring on domestic air and rail routes 'where serious problems of peak season congestion, overcrowding and overbooking occur' (Lavery 1989: 91). The nature of transport problems for overseas tourists in China has been well expressed by Cook (1989: 66):

The bicycle was the only form of transportation I could count on. A 100-mile bus ride took seven hours due to treacherous roads that were often only wide enough for traffic to travel in one direction at a time. Flight delays of two or three hours are the norm on the government-owned airlines, which in some cases have seats that are too small to fit the average American. Although my trains ran on schedule, they were old and dirty and seemed unsafe.

Guangrui (1989) has argued that transport barriers to and within China are now the greatest limitation on the expansion of inbound tourism. Undoubtedly, there has been some expansion in the transport network. For example, between 1978 and 1988 the Civil Aviation Administration of China (CAAC) increased its capacity over eight times and in 1988 transported 14 million passengers (Tisdell & Wen 1991). However, substantial problems still exist with airline and train availability. In order to try to overcome some of the difficulties passengers have been experiencing, the CAAC announced in November 1988 that it would be broken up into six regional state owned airlines. This was done to encourage competition. In addition, the new airlines are purchasing new aircraft in order to establish new domestic and international routes and improve business. While the vast bureaucratic edifice of the Ministry of Railways has refused to consider being corporatised or broken up into more efficient regionally based units, the Ministry has embarked on a rolling stock construction programme that is designed to alleviate the shortage of tourist class carriages and sleeping cars (Lavery 1989). Furthermore, while Guangrui (1989) notes that sufficient rooms are now available in China to meet tourist demands, at least at the five star level, the economic value of accommodation is negligible unless tourists can reach it. As Tisdell and Wen (1991: 63) observed, China is a developing country: 'one would therefore expect it to encounter difficulties with its transport system similar to many other less developed countries. But... a transport system which is developed to cater for foreign tourists may result in a transport infrastructure which lacks flexibility or adaptibility in relation to local needs'.

Beyond Tiananmen Square: future prospects for tourism in China

The sight of tanks rolling into the Square; the violent battles between students and troops; the steadfastly uncompromising attitude of the Chinese authorities; it was all watched by the world on prime-time television. And most people living in free societies felt revulsion and anger; those planning holidays to China cancelled, while those with a vague notion of visiting the country put it on hold for the distant future—if ever (Graham 1990: 25).

The massacre of Chinese students and civilians in Tiananmen Square put a temporary end to international tourism in China. As history is rewritten in China, however, and as the events of Spring 1989 become back-page news around the world, tourists will return to China. In fact, the number of travellers to China is expected to increase dramatically throughout the 1990s (Cook 1989: 64).

The day of the events at Tiananmen Square, 4 June 1989, is a pivotal date in Chinese political history and in its relations with the outside world. The political protests at Tiananmen Square and throughout many of China's cities dramatically impacted the country's tourism industry. By late 1989 many of Beijing's hotels were almost empty. Occupancy levels in the hotels were 'below 30 per cent at a time when closer to 90 per cent would have been expected... 300 tour groups totalling 11 500 people were cancelled in May' (Lavery 1989: 96). As Gartner and Shen (1992: 47) noted, 'occupancy rates of 15 per cent were considered high in the months shortly after the conflict'.

The low occupancy rates reflected many hotels' reliance on business travellers. Business visits were affected by both perceptions of stability which affected business confidence and also by the formal and informal sanctions that were imposed on corporations conducting business in China. However, the perception of risk affects all aspects of the tourism market.

In 1988 China earned US$2220 million from foreign tourists but this fell by US$430 million the following year due to the effects of the political unrest during May and June (Tisdell & Wen 1991). While a substantial loss of foreign exchange was experienced, it was nowhere near as bad as some commentators had forecast (Table 5.6). For example, *Travel and Tourism Analyst* estimated that 'receipts from foreign tourists will fall by 75 per cent in 1989, reducing earnings to around $550 mllion, or, to put it another

Table 5.6: China's international tourism receipts, 1978–1991

Year	Receipts US$million	% Growth rate
1978	262.90	-
1979	449.27	70.9
1980	616.65	37.3
1981	784.91	27.3
1982	843.17	7.4
1983	941.20	11.6
1984	1 131.34	20.2
1985	1 250.00	10.5
1986	1 530.85	22.5
1987	1 861.51	21.6
1988	2 246.83	20.7
1989	1 860.48	-17.2
1990	2 217.58	19.2
1991	2 844.97	28.3

Source: National Tourism Administration of the People's Republic of China 1992: 102

way, recording a loss of $1.9 billion over expected levels' (Lavery 1989: 96). Following the political unrest of mid-1989, the Taiwanese market was unaffected, the Japanese are coming back but the insurance conscious United States market is still substantially affected.

Research by Roehl (1990) on United States travel agents and Gartner and Shen (1992) on mature travellers, indicated a negative shift in attitudes towards visiting China as a result of the events at Tiananmen Square. Given time and a run of favourable images in the travel press and the general media, China's tourist image may slowly revert to that held before the political unrest of 1989. Nevertheless, overseas attitudes towards the Chinese occupation of Tibet (Klieger 1992), human rights issues, and the transfer of Hong Kong to Chinese sovereignty will clearly continue to colour foreign tourist's perceptions of China as a destination and therefore influence their decision making.

Despite the significance of safety and political issues, the country's cultural attractions 'will prove irresistible lures in the long-term' to tourists (Graham 1990: 26). However, even as tourists return, there will still be a glut of hotel accommodation. For example, in Shanghai nearly forty new hotels were either ready or nearing completion early in 1990. There were almost 13 000 rooms in twenty-six joint venture hotels at the end of 1990, almost double the number at the end of 1989. At the end of 1991, the number of rooms moved to an estimated 18 000 (*Asia Travel Trade* 1990o: 29). Nevertheless, as China improves its communication, travel, service and budget travel infrastructure, more tourists will be able to visit destinations away from the current centres (Cook 1989).

Can China realise tourism with a Socialist face?

Considerable emphasis has been given by the Chinese authorities to the development of a 'Chinese-style' form of tourism which promotes its indigenous attractions, culture, and tourism resources in a manner which meets the goals of Chinese State Socialism. China has the avowed goal of achieving a 'double harvest' from tourism 'in both the economic and political spheres', whereby 'China should... aim to promote tourism activities that are beneficial to the spiritual and physical well-being of both tourists and host community. Like all other economic undertakings under socialism, tourism should be a component of the entire national economic policy' (Dichen & Guangrui 1983: 79). Nevertheless, substantial development issues still remain.

In many ways the social, economic and physical development problems of China are similar to those facing other countries in Asia and the Pacific. As Guangrui (1989: 62) reported:

Unplanned development, excessive utilization, and the neglect of environmental protection while pursuing immediate objectives or one's own sector's interests, have led to destruction and pollution of tourist resources. Overcommercialization, cheating and counterfeiting have 'cheapened' many forms of art and the image of the destination as a whole, and also offended overseas visitors. Though some of the problems were unavoidable to begin with, they should now be looked at and the necessary measures taken to minimize the negative effects of tourism while maximising the gains—economically, socially and physically.

China needs to find appropriate solutions to the problems posed by rapid tourism development. However, neither complete state control nor unbridled capitalism have the answer. Given the experience of inappropriate and unbalanced development of tourism infrastructure discussed above, particularly in the accommodation sector, greater account needs to be given by tourism authorities at all levels of market forces. As Tisdell and Wen observed 'market mechanisms may fail... to take account of adverse environmental spillovers from tourist development. But the current situation is unsatisfactory since neither the market nor central authorities are providing discipline, coordination and direction of tourist development' (1991: 63).

The slowdown in tourism growth following Tiananmen Square has given China's tourism policy-makers an opportunity to re-evaluate the direction which Chinese tourism has taken. Indeed, Reynolds (1990: 115) observed, 'The realities of modern mass travel may force the Government to reassess the country's position as a tourist destination in the world market-place'. The restructuring of the domestic aviation industry and the continuing support of the modernisation policy clearly indicates the seriousness that some authorities have paid to enhancing China's competitiveness as a destination. Although inbound tourism is recovering steadily because of the maintenance of the 'open door' policy; an improved image through, for example, the hosting of the 11th Asian Games in Beijing in September 1990 and the restoration of law and order and the lifting of martial law, continued political uncertainty may well stymie growth in a fragile tourism market (Hart 1990; Parker 1992b). However, some promotional efforts, such as Visit China Year 1992, were substantially misdirected.

The concept of declaring 1992 'Visit China Year' follows the success of such events throughout eastern Asia but particularly in the ASEAN countries (see Chapter 4), and the need to improve the country's tarnished reputation following the unrest of 1989. However, the Year was 'hastily planned, less than a year in advance' (Parker 1992a: 47), and the budget was so small (US$2 million for promotion) that the National Tourism Authority ruled out any paid advertising overseas (Parker 1992c). As Parker (1992a) observed, most tourists only learned about Visit China Year after they arrived.

As with a number of countries in the Asia–Pacific region, Chinese tourism authorities need to reconcile the conflicting demands of tourism development. The National Tourism Administration hopes to boost China's earnings from foreign exchange from its target of US$2 billion for 1990 to US$3.5 billion for 1995 (Tisdell & Wen 1991). However, development rarely occurs without its perceived costs. 'Some top policymakers remain uneasy with some of the political ramifications of increased social mobility and integration of China with the rest of the world' (*Far Eastern Economic Review* 1992b: 46). The increased dependence on tourism as a source of economic growth means that it would be extremely difficult for China to halt tourism development. Tourism represents both an exchange of ideas as well as an exchange of people. The social and political effects of international tourism on Chinese society will last much longer than the temporary sojourns of Western tourists.

Suggestions for further reading

A good overview of China's economic development and its growing inter-dependence with the Pacific economies is to be found in Ariff (1991), Garnaut (1990), and in the standard work on modern Chinese history by Hsü (1990) *The Rise of Modern China*, especially Chapters 35 to 40 which discuss the four modernisations, the building of socialism with Chinese characteristics, the impact of the open-door policy, and the events at Tiananmen Square.

Students are fortunate in being able to examine a well-developed body of academic literature on tourism in China. Richter (1989) (Chapter 2 About Face: The Political Evolution of Chinese Tourism Policy, pp. 23–50), Reynolds (1990), Guangrui (1989), and Oudiette (1990), all provide excellent overviews of tourism in China. In addition, a 1990 special theme issue of *Geojournal* (vol. 21, no. 1/2) contains seven articles on the Chinese tourist industry, with four at a regional level, including Tibet, Xi'an, and North Xinjiang.

Early assessments of tourism in China following the commencement of the four modernisations and the open-door policy can be found in Richter (1983), Choy & Gee (1983), Guangrui (1985), Uysal *et al.*, and Choy *et al.* (1986). The difficulties surrounding tourism development in China are discussed in Hairui (1987), Schrock *et al.* (1989), Zhao (1989), and Tisdell & Wen (1991). The effects of the protests at Tiananmen Square and elsewhere in China on inbound visitation have also been well covered, see Lavery (1989), Roehl (1990), Gartner & Shen (1992), and Klieger (1992). For a more recent analysis of international tourism to China see Yu (1992).

Discussion and review

Key concepts

'Open door policy', foreign investment, socialist market economy, foreign exchange, 'compatriots', political unrest, Tiananmen Square, ideology, tourism administration, four modernisations, social impacts, education and training, accommodation sector, joint ventures, cultural tourism, special interest tourism, transport network.

Questions for review and discussion

1 How has the political situation in China influenced inbound tourism growth?
2 What are the major problems which China has faced in the development of tourism infrastructure?
3 What are the major problems that have emerged in relation to foreign investment in the Chinese tourism industry?
4 Will China's cultural attractions 'prove irresistible lures in the long-term' (Graham 1990: 26) to foreign tourists?
5 Is it correct to decribe China as the sleeping tourist giant?

6 Australia and New Zealand: the formation of a joint market

> Traditionally both Australia and New Zealand have relied upon each other for most of their inbound traffic. But there is a limit to the growth opportunities in tourism if we become too caught up in our regional market of some 20 million people—Sir Frank Moore, Chairman, Australian Tourism Industry Association (1991)
>
> The new chapter we have opened in our bilateral economic and trade relationship will strengthen our ability to participate in the dynamic growth of the world economy and particularly in the Asia/Pacific region, of which we are part—Joint statement by the Prime Ministers of Australia and New Zealand on the occasion of the conclusion of the 1988 review of the Australia New Zealand Closer Economic Relationship (Department of Trade and Industry 1988: 6)

Long perceived as tourist generating regions rather than destinations in their own right, Australia and New Zealand have recently become significant inbound destinations (see Figure 6.1). Tourism is now a major export industry. The Government in both countries has placed substantial emphasis on tourism as a source of foreign exchange and a mechanism for regional development and employment generation during a period of substantial economic restructuring (Forsyth & Dwyer 1991a). The annual arrivals to Australia and New Zealand are relatively low in international terms, with Australia receiving approximately 2.5 million visitors in 1992 and New Zealand one million, although the growth of inbound tourism to Australia was one of the highest in the developed world in the 1980s. From 1980 to 1989 Australian visitor arrivals grew 130 per cent at an average annual growth rate of 9.7 per cent. At the same time, visitor arrivals to New Zealand grew 94 per cent at an average rate of 7.6 per cent per annum. The strength of these figures is reinforced when we note that total world

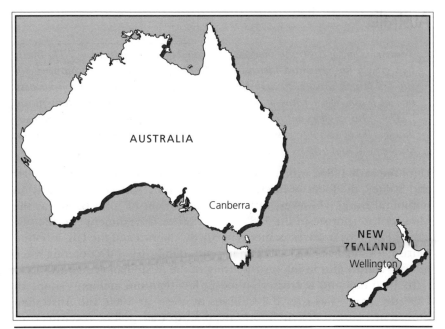

Figure 6.1: Australia and New Zealand

arrivals for the same period grew by 42 per cent with an average increase of 3.9 per cent (New Zealand Tourism Board 1991).

The two countries are undergoing substantial economic and social restructuring as they adapt from highly protected and primarily British and North American trade driven economies to an increasingly Asian and Pacific outlook with reduced trade barriers. Trade between the two countries is extremely significant and has increased rapidly in recent years under the Closer Economic Relations Trade agreement which came into effect in 1983 and which is now being extended into service industries such as aviation and tourism. Australia is New Zealand's most important inbound tourist market while New Zealand has only recently been replaced by Japan as Australia's largest source of visitors.

This chapter will discuss the inbound and outbound tourism markets of both countries. The growth of international tourism in Australia and New Zealand has been accelerated by the Closer Economic Relations Trade Agreement (CER) between the two countries and the deregulation of the domestic and trans-Tasman aviation markets. Aviation deregulation in Australia and New Zealand has been matched by an increasingly market-oriented approach to tourism development which has lead to substantial restructuring of government tourism agencies. Like other countries in the region, the growth of international tourism has been matched by concerns about its negative impacts. Therefore, government is faced with difficult decisions over the appropriate rate and nature of tourism development.

stralia

> *Tourism is one of Australia's biggest and fastest growing industries... The industry's growth has generated increased employment opportunities, encouraged substantial private investment and enhanced the nation's balance of payments position at a time when many of our traditional exports face an uncertain future. ...The industry offers outstanding prospects for future growth. It is an industry that has the potential to make a significant contribution to the nation's economic development and help secure our future prosperity (Simmons 1991: 1).*

Until the early 1980s, with a few notable exceptions such as the Gold Coast and Sydney, the focus of international tourism in Australia was clearly on outbound travel. However, with the appointment of John Brown as the Minister for Tourism in the 1983 federal Labor Government and the success of Paul Hogan advertisements in North America and the UK, inbound tourism was finally perceived as an important industry and a potentially significant contributor in the restructuring of the Australian economy.

In 1980 inbound tourism resulted in less than one million visitors. In 1990 the figure was over 2.2 million. By the year 2000, the Australian Bureau of Tourism Research forecasts that Australia will be receiving over five million visitors per annum, while the Australian Tourism Industry Association has estimated that the figure will be 7.5 million. Furthermore, the Australian Tourist Commission has predicted that tourism will generate

Table 6.1: Contribution of tourism to the Australian economy, 1990/91–1991/92

Item	1990–1991	1991–1992
Tourism Expenditure (A$million)		
International	7 200	8 200
Domestic	17 900	18 400
Total	25 000	26 600
Employment Generated		
International	130 000	144 000
Domestic	320 000	322 000
Total	450 000	466 000
Contribution to GDP (%)		
International	1.6	1.8
Domestic	3.8	3.8
Total	5.4	5.6

Source: Bureau of Tourism Research 1992

'200,000 new jobs in the next decade and generate between A$20 billion and A$30 billion in income from overseas' (Edwards & Murphy 1992: 33).

Tourism is a major contributor to economic development and employment generation in Australia. Tourism accounted for an estimated 10 per cent of all new positions, part -time and full-time, created annually in Australia from 1982 to 1989 (Economist Intelligence Unit 1990e). In the late 1980s tourism was estimated to provide approximately 448 000 jobs, employing 5.8 per cent of the workforce. In 1990–1991 the total had risen marginally to 450 000 while in 1991–1992 the figure was 466 000 with nearly all of the employment growth being generated by inbound tourism (Table 6.1).

Tourism is Australia's biggest export earner and accounts for approximately 5.6 per cent of GDP. Domestic tourism accounts for almost three-quarters of tourist expenditure. The Federal Government emphasises inbound tourism because of the potential foreign exchange earnings and contribution to the balance of payments. For example, in the 1988–1989 financial year, tourism accounted for A$6.1 billion of foreign exchange earnings. However, as Faulkner (1990: 37) observed, 'while tourism is improving Australia's balance of payments by virtue of the substantial contribution international visitors make to export income, this contribution is being offset by the impact of increased overseas travel by Australians on the country's import bill'.

The outbound market

Australian outbound travel has continued to grow during the 1980s but has reflected the impact of the downturn in the Australian economy, particularly the substantial depreciation of the Australian dollar in 1984 and the recessions of 1982–1983 and 1990–1992 (Faulkner 1990). Short-term departures by Australian residents has grown from 1.2 million in 1980 to 2.1 million in 1991 (Table 6.2). The major purpose for outbound travel is holiday (54 per cent) with visiting friends and relatives the next most important reason (22 per cent). 'In the face of increasing cost for overseas travel, consumers responded with product substitution. Destinations in the Asia–Pacific region grew at the expense of Europe where the depreciation of the dollar was most obvious' (King 1991: 85). The rapid increase in airline capacity in the Pacific Rim associated with the growth of inbound tourism has enhanced the price competitiveness of closer destinations such as Bali, Fiji, Hawaii and New Zealand.

The inbound market

Short-term arrivals of overseas visitors in Australia has increased from 904 600 in 1980 to 2.37 million in 1991 (Table 6.3). During the mid-1980s Australian inbound tourism numbers were increasing at approximately 25 per cent per annum. In the 1988–1989 financial year this figure fell substantially to -3.3 per cent partly because of the effects of the domestic pilots' strike but also because the figures for 1988 were above average as a

Table 6.2: Short-term departures of Australian residents, 1980–1991 (000's)

Purpose	1980	1985	1989	1990	1991	%
Convention	27.8	34.1	47.7	55.3	42.6	2
Business	133.4	182.3	302.2	306.9	305.1	15
VFR	235.1	287.9	387.6	439.2	453.6	22
Holiday	706.3	891.4	1 085.5	1 193.9	1 124.1	54
Other	101.0	116.3	166.8	174.6	174.0	8
Total	**1 203.6**	**1 512.0**	**1 989.8**	**2 169.9**	**2 099.4**	**100**

Source: Australian Bureau of Statistics in Bureau of Tourism Research 1992

Table 6.3: Australian short-term arrivals of overseas visitors by country of residence, 1980–1991 (000's)

Country of Residence	1980	%	1985	%	1989	%	1990	%	1991	%
Canada	28.5	3.2	40.9	3.6	54.2	2.6	53.7	2.4	53.4	2.3
USA	111.4	12.3	196.5	17.2	260.7	12.5	250.7	11.3	271.8	11.5
UK and Ireland	131.5	14.5	158.9	13.9	285.1	13.7	288.3	13.0	273.4	11.5
Europe	112.3	12.4	142.0	12.4	245.6	11.8	260.1	11.7	257.4	10.9
Japan	48.8	5.4	107.6	9.4	349.5	16.8	479.9	21.7	528.5	22.3
Asia	89.9	9.9	163.4	14.3	321.0	15.4	348.1	15.7	373.8	15.8
New Zealand	307.1	33.9	245.3	21.5	449.3	21.6	418.4	18.9	480.6	20.3
Other	75.1	8.3	88.0	7.7	114.9	5.5	115.7	5.2	131.5	5.5
Total	**904.6**	**100.0**	**1 142.6**	**100.0**	**2 080.3**	**100.0**	**2 214.9**	**100.0**	**2 370.4**	**100.0**

Source: Australian Bureau of Statistics in Bureau of Tourism Research 1992

result of the Australian Bicentennary celebrations and the Brisbane Expo (Faulkner 1990; Jeffrey 1990b). In the early 1990s inbound growth has been around the 7 per cent mark.

Australia's visitor profile is becoming increasingly Asian dominated, a trend that is being reinforced by the level of Australia–Asian trade, the opening of new aviation routes, and the rate of Asian investment in the Australian tourism industry (Garnaut 1990). The priority markets for the Australian Tourism Commission in the early 1990s were Germany, Switzerland, Sweden and England in Europe; Hong Kong, Singapore, Thailand and Japan in Asia, and Canada and the USA (Economist Intelligence Unit 1990e). In 1990 Japan replaced New Zealand as the largest source of visitors and although New Zealand will continue to be an important source of tourists, Japan and East Asia will probably become the dominant tourist-generating region for Australia before the end of the century.

The primary purpose of visit for short-term travellers to Australia is holiday (60 per cent) with visiting relatives as the next most important reason (20 per cent) (Table 6.4). The latter was proportionately more significant in the 1970s and early 1980s, however, as travel with Asia has opened up, the inbound markets associated with immigration to Australia, particularly Britain and southern Europe, have declined in importance.

The average length of visitor stay has been steadily increasing. In 1986, the average was 26 nights, 28 nights in 1988 and 29 nights in 1991 (Table 6.5). Corresponding with an increased length of visitor stay has been growth in total visitor expenditure. In 1988 visitors spent an average of A$1702 per head on goods and services while in Australia, compared with $1819 in 1991. However, the average daily expenditure only increased marginally between 1988 and 1991 (Bureau of Tourism Research 1992).

Overseas visitor stays are concentrated in Queensland and New South Wales. This is largely due to the popularity of attractions such as the Sydney Opera House, the Great Barrier Reef, the Gold Coast and the gateway function of Sydney. However, it is also indicative of the international air routes which have been opened up in recent years. For example, Cairns

Table 6.4: Australian short-term arrivals of overseas visitors by purpose of visit, 1980–1991 (000's)

Purpose	1980	1985	1989	1990	1991	%
In transit	67.3	79.6	78.6	70.2	70.3	3
Convention	17.6	20.1	25.4	32.5	42.8	2
Business	112.7	158.0	230.8	231.1	221.9	9
VFR	263.9	287.1	459.9	456.0	473.9	20
Holiday	360.2	500.0	1 107.0	1 233.7	1 414.6	60
Other	82.9	97.8	178.6	191.4	146.9	6
Total	**904.6**	**1 142.6**	**2 080.3**	**2 214.9**	**2 370.4**	**100**

Source: Australian Bureau of Statistics in Bureau of Tourism Research 1992

Table 6.5: Australian international visitor survey, 1991 (000's)

Country of Residence	USA and Canada	Japan	Other Asia	New Zealand	UK and Ireland	Other Europe	Total
Average expenditure (A$)	1 945	1 329	2 169	1 281	2 431	2 529	1 819
Average expenditure per day (A$)	67	166	59	64	41	54	63
Average number of nights	29	8	37	20	59	47	29
Total number of nights (million)	9.0	4.3	12.8	9.0	15.3	11.5	65.2
Region of Stay (Nights) (%)							
New South Wales	36	32	43	35	34	31	36
Victoria	13	8	23	17	17	20	18
Queensland	27	46	13	31	21	22	24
South Australia	5	4	3	3	7	8	5
Western Australia	9	5	14	10	14	9	11
Tasmania	1	2	1	1	2	2	2
Northern Territory	5	2	1	1	3	6	3
Australian Capital Territory	3	1	2	1	2	2	2
Australia	100	100	100	100	100	100	100

Source: Bureau of Tourism Research 1992

airport in North Queensland has more international than domestic arrivals. Similarly, there have been substantial increases in direct international arrivals at Hamilton Island, Brisbane, and Coolangatta airports.

Australia's relationship with the Pacific Rim is crucial for its future tourism growth. The Australian Tourist Commission believe that by the end of the century, Asia and Japan will account for nearly half of all arrivals in Australia (Jeffrey 1990b). As in other Asia–Pacific countries, the Japanese market has grown substantially in the past decade. In 1984 Leiper forecast that by 1988 Japanese arrivals would total at least 118 000 and possibly 247 000 representing annual growth rates of between 10 per cent and 30 per cent. However, in 1988–89 363 049 Japanese visited Australia with 528 500 Japanese arrivals in 1991 (Australian Tourist Commission in Economist Intelligence Unit 1990e; Bureau of Tourism Research 1992). As Chapter 2 indicated, nearly every Japanese outbound tourist market rates Australia as their most preferred travel destination. However, at present Australia has focused on the Japanese honeymoon, single women and silver (retired) markets. The honeymooners and single women appear to favour North Queensland and the Great Barrier Reef, the Gold Coast and Sydney as their preferred destinations. The Gold Coast and North Queensland in particular compete with other Pacific destinations such as Hawaii and Guam.

Since 1985 visitation from Asia (excluding Japan) was second only to Japan and increased by an average of 16 per cent per annum. This was above the rate of growth for arrivals from all other countries, which averaged 14 per cent per annum over the same period. Asian visitors to Australia tend to be younger than visitors in general, and often have an educational emphasis in their travel. Furthermore, they tend to have fewer stopovers than visitors to Australia in general and approximately two-thirds of them are fluent in English. Asian visitors are less likely to travel on package or group tours than the Japanese but they are still substantially above the average figure. 'In 1990, 19% of visitors from Asia came on an inclusive package tour and 14% came on a group tour compared with 12% and 4% of non-Asian, non-Japanese visitors' (Bureau of Tourism Research 1991a: 6). The Asian market continues to be attractive to Australia because of their higher spending pattern and the continued prospects for high growth (Bureau of Tourism Research 1991a, b).

Tourism development issues

Whatever the financial benefits of tourism, there are costs at a local level that include infrastructure levies for extra water, sewerage, power and water services, and the cost of dealing with social problems caused by housing shortages and increased crime (Edwards & Murphy 1992: 36).

The rapid growth of inbound travel has placed substantial pressures on the provision of tourism infrastructure and the ability of destinations to adapt to the demands of international tourism. Tourism has contributed markedly to employment generation and economic development in a number of regions. However, the full costs and benefits of tourism are often not examined. For example, while tourism does appear to generate jobs there are concerns over the characteristics of the tourism labour force. Many positions are part time and/or short term, unskilled and poorly paid, and women are taking a disproportionately large number of such unskilled positions (Industries Assistance Commission 1989; Craik 1991). 'The industry is determined to de-unionise its workforce, arguing that the abolition of penalty rates and other award conditions is necessary to make Australia competitive' (Edwards & Murphy 1992: 35). Nevertheless, the high unemployment rates in some parts of Australia has meant that criticism of the employment profile of tourism has remained relatively low-key.

The environmental impacts of tourism are also emerging as a major tourism planning issue in Australia, particularly in light of demands for the development of sustainable forms of tourism development (Hall 1991; Tourism Working Group 1991). Concern has focused on the increasing numbers of people at attractions and the ability of tourism resources to withstand trampling, and the development of associated tourism infrastructure (for example, tourists walking through national parks and the increase of marine pollution in such attractions as the Great Barrier Reef). Australian national park authorities, which have used tourism to provide an economic value for their conservation activities, now face a major management problem in terms of the provision of facilities to visitors and the maintenance of high-quality visitor experiences while still carrying out their conservation objectives (Hall 1992c, 1992d).

Cultural and heritage attractions such as festivals, museums and art galleries, historic sites, and Aboriginal art and culture, have become major attractions for overseas tourists (Hall 1991; Brokensha & Guldberg 1992). However, concerns have been raised as to the extent that culture and heritage may become a tourist commodity rather than a living entity (Craik 1991; Hall & Zeppel 1990). There is a fear from many Aboriginal groups that contact with tourists may devalue Aboriginal culture and lead to further social breakdown in some communities. For example, Mr S. Brennan from the Bureau of the Northern Land Council commented that the Gagudju people in the Kakadu region of the Northern Territory 'do not like the idea of being a bit like a zoo, feeling that they are on display for tourists to come and see what an Aboriginal person looks like in his environment, to see whether he still walks around with a spear. They certainly do not like that concept of tourism' (in Senate Standing Committee on Environment, Recreation and the Arts 1988: 28–9).

Concerns over the social impacts of tourism are not just associated with the Aboriginal community. Tourism is held responsible for localised inflation, crowding, and loss of amenity at many destinations, while increases in crime and prostitution have been associated with tourism development in such locations as the Gold Coast and Cairns (Jones 1986; Clark 1988). In

Cairns, the demand for land for tourism developments and the slump in world sugar prices in the 1980s has meant that much of the land under sugar cane is being lost to tourism. One of the city's two sugar mills, the Hambledon sugar mill, closed in 1991 and if the other mill were to close the local economy would become almost completely dependent on tourism (Edwards & Murphy 1992). In the case of major destinations such as the Gold Coast and Cairns, substantial disquiet has also emerged over the amount of foreign ownership of tourist accommodation and attractions, particularly Japanese ownership. Tourism in this instance therefore, offers a potential two-edged sword; on one side, the prospect of employment and infrastructure generation, on the other, a possible loss of local control and income.

Foreign investment
Foreign investment in the Australian tourism industry has increased dramatically over the past decade. Total expected foreign investment associated with tourism and related industries has increased from $440 million in 1985–1986 to $4997 million in 1988–1989. This represents, as a proportion of expected foreign investment in all sectors of the Australian economy, an increase from 4.4 per cent in 1985–1986 to 15.6 per cent in 1988–1989 (Dwyer, Findlay & Forsyth 1990). In the accommodation sector, 15.5 per cent of rooms are foreign owned, with 49.5 per cent of rooms in five-star accommodation foreign owned. In the Gold Coast and Cairns, where much of the foreign ownership is concentrated, 28 per cent of rooms, and approximately two-thirds of five-star rooms are foreign owned (Forsyth & Dwyer 1991b).

Japan has been by far the major source of foreign investment in tourism. Expected Japanese foreign investment in the tourism industry in 1988–1989 was around nine times as great as that of Hong Kong, the next highest country. 'Estimates show that about 70% of current and proposed project value is Japanese funded' (Bull 1990: 328) (A$3516 million out of a total of A$4997 million in 1988–1989), with over 90 per cent of Japanese investment concentrated in Queensland (69 per cent of total Japanese investment) and New South Wales (23 per cent) (Dwyer, Forsyth & Findlay 1990). Nevertheless, it must be emphasised that the Japanese are not the only foreign investors in the Australian tourism industry. Substantial property portfolios are also held by American, British, Hong Kong, New Zealand and Malaysian based companies with investment from ASEAN countries becoming increasingly significant (Dwyer, Findlay & Forsyth 1990; Forsyth & Dwyer 1991b).

Foreign investment has become a significant issue on the Australian political agenda because of concerns, particularly over Japanese investment, as to the perceived loss of national control over tourism resources and the potential flight of capital overseas. The Japanese have shown an interest in the Australian tourism market for a number of reasons including a favourable exchange rate, the desire to export capital from Japan,

Australia's relatively stable economic and political environment, and the strong interest of Japanese travellers in Australia (Smith, T. 1988; Hall 1991) (See Chapter 2). Japanese investment is generally regarded by the Australian tourism industry as being essential to the long-term development of the Australian tourism product. However, substantial opposition towards Japanese and Asian investment exists in Australia because of a perception among some people that the Japanese are dominating the economy, although it must also be recognised that opposition to Japanese investment also retains distinctly racist overtones that could damage the inbound tourism industry. 'We must act quickly to overturn negative public opinion such as recent publicity given to a reported groundswell against Japanese investment in Australia which has been interpreted by the Japanese in a much wider sense. They believe that because we do not want them investing in our country that we do not want them visiting here either' (Sargeant 1988: 53). Nevertheless, concerns over foreign investment do indicate the desire of destinations to retain a sense of identity.

Direct foreign investment does lead to a dilution in the control of the tourism industry by Australians. 'However the government retains the ability to impose strategic controls on the industry should it believe the industry is not being operated in Australia's interest' (Forsyth & Dwyer 1990), but, as Bull (1990: 331) has pointed out 'To prohibit, or directly limit, overseas investment in tourism in Australia would... probably be damaging unless highly selective. It may also lead to retaliation overseas adversely affecting Australian external investment'.

The government response

There is an emerging trend among tourism agencies in Australia towards an increasing emphasis on advertising at the expense of research, strategic marketing and other activities which provide the ingredients of a more balanced and rational approach to the development of the tourism industry (Faulkner 1991: 2).

Government in Australia faces a paradox. On one side, it has to meet demands from concerned environmental and social groups on the negative impacts of tourism, while on the other, it has to satisfy industry demands for deregulation of the tourism and travel industry and place greater emphasis on marketing and promotion. Although concerns regarding the negative social and environmental aspects of tourism have been raised at the federal level, the prime responsibility for planning and development issues lies with the states. State government involvement in tourism is marked by an increasing attention to promotion and marketing of tourist product and the states as destinations rather than the development implications of tourism for the wider benefits of society. The Victorian, New South Wales and Queensland Tourist Commissions have all expanded their promotion campaigns and marketing divisions at the expense of planning and development functions. The focus of the states, as well as some sections of the Federal Government, is on tourism numbers rather than the net benefits that tourism can bring to a destination. For example, in July 1991 the Queensland Tourist and Travel Corporation axed 41 positions and stripped 'the QTTC of its research, industry planning and public relations units. The Corporation also switched the focus to promotion and advertising in what was described by its chairperson, Peter Laurance, as a 'rebirth' with the organisation's prime responsibility being to get 'bums on seats and in beds' (in Massey 1991: 29). 'Mr Laurance said the changes were part of a strategy to double interstate visitor numbers to Queensland to 7 million and boost overseas visitors from 4.5 million last year to 13 million by 2000' (Massey 1991: 29).

The focus on tourist numbers and promotion to attract inbound visitors is also evident in New South Wales. Since the early 1980s substantial changes to the focus and structure of government tourism administration, marketing and promotion in New South Wales have occurred. In 1982 the State Government amalgamated the former Departments of Tourism, and Sport and Recreation to form the Department of Leisure, Sport and Tourism in order to provide for 'more effective and efficient co-ordination and management' (Tourism Commission of New South Wales 1985: 1). The restructuring process was continued in 1985 by the establishment of the Tourism Commission of New South Wales (TCNSW) as a corporation under its own act of Parliament. As in other states and at the Commonwealth level, the creation of a Commission was due to a perception by government that 'the further development of the tourism industry... would be greatly facilitated by the establishment of a commercially oriented organisation solely responsible for the co-ordination of this important industry' (Tourism Commission of New South Wales 1985: 1). As Hollinshead (1990: 46) observed that 'the 1985/86 annual report of the New South Wales Tourism Commission is as much a manifesto of entrepreneurial interest as it is an exposition of legislative responsibility'.

Changes in the bureaucratic structures of tourism agencies can reflect substantial shifts in policy direction which can have substantial impact throughout the tourism industry and the wider community. For example, one of the most significant aspects of tourism in New South Wales over the past decade has been the substantial reorientation of the Commission's marketing strategy. Under the Labor Government which held office for most of the 1980s, the marketing strategy focused on the development of 'a comprehensive planning framework to co-ordinate the planning and development of tourism in... nominated priority areas' (Tourism Commission of New South Wales 1987a: p.vii; 1987b). In contrast, the approach under the Liberal–National party coalition, which first assumed office in 1988, has been marked by an increased emphasis on 'efficiency' and the redefinition of the role of regional tourism structures.

The new marketing strategy under the Liberal Government led to a substantial reallocation of the Commission's resources away from rural regions to the promotion of the New South Wales tourist experience and

Sydney as the gateway to the state (Tourism Commission of New South Wales 1988). The emphasis on marketing and promotion over planning and development was made apparent in the announcement in August 1991 that the Commission would cut staff numbers in the corporate service, planning and development, and policy research divisions with the money from the staff cuts being allocated to marketing. The changes in the Tourism Commission of New South Wales followed those in Queensland a week earlier and were clearly motivated by a common attitude towards the role of government agencies in tourism which emphasised promotion over planning. As Moffet (1991: 24) reported: 'The general manager of the NSW Tourism Commission, Mr Paul Crombie, said yesterday that, like the QTTC, the commission had decided to focus on marketing in an attempt to boost tourism and fill the plethora of hotels which have opened in Sydney in recent times'. Similarly, Simon Baggs, the Director of Marketing with the Commission, described the organisation as primarily a marketing organisation, in spite of the fact the front page of the Commission's *1990/1991 Annual Report* clearly stated that the agency has the task of 'maximising the economic, social and cultural benefits of tourism for the people of New South Wales' (1991: 1). 'There was a lot of blood on the carpet, we abolished 30 jobs. In a way that will fund the Sydney push. That's the painful side, but it's reality. We're not at all protected from the real world' (Simon Baggs quoted in Burbury 1991).

The transfer of funds from policy, planning and research areas towards the promotional functions of state government agencies led the Director of the Bureau of Tourism Research (Australia's national tourism research agency jointly funded by the State Government and Federal Governments), Dr Bill Faulkner, to publicly comment on the emergence of 'advertising fundamentalism' whereby research programmes were being downgraded in order to spend more money on advertising. As Faulkner (1991: 2) commented: 'It is unlikely that research into, for instance, the environmental and social impacts of tourism would be carried out under the market forces regime, even though problems in these areas could eventually render the tourism product of particular regions unsaleable'.

That Dr Faulkner hit a raw nerve with his comments was perhaps indicated by the reply of the New South Wales Minister of Tourism, Mr Simon Yabsley, who stated, 'To accuse the commission of "advertising fundamentalism" merely highlights deficiencies in Mr Faulkner's own research into this subject' (Yabsley 1991). The Minister's comments reflected a deep division as to the role and nature of government involvement in tourism in Australia and as to the future nature of tourism development.

Despite being a developed country, Australia is in danger of becoming overly focused on numbers of inbound tourists rather than the best available return from tourism given its various benefits and costs. In doing this, Australia is in danger of reproducing some of the errors of its northern neighbours. Australia may sacrifice long-term gain for immediate short-term results in its search for foreign exchange, employment generation and positive balance of payments figures. As the next section illustrates, New Zealand has also placed emphasis on attracting inbound visitors at the potential expense of a longer-term view of tourism development.

New Zealand

Tourism earns more for New Zealand than any other single industry. Its earnings can increase dramatically, revitalising the New Zealand economy.

Tourism has the potential to be the most successful industry in New Zealand (New Zealand Tourism Board 1991: 24).

As in Australia, inbound tourism has become a major industry in the past decade and is seen by the New Zealand Government as a means to improve the country's balance of payments problems. Since 1989, tourism has surpassed meat, wool, dairy products, forestry and manufacturing as a source of foreign income. Tourism is New Zealand's biggest foreign exchange carrier generating some NZ$2.6 billion for the year ending March 1991. In addition, tourism directly contributes NZ$3.3 billion or 5.2 per cent of GDP (New Zealand Tourism Department 1991a).

New Zealand has experienced substantial growth in inbound tourism in recent years on the back of a declining New Zealand dollar, deregulation of the country's domestic aviation industry, improved marketing and promotion of the country overseas, and the addition of international airline routes to countries such as Korea, Taiwan, and Japan. The New Zealand Tourism Board, the quasi-government authority responsible for overseas tourism promotion, has set a series of ambitious targets for inbound tourism for the remainder of the decade. To the year ending June 1992, New Zealand had received 1 023 163 international visitors (New Zealand Tourism Board 1992a). The Board's goal is to attract 1.3 million visitors by the end of 1993 and 1.6 million by the end of 1995, an increase of 45 per cent on present visitor numbers. However, the Tourism Board's most ambitious, and controversial, target is that of attracting three million visitors to New Zealand by the year 2000 (New Zealand Tourism Board 1991). A figure, which although estimated to have substantial economic benefits including predicted generation of NZ$5.7 billion worth of foreign exchange (Chamberlain 1992), is also regarded by some as having substantial negative social, economic and environmental impacts.

The restructuring of government involvement in tourism

A significant aspect of New Zealand tourism in recent years has been the changing role of government involvement in tourism. Two government organisations are directly involved in tourism: the New Zealand Tourism Board (NZTB) which is responsible for international marketing and promotion, and the Ministry of Tourism which is responsible for policy advice to government. The two organisations were created in 1991 out of the New Zealand Tourism Department (NZTD), which was itself formed in July

1990 from the restructured New Zealand Tourist and Publicity Department (NZTP) (Ministry of Tourism 1991; Pearce 1992). As Chamberlain (1992: 91) observed: 'reforming, renaming, restructuring, re-logoing and relaunching tourism is an ingrained tradition' in New Zealand. The reorganisation of government involvement in New Zealand tourism has parallels with the Australian experience where government involvement is primarily being oriented towards marketing and promotion, while the development of infrastructure and product is increasingly left in the hands of the private sector.

In the final corporate plan for the NZTD the Minister of Tourism, John Banks, stated that the creation of the NZTB and the Ministry for Tourism reflected 'the culmination of a direction which has been emerging in previous department plans—the building of an effective relationship with industry in marketing New Zealand as a visitor destination', with the government's overall outcome for tourism being, 'To achieve the highest levels of overseas earnings and employment creation attributable to tourism growth, consistent with the sustainable development of New Zealand as a visitor destination and with maximising the long term benefits to the nation' (New Zealand Tourism Department 1991b: 2).

The New Zealand Tourism Board was established in December 1991 to 'revitalise New Zealand's marketing effort in its international markets' and to 'work closely with the private sector to accelerate the growth of visitor arrivals and increase the length of stay and the amount of money visitors spend in New Zealand' (New Zealand Tourism Board 1992b). Under the Board's Act, the functions of the NZTB are to 'develop, implement and promote strategies for tourism' and 'advise the government and the New Zealand tourism industry on matters relating to the development, implementation, and promotion of those strategies' (New Zealand Tourism Board 1991: 6). With a mission statement, which sets the role of the NZTB 'to ensure that New Zealand is developed and marketed as a competitive tourism destination to maximise the long term benefits to New Zealand' (New Zealand Tourism Board 1991: 7).

The emphasis of the Board is clearly on overseas marketing and promotion. As part of the government restructuring of tourism, the NZTB cut staff in New Zealand from 120 to 75 and boosted overseas staff numbers from 47 to 75 in February 1992 (Vasil 1992). Eighty per cent of the Board's financial resources have now been concentrated on overseas marketing, compared with 60 per cent under the NZTD's budget for 1990–1991. The number of overseas offices of the NZTB has been (re)expanded from eight to fourteen and half of the Board's staff are now located off-shore (Cheyne-Buchanan 1992; New Zealand Tourism Board 1992b, c). The development of the 'New Zealand Way' brand between the NZTB and Tradenz, a New Zealand Government overseas business promotion organisation, is also designed to improve the profile of New Zealand products in the international market-place. As Cheyne-Buchanan (1992: 52) observed: 'The emphasis on overseas market resources reflected the Board's strategy to increase the number of visitors and the time and money they spend in New Zealand'.

The outbound market

Short-term departures by New Zealand residents have shown a marginal increase over the period 1990–1992 (Table 6.6). The slow rate of growth in outbound travel is primarily due to poor domestic economic conditions, although the deregulation of trans-Tasman aviation will undoubtedly have a influence on outbound travel to Australia and Asia. Australia is by far the major outbound destination, followed by the USA and the UK. Given its geographic proximity, the substantial VFR market, and the impact of aviation deregulation, Australia will continue to be the primary overseas destination for New Zealanders although short-term breaks will become an increasingly significant holiday market. In addition, the opening up of direct air routes to Asian destinations and improved beyond rights for New Zealand carriers in Australia will lead to greater outbound travel to Asia.

Despite the attention of government on inbound tourism, domestic travel is still the mainstay of the country's tourism industry (Pearce 1990, 1992, in press). In the year ending March 1990, New Zealanders made a total of 10.3 million trips within New Zealand, staying an average of four nights away from home. Although domestic travel suffered a decline in total trips and total person nights from 1987 to 1990 due to economic recession, the contribution of domestic tourism to GDP increased substantially over the same period from NZ$1.3 billion in 1986/1987 to NZ$2.1 billion in 1988/1989. In the year ending March 1990 domestic tourism

Table 6.6: New Zealand short-term departures, 1990–1992

Main destination	1990	1991	1992
Australia	372 957	374 596	401 168
USA	76 159	81 626	66 617
UK	52 189	50 587	47 166
Japan	9 539	9 840	10 899
The Netherlands	4 372	4 540	4 096
South Africa	1 215	1 440	1 454
Cook and Niue Islands	14 873	14 097	13 611
Fiji	27 654	30 096	30 665
Western Samoa	10 177	9 385	9 809
Other	135 039	153 297	168 154
Total	**713 959**	**738 434**	**761 091**

Note: Short-term is a period of less than twelve months, data extracted from random sample

Source: Migration Section, Department of Statistics 1993

Table 6.7: International visitor arrivals to New Zealand, 1990–1992 (year ended August) (000's)

Arrivals	1992	% Change	1991	% Change	1990
Australia	356.9	5	339.7	0	339.0
Americas	165.8	-5	173.6	-1	175.7
USA	131.8	-3	136.0	-1	137.6
Canada	27.5	-15	32.4	0	32.6
Other	6.5	27	5.1	-7	5.5
Europe	195.2	15	170.3	6	161.3
UK	95.8	11	86.1	1	85.1
Ireland	1.8	15	1.5	3	1.5
Nordic	15.5	6	14.7	-2	15.0
Germany	42.1	31	32.1	22	26.2
Switzerland	12.2	8	11.3	13	10.0
The Netherlands	9.0	22	7.4	3	7.2
Italy	3.8	17	3.2	5	3.1
France	5.0	29	3.9	-4	4.0
Other	10.1	0	10.1	9	9.2
Japan	132.2	23	107.4	1	106.0
Asia	103.2	30	79.4	1	78.7
Taiwan	21.8	95	11.2	-27	15.3
Hong Kong	19.1	9	17.5	10	15.8
Singapore	18.3	14	16.0	11	14.5
Malaysia	9.3	2	9.1	-1	9.2
South Korea	10.6	101	5.3	31	4.1
Indonesia	6.3	20	5.3	9	4.8
Thailand	8.9	39	6.4	33	4.8
Other	8.9	3	8.6	-15	10.2
Other	80.8	-3	83.6	-21	105.3
Middle East	3.9	16	3.3	-11	3.7
Africa	4.0	33	3.0	-19	3.8
Pacific Islands	39.7	5	37.9	-7	40.7
Total	1 034.1	8.4	953.9	-1.3	966.0

Source: Market Research, New Zealand Tourism Board/Department of Statistics in New Zealand
Tourism Board 1992d

expenditure totalled NZ$2.579 billion with a mean expenditure per trip of NZ$250 and a mean expenditure per day of NZ$60. In contrast, international visitor expenditure totalled NZ$1.672 billion (New Zealand Tourism Department 1991c). Given the restructuring of government involvement in tourism in New Zealand, it is apparent that the emphasis of government and the New Zealand Tourism Board will be on inbound travel. Nevertheless, following the emergence of New Zealand out of recession, domestic travel will remain the backbone of the country's tourism industry, especially outside the metropolitan areas and Queenstown for a number of years to come.

The inbound market

Inbound tourism to New Zealand grew rapidly during the mid 1980s but, as in Australia, growth rates slowed down substantially at the end of the decade (Hamilton 1988). Inbound tourism began to grow rapidly again in the 1990s following the setbacks of the Gulf War and the Australian domestic aviation dispute, and an increased overseas marketing campaign by the New Zealand Tourism Board. To the year ending August 1992 total international visitor arrivals to New Zealand were up 8.4 per cent from 1991, following a 1.3 per cent drop over the previous twelve month period (Table 6.7). Growth in visitor arrivals to New Zealand in 1992 has been strong, particularly in the Japanese and Asian markets, with growth in European visitors also being above the average for all markets. Visitor numbers from Japan are up approximately 22 per cent, Germany 30 per cent, Taiwan 94 per cent and South Korea 101 per cent (New Zealand Tourism Board 1992d).

The major reason for travel to New Zealand is holiday (52.7 per cent) followed by visiting friends and relatives (24.9 per cent) (Table 6.8). As in Australia, immigration patterns have greatly influenced the visiting friends and relatives (VFR) market. The major VFR sources are Australia, with almost 40 per cent of all visitors in this category. Europe, especially the UK, and the Pacific Islands are also major VFR markets. The major sources of holiday visitors are Japan (87.5 per cent of all Japanese travellers) and Asia (66.2 per cent). It is expected that the Japanese market will continue to be largely holiday oriented although the increased migration from Hong Kong and other East Asian countries into New Zealand may have a substantial impact on the VFR pattern.

The ratio of VFR to holiday travellers has a marked effect on patterns of visitor spending and the gross economic impact of inbound tourism. In 1989–1990 the most significant market in terms of total travel expenditure was Australia (NZ$446 million), although Australian visitors have one of the lowest mean expenditures per person (NZ$1500) because so many stay with friends and relatives (Table 6.9). Holiday-oriented visitors such as the Japanese have by far the highest mean expenditure per day (NZ$200) (New Zealand Tourism Board 1991) while the highest mean total expenditures per person are derived from German (NZ$2900) and Singaporean tourists (NZ$2700).

Table 6.8: International visitor arrivals to New Zealand, 1992, primary reason for visit (year ended August)

Arrivals	Total	% Holiday	% VFR	% Business
Australia	356 949	35.6	37.2	16.7
Americas	165 795	63.9	14.4	9.0
Europe	195 236	53.1	30.5	7.4
Japan	132 168	87.5	2.2	4.2
Asia	103 215	66.2	13.3	8.6
Other	80 801	30.6	29.6	7.2
Total	**1 034 142**	**52.7**	**24.9**	**10.6**

Source: Market Research, New Zealand Tourism Board/Department of Statistics in New Zealand Tourism Board 1992d

Table 6.9: Overseas visitor expenditure in New Zealand (year ended March 1990) (NZ$)

Market	Total travel expenditure (Millions)	Mean expenditure per person	Mean expenditure per day
Australia	446	1 500	100
USA	254	1 900	130
Japan	252	2 600	200
UK	168	2 300	80
Canada	60	1 900	80
Germany	67	2 900	90
Singapore	35	2 700	130
Other	390	2 300	70
Total*	**1 672**	**2 000**	**90**

*May not be the sum of rows due to rounding

Source: NZTD International Visitors Survey 1989/1990 in New Zealand Tourism Board 1991: 11

The future

Forecasts for visitor growth, based on past trends, indicate that we would nor-
mally expect to receive approximately two million visitors by the end of the decade.
However the Board is aiming for three million visitors.

   This gap of approximately one million is our opportunity. It can happen if we
all work together. The vision can become the reality (New Zealand Tourism
Board 1991: 24).

As noted above, the NZTB has adopted a target of three million visitors to
New Zealand by the year 2000. Table 6.10 illustrates the forecasts and targets for visitor arrivals for the main inbound markets. As with the forecasts
for Australian inbound travel, achieving the three million target will be
greatly dependent on continued tourism growth in the Pacific Rim, particularly Australia, Japan and East Asia. Although the forecast for the year
2000 is just under two million arrivals which requires a growth rate of 8 per
cent over the decade, the three million visitor target requires 12 per cent
growth per annum. The three million target was first raised as a result of
the Tourism 2000 Task Force which recommended the establishment of
the NZTB (Cheyne-Buchanan 1992). 'The target came in for some criticism for not being market or segment specific enough, and for focussing
on numbers rather than achieving growth through performance... However, it is argued that it merely requires the market to repeat the upper
end of the growth levels of the last few years to achieve this' (Economist
Intelligence Unit 1990f: 66).

   In addition to the target of three million visitors by the year 2000, the
NZTB is also working towards targets of NZ$5.6 billion in foreign
exchange earnings, 120 000 extra jobs in tourism, and NZ$6 billion of new
investment in tourism infrastructure (New Zealand Tourism Board 1992b:
6). In order to achieve these targets, the Minister of Tourism has stated
that NZ$10 billion will be necessary for infrastructure development, the
majority of which will have to come from overseas (Cheyne-Buchanan
1992). Chamberlain (1992) has suggested that the current overseas marketing strategy of New Zealand and the restructuring of government
involvement in tourism are part of a 'quick results opening gambit' with little consideration of the subsequent impacts of such a strategy. Indeed,
Cheyne-Buchanan observed that neither the New Zealand Tourism Board
nor the Ministry of Tourism are making a concerted effort to address environmental planning issues:

   Within the New Zealand Tourism Board especially, most of the funds
   available are going into marketing and promotion. The policy makers
   themselves may raise the issues of environmental protection planning, but nothing is actually being done about it in the short term...
   Surely if and when New Zealand gets the extra two million tourists
   talked of, it will be essential to consider environmental factors,
   especially if talking about New Zealand being a quality destination,
   able to compete with other international destinations (1992: 68).

Table 6.10: New Zealand forecasts and targets for visitor arrivals (000's)

Market	1990 Actual	1992 Forecast	1992 %	1992 Target	1992 %	1995 Forecast	1995 %	1995 Target	1995 %	2000 Forecast	2000 %	2000 Target	2000 %
Australia	342	369	4	390	7	438	6	538	11	593	6	818	9
Japan	108	121	6	130	10	170	12	200	15	310	13	500	20
Germany/Switzerland	41	57	18	63	24	87	15	127	26	155	12	252	15
USA	140	145	2	154	5	170	5	246	17	228	6	436	12
UK	87	93	3	96	5	114	7	123	9	153	6	175	7
Canada	34	38	6	39	7	43	4	51	9	55	5	73	7
Taiwan	13	NA	-	14	4	NA	-	35	36	NA	-	100	23
Singapore	15	16	3	21	18	18	4	31	14	23	5	46	8
Malaysia	10	NA	-	13	14	NA	-	23	21	NA	-	60	21
Other Asia	40	NA	-	50	12	NA	-	80	17	NA	-	190	19
Other Europe	42	NA	-	47	6	NA	-	70	14	NA	-	138	15
Other	105	NA	-	106	1	NA	-	114	3	NA	-	146	3
Total	977	1 056	4	1 123	7	1 302	7	1 638	13	1 912	8	2 934	12

Notes

NA = No forecasts available for these markets

% = Compound growth per annum

Other Europe includes France, The Netherlands, Italy, Ireland, Austria, Eastern Europe, Denmark, Sweden, Norway, Finland, Iceland and other Western Europe.

Other Asia includes China, South Korea, Hong Kong, India, Brunei, Indonesia, The Philippines, Thailand, and other Asia.

Source: New Zealand Tourism Board 1991: 14

Despite the use of New Zealand's 'clean, green image' as a marketing and promotional tool, the environmental and social impacts of such a large increase in tourism visitation have not been adequately discussed. Although the Tourism Board 'accepts the principles of sustainable management and environmentally sensitive development' (New Zealand Tourism Board 1991: 17), they do not have any direct responsibility for the effects of inbound tourism. Instead, policy advice for tourism rests with the Ministry of Tourism, while planning responsibilities lie with the Department of Conservation and regional and local councils.

Research undertaken by the Ministry of Tourism (1992a) indicated that residents of fifteen selected New Zealand cities and towns were generally supportive of tourism. Nevertheless, concern over the effects of tourism has already arisen from sections of the Maori community (Hall, Mitchell & Keelan 1993) and the growth in visitor numbers is placing seasonal pressure on some destinations and attractions such as the national park system (Hall & McArthur 1993). For example, in reference to the New Zealand Tourism Board's three million visitor target, Molloy (1993) commented, 'We know that 55% of all current tourists visit a national park during their stay; it is inconceivable with such an increase in visitor numbers that current standards of estate management will be able to be maintained without a significant increasing in resourcing'.

Given the significance of the 'clean, green' image to attracting overseas tourists, it is essential to manage heritage attractions in a manner which maintains the quality of the visitor experience. At a legislative level, the new Resource Management Act is designed to ensure the sustainability of resources through its focus on the effects of human activities, including tourism, and the development of preventative measures to ensure environmental standards are met (Ministry of Tourism 1992b). However, the general principles and quality controls for sustainable tourism in New Zealand are still to be determined. As the Ministry of Tourism (1992c: 10) commented: 'the industry needs to recognise that in its day to day actions it is inevitably involved in a wide range of resource management activity. Tourist operations will increasingly have to reflect concepts of eco-efficiency. Sound environmental practices will help ensure on-going bottom line profit'.

Investment is also required to provide the accommodation and infrastructure needed to meet the increased tourism growth. The NZTB (1991: 17) has noted that in order to maintain current rates of growth to the year 2000, New Zealand will need investment of more than NZ$3 million. The three million visitor target will clearly require substantially more investment funds. Given a lack of domestic investment, the NZTB is actively searching for foreign investment, particularly from Japan, Taiwan, Korea, Hong Kong and Malaysia, in order to develop tourism infrastructure. However, as in Australia, there is a degree of resistance to Asian investment which may impact on visitor perceptions of host communities.

Nevertheless, the projected growth in inbound tourism, the improving health of the New Zealand economy, and the positive benefits of CER all augur well for investment and tourism development.

Closer economic relations (CER) and the development of a joint tourism market

A single market requires the abolition of all restrictions on travellers and on the transport of goods and services within the area, that is, the abolition of the customs control at the frontier... There can be little doubt that the removal of trans-Tasman restrictions... would increase this form of arbitrage (Sir Frank Holmes in Lloyd 1985: 28).

In 1983 the Australia New Zealand Closer Economic Relations Trade Agreement (CER) came into force. The goal of CER is to establish a single trans-Tasman market within which tariff and other trade barriers are abolished, relevant business laws and administrative practices are harmonised, and free trade encouraged in goods and services. Since 1983, New Zealand has become Australia's fourth largest market and Australia is New Zealand's most important trading partner. Trade between the two countries has increased from NZ$2600 million in 1983 to NZ$5960 million in 1989–1990 (Murphy & Reid 1992). Although initially only affecting goods, CER has now been extended to include aviation and tourism.

The extension of CER to include aviation services and merge the Australian, New Zealand and trans-Tasman aviation markets into a single deregulated market has considerable benefits for tourism not only between the two countries but also in promoting Australia and New Zealand as a single destination package. According to the joint study commissioned by the two governments into the formation of a single Australasian aviation market (Commonwealth of Australia and Government of New Zealand 1991), both countries would benefit through lower fares and more flights, but with a larger gain to Australia because it is a bigger market.

Under the study's model, any benefits to consumers from a removal or relaxation of barriers would come in the form of reduced fares and in the improvement of the quality of air services. A 'net welfare gain' was also calculated by subtracting the costs incurred by the airlines in producing the additional output stimulated by the changes. The results of the single market model suggested that the entry of Ansett Airlines onto the Tasman, and limited added competition from Qantas and Air New Zealand on the domestic Australian market would generate a net welfare gain of A$53 million. The total consumer gains would be A$93 million but airline profits reduced this by A$40 million, with Australia gaining A$35.9 million, New Zealand A$9.7 million, and other countries, A$7.1 million (Commonwealth of Australia and Government of New Zealand 1991; Smith 1991).

At the same time as trans-Tasman aviation has been liberalised, expanded beyond rights have also become available to Australian and New Zealand airlines. The rights are especially valuable to New Zealand because of the larger Australian market and should bring in significantly more arrivals to New Zealand (Kissling 1993). Air New Zealand will be progressively entitled to pick up and set down passengers and cargo in Australia en route between New Zealand and up to nine cities in Asia and Europe (Field 1992). The opening up of trans-Tasman passenger services will enable Ansett Airlines to integrate their Australian and New Zealand operations and provide an improved service for their newly developed routes into East Asia, therefore strengthening the promotion of Australia and New Zealand as a joint destination package in the high growth Asian market.

The New Zealand Tourism Industry Federation and the Australian Tourism Industry Association have been lobbying their respective governments to create a single entry destination between the two countries since 1990 (Coventry 1990). The two groups have also engaged in joint marketing campaigns and the Australian Tourism Commission and New Zealand Tourism have conducted a joint market segmentation study in Asia, Europe and North America. However, there is considerable debate over whether the two destinations should be marketed jointly. Organisations such as Air New Zealand and the McDermott Miller Group have been arguing for the development of a 'Destination South West Pacific' concept, including Australia and New Zealand, which would establish a regional tourism alliance in much the same way as 'Visit ASEAN Year' and the European Travel Commission (McDermott Miller Group 1991). Although the development of joint marketing campaigns seems inevitable, particularly as the extension of CER virtually establishes a single domestic tourism market, the desire to maintain national identity will probably override regional promotion in the short term. Nevertheless, as Australia and New Zealand become further economically and politically integrated, the development of regional product will become increasingly commonplace.

The future of tourism in Australia and New Zealand

No one really wants to question the biggest dream of all—of a great and ever-growing Australian tourist industry that will solve the nation's economic problems... The shining benefits have been proclaimed but many of the problems and risks remain hidden (Edwards & Murphy 1992: 32).

As this chapter has indicated, Australia and New Zealand have placed substantial emphasis on the potential economic benefits of inbound tourism as part of their national economic development strategies. Inbound tourism has become a major mechanism for both governments in overcoming balance of payments and overseas debt problems. Tourism is also seen as a means to generate employment and promote economic development, particularly in those marginal rural areas that have been most affected by the decline in returns on agricultural produce.

In both Australia and New Zealand, government involvement in tourism has been restructured to emphasise overseas marketing and promotion. Although this may produce substantial short-term benefits in the form of increased international arrivals, broader planning and policy issues regarding the environmental and social impacts of tourism are often inadequately addressed. Given the high rates of inbound growth sought by both countries, the development of further infrastructure is also a necessity, especially in the transport and accommodation sectors. Although both countries face the prospect of negative reactions to Asian, particularly Japanese, investment, the low rates of domestic investment in the tourism industry means that foreign investment is essential if the infrastructure is to be in place for the forecast increases in visitor arrivals.

The deregulation of the trans-Tasman aviation market and the growth in Asian visitation to Australia and New Zealand means the prospects for inbound tourism look bright. The expansion of air links with Asia and improvements in aviation technology make both countries increasingly attractive for Asian visitors. In terms of outbound travel, short haul destinations will continue to take an increasing market share at the expense of long haul destinations such as Europe, therefore enhancing the linkage to Asia and the Pacific. Despite the optimism surrounding inbound travel to Australia and New Zealand, several threats to continued growth emerge. First is the importance attached by government and sections of the tourism industry on numbers of visitors rather than the benefits which visitors bring. Second is that given the significance attached to rapid growth scenarios for tourism, suitable infrastructure may not be available. Third, large increases in tourism may have undesirable social and environmental impacts at a number of destinations, therefore damaging the environmental and cultural features which are important factors in the two countries' positioning in the international tourism market. The governments of both countries have emphasised the need for sustainable tourism development. The problem now is to transform words into action.

Suggestions for further reading

The best accounts of the shift towards Asia in Australian and New Zealand trade are to be found in the influential report on *Australia and the Northeast Asian Ascendancy* by Garnaut (1990), and Bollard *et al.* (1989) *Meeting the East Asia Challenge: Trends, Prospects and Policies*. On the implications of CER for trade, aviation and tourism, students should consult Lloyd (1985), Department of Trade and Industry (1988), and Commonwealth of Australia and Government of New Zealand (1991).

Excellent overviews of the tourism industry in Australia and New Zealand are to be found in reports by the Economist Intelligence Unit (1990e, 1990f). Volume 29, number three of *Geojournal* (1993) is a special theme issue on tourism in Australia and New Zealand entitled 'Antipodean

Tourism Economy'. The special issue contains eleven articles on various aspects of tourism in the two countries and provides a good introduction to contemporary tourism research in the region. Another collection which includes material from both countries is Hall and McArthur (1993) *Heritage Management in New Zealand and Australia: Visitor Management, Interpretation and Marketing*, which looks specifically at issues in the management of cultural and nature-based tourism.

The two leading texts on tourism in Australia are Hall (1991) *Introduction to Tourism in Australia: Impacts, Planning and Development* and Craik (1991) *Resorting to Tourism: Cultural Policies for Tourist Development*. Other material which students should consult in attempting to gain an overview of tourism issues in the country include Dwyer *et al.* (1990), Industries Assistance Commission (1989), Faulkner & Fagence (1988), and Faulkner (1990). Students seeking information on current statistical trends should consult the excellent set of regular publications of the Bureau of Tourism Research in Canberra, while the most recent national government policy statement regarding tourism is contained in Commonwealth Department of Tourism (1992) *Tourism Australia's Passport to Growth: A National Strategy*.

The leading text on tourism in New Zealand is Collier (1991) *Principles of Tourism*. Chapter 8 of Pearce (1992) *Tourist Organizations*, gives a useful short account of tourism in New Zealand, particularly in terms of government restructuring of involvement in tourism, while Pearce (1990) discusses the broader effects of restructuring on tourist flows. For statements regarding tourism policy students should consult the publications of the New Zealand Ministry of Tourism and the New Zealand Tourism Board, in the case of the latter see *Tourism in New Zealand: A Strategy for Growth* (1991) and *Tourism in the 90s* (1992b).

Discussion and review

Key concepts
Bilateral economic and trade relationships, foreign exchange, regional development, employment generation, economic restructuring, Closer Economic Relations Trade Agreement (CER), aviation deregulation, tourist generating regions, purpose of visit, Japanese market, package tours, Asian market, environmental impacts, sustainable tourism, heritage tourism, social impacts, Aboriginal culture, foreign investment, role of government in tourism, short-term departures, visiting friends and relatives (VFR) market.

Questions for review and discussion
1 What are the implications of the Closer Economic Relations Trade Agreement (CER) between Australia and New Zealand for tourism?
2 What are the major determinants in the rapid growth in Australian inbound tourism during the 1980s?

3 Why has foreign investment become a significant issue on the Australian political agenda?
4 How and why has government involvement in tourism in Australia and New Zealand been changed since the mid-1980s?
5 What are the major threats to continued inbound tourism growth in Australia and New Zealand?

7 The South Pacific:
the tourism periphery

> Conventional tourism is a vehicle for 'metro-
> politanization' of islanders either through
> 'westernization' or 'Japanization', which
> may be quite different from a 'Pacific way' to
> 'modernization' more in tune with local cul-
> ture and needs (Minerbi 1992: 1).

The South Pacific is perceived by many as a tourist paradise. The name
conjures up pictures of palm trees, sandy beaches, and crystal clear sea.
However, behind the tourist brochure images lurk many problems for the
developing nations of the Pacific. Pacific Island nations have very few economic resources. Because of their colonial history, small size, and distance
from major markets, they have an extremely small indigenous capital base.
They are therefore reliant on foreign powers to provide capital for economic development and the transport links that enable the export of
goods and services.

In global terms, the South Pacific island region accounts for only
approximately 0.15 per cent of the world's international tourism arrivals,
with an estimated 508 000 arrivals in 1989, with two-thirds of that figure
being taken up by Fiji (42 per cent) and Tahiti (26 per cent) (Yacoumis
1990). In spite of its small size in global terms, tourism is one of the main-
stays of the region's economy and is a major employment provider for
many of the countries in the region (Milne 1990b, 1991, 1992a). The projected growth in intra-Pacific travel and increased interest in cultural and
heritage tourism is seen as holding good prospects for further tourism
growth and lessening dependence on external aid.

Rather than provide an analysis of each Pacific island state, this chapter
will provide an overview of the significance of tourism for the nations of
the South Pacific and some of the concerns which surround tourism development. The chapter will commence with an examination of the problem
of economic development in Pacific island microstates and the question of

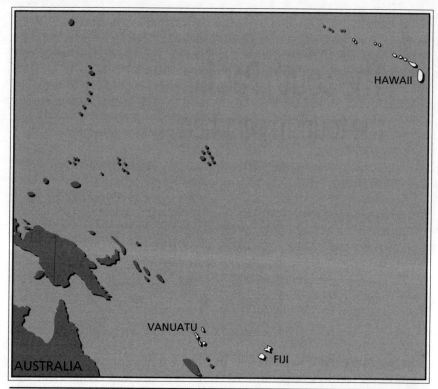

Figure 7.1: The South Pacific

whether tourism constitutes a new form of plantation economy. A number of issues arise out of the dependency of Pacific island nations on external powers for tourism development. In addition to concerns over the implications of foreign investment, discussion will focus on aviation, socio-cultural impacts, and the importance of political stability. Case studies of the nations of Fiji and Vanuatu are then used to illustrate broader themes of Pacific island tourism. The chapter concludes with a discussion of the search for 'alternative' tourism strategies in the Pacific region and further consideration of whether tourism is a new form of plantation economy.

The problem of economic development in Pacific island microstates

The small island nations or island microstates (IMS) of the Pacific Ocean lie at the margins of the world economy and face massive problems of economic and social development (see Wilkinson 1987, 1989). The Pacific nations are highly dependent on foreign aid and investment programmes, from the USA in the northern Pacific and from Australia and New Zealand in the South Pacific, although Japan has become a major aid provider in recent years (see Chapter 2). Because of this dependence they have relatively little power to influence the economic and political direction of the Pacific, except for isolated instances such as fisheries policy.

The Pacific islands have few natural resources which can be exploited and those that exist, such as fish, timber, and phosphate, are rapidly dwindling due to the lack of economic alternatives and development options. Given slow rates of economic development and increasing population pressures, greater importance has been attached by Pacific island governments to service sector activities such as tourism and international finance, the latter through the introduction of tax havens (see Caulfield 1978). 'For island states that have very few resources, virtually the only resources where there may be some comparative advantage in favour of [island microstates] are clean beaches, unpolluted seas and warm weather and water, and at least vestiges of distinctive cultures' (Connell 1988: 62). While many Pacific islands appear to have competitive advantages in natural resources, they generally lack the capital required to develop tourism products and supply the physical resources to tourist generating regions in the form of accommodation, marketing, and transport. Therefore, foreign investment and ensuing ownership is required in order to develop a tourism industry.

In commenting on tourism development in Papua New Guinea, Lea (1980) described tourism as 'the last resort'. In the 1990s it is apparent that with the lack of an alternative many Pacific nations have decided to embrace tourism as a key component of economic development strategies despite long-held concerns over foreign ownership, uneven development and negative socio-cultural and environmental impacts (Farrell 1977; Finney & Watson 1977; Rajotte & Crocombe 1980; Rajotte 1982; Britton & Clarke 1987; Milne 1990a, 1992a). As Connell noted, 'transnational corporations... once feared, are more widely welcomed, because of their promise of economic growth and employment' (1988: 13).

The new plantation economy: the economic and social impacts of tourism

Tourism may add to the numbers of jobs available and it may increase the trappings of modernity with modern buildings and new services, but if it does not contribute to the development of local resources, then it differs little from the traditional agricultural plantation (Matthews 1978: 80).

Matthews (1978: 79) described tourism as potentially being a new colonial plantation economy in which 'Metropolitan capitalistic countries try to dominate the foreign tourism market, especially in those areas where their own citizens travel most frequently'. Air services, bus companies, hotels, resort developments, recreational facilities such as golf courses, and food and beverage are all potential markets related directly to tourism which may become owned by foreign interests. The elements of a plantation tourism economy (Best 1968) are that:

- tourism is structurally a part of an overseas economy
- it is held together by law and order directed by the local élites
- there is little or no way to calculate the flow of values.

In the case of the Pacific, it has been argued that tourism development, along with other foreign economic services such as tax havens, demonstrates elements of a plantation economy (Britton 1982a, b, 1983; Connell 1988), in which the island nations are nothing more than the place of production in a system of trade and production in which control lies with the demand for produce in the First World and with the merchants (Girvan 1973: 17). Within the plantation economy, overseas interests are critical for creating both the demand and supply of the tourist product. For example, Britton (1987a: 131) argued that 'without the involvement of foreign and commercial interests, Tonga has not evolved the essential ties with metropolitan markets and their tourism companies. It would seem that Tonga's tourist industry has paradoxically suffered because the country was not exploited as a fully-fledged colony'. The potential implications of dependence on overseas interests for tourism development has been highlighted by Connell (1988: 63):

> The goods (especially food and drinks) consumed by tourists are often imported, hence the most positive role of tourism is in employment in the services, handicraft and construction industries, rather than in direct income benefits. Even payments made within the IMS are exported; sources of leakage include foreign ownership, employment of foreigners (hence repatriated incomes) and imported materials. The high energy costs of modern tourism are also a significant cost factor, and a possible constraint to future development in more remote states.

The dependence on tourism of Pacific island microstates is also regarded as having a number of other negative economic and social impacts. For example, several authors have questioned the employment benefits of tourism in developing countries (such as Finney & Watson 1977; Britton 1983, 1987a; Bastin 1984; Cater 1987; Connell 1988; Lea 1988). It is true that employment in the tourism industry is often marked by low payment levels, a low skills base, and seasonal unemployment. However, in the case of many Pacific nations there are few or no other employment alternatives in a rapidly growing population. Therefore, the labour intensive nature of many hotel and resort developments is seen by island governments as an important employment generator and, hopefully, a mechanism for improving the business skills of the indigenous population. Furthermore, indirect employment is also provided in construction of hotel and tourism facilities and through linkages with other sectors in the economy.

Impacts on agriculture

International tourism has also been criticised for its impacts on agriculture. Criticisms have centred on three main factors. First, the loss of the best coastal agricultural land to tourism and access to reefs and shorelines for fishing. Second, the effect of withdrawal of labour on agricultural production. Third, the importation of food rather than utilising local resources.

There have been a number of occasions in the Pacific islands where resort developments have been sited on land suitable for agriculture. The tourist requirements of sun, sand and surf have in the past often overridden local community needs. However, the increased activism of traditional land-owners has meant that compensation and/or part-ownership of new developments by local communities is becoming increasingly common. For example, a Hawaiian judge 'ruled in favor of Paa Pono Miloli'i, a community group represented by the Native Hawaiian Legal Corporation, against a developer and required a hearing to properly establish the impact of recreational fishing from a proposed marina... on Hawaiian fishermen' (Minerbi 1992: 53).

Labour withdrawal from agricultural production has not been a major issue in most South Pacific islands. The rate of population growth has been such in recent years that traditional subsistence agriculture has continued beside tourism. Withdrawal has only occurred where the employment benefits of tourism have outweighed agricultural returns, although the cultural dimension of indigenous crop cultivation such as taro is a consideration in employment demands on certain families. In fact, the use of indigenous foods in hotels and resorts is now undergoing something of a revival as local produce is promoted as part of the cultural element of tourism. Arndell (1990) has reported substantial success in improving agricultural–tourism industry links in Fiji and the launch of a promotional campaign 'get a taste of tropical Fiji' to encourage the use of local produce.

Impacts on culture

International tourism is also criticised for severely impacting the cultures of the Pacific islands. Tourism has undoubtedly done great damage to a number of island cultures, particularly through the development of particular images and stereotypes such as the 'romantic' South Pacific which has determined many tourist expectations. However, it is often difficult to distinguish the impacts of tourism from other effects of Western society. It should be noted that Western missionaries have had a far more substantial impact on Pacific culture than tourism has ever had. Although tourism has been held responsible for the fabrication of 'airport art' and 'performances of fake folklore' (de Kadt 1979: 14), interest in cultural tourism has provided impetus for maintaining or reviving cultural traditions such as carving and dance, which in the case of the latter was forced underground by missionaries in many of the islands. In addition, the conservation of material culture in museums and cultural centres is also receiving support it would not otherwise receive, because of tourist interest in cultural heritage (Tourism Council of the South Pacific 1990a).

Aviation

Transport is crucial for tourism development. Although cruise ships have provided tourist access for much of this century and are still regarded as an important feature of Pacific island tourism, the majority of tourist arrivals in the South Pacific come by plane (Kissling 1990). As Densai (1976: 148) observed with regard to small island economies, 'the supply of tourists to a country is governed by air services'.

Almost every country in the South Pacific has an international airline, although nearly all operate with an extremely small fleet and route networks extend only to neighbouring islands or to Australia and New Zealand. Inbound tourism has created the greatest demand for airline services. Of the fifteen international airlines based in the South Pacific, four operate almost 80 per cent of aircraft (Qantas, Australian Airlines, and Ansett Airlines in Australia; and Air New Zealand and Ansett Airlines in New Zealand) (Bywater 1990). The existence of a national carrier for many countries in the region is a prestige factor (Britton & Kissling 1984), but it should also be recognised as a mechanism by which countries can protect themselves against disruption to their tourism industry by the rescheduling of international carrier flights.

One of the characteristics of airlines in the region is the increasing level of cross-ownership and Asian investment. For example, Qantas, along with Japan Airlines and American Airlines, owns a major shareholding in Air New Zealand, while Qantas and Air New Zealand also have holdings in Air Pacific, and Ansett Australia in Polynesian Airlines (Bromby 1990; Bywater 1990). The high level of cross-ownership is an increasing factor in international aviation, but the non-South Pacific ownership is a more recent factor and is a reflection of the substantial growth in inbound tourism to the region. However, the greatest problem for the Pacific states is the securing of regular flights from the major tourist generating regions of Australia, New Zealand, North America and, increasingly, Asia and Japan.

Air New Zealand, Qantas and Canadian International Airlines are the long-haul trunk route operators that matter most to the Pacific Islands. Qantas has commenced service to the Solomon Islands (although in competition with Solomons Airlines), Qantas has maintained Fiji and Tahiti as transit points between Australia and the USA, while Air New Zealand has extended its services to include Fiji, the Cook Islands and Western Samoa within its trans-Pacific routes. However, the provision of aviation services in the South Pacific is extremely volatile (Britton & Kissling 1984; Milne 1992a, b). For example, the withdrawal of Hawaiian Airlines from New Zealand in 1990, left Air Rarotonga without an international service and increased the dependency of the Cook Islands tourism industry on the New Zealand carrier for that particular market (Bromby 1990). Tourism in Tahiti has also been substantially affected by foreign airlines cutting services. In 1990 United States carrier Continental stopped its services to Tahiti, and Qantas cut seat capacity. The result was a 15 per cent drop in tourist arrivals. The head of Air Tahiti, Christian Vernaudon, noted that 'All major United States tour operators who used to sell Tahiti stopovers stopped doing so... In 1987 we had 45,000 US tourists. This year it is down to less than 15,000. It is completely crazy... Strategically, hotel owners need to know they will have a sufficient availability of seats all year long from major markets' (in *Islands Business* 1990a: 38).

The hub and spoke configuration that is an increasing feature of global aviation will have a large impact on the level of visitation of South Pacific destinations. Fiji has been more fortunate than other Pacific islands in terms of tourism development because it sits astride the main air route between Hawaii, and Australia and New Zealand. As Densai (1976: 148) noted, 'although Papua New Guinea is on the path of Australian tourists travelling to the Far East, tourism has bypassed it; airlines prefer instead to stopover in Singapore and Bangkok'. However, as the next section indicates, even though Fiji is the most substantial hub in the South Pacific outside Australia and New Zealand, its tourism industry has had major difficulties in sustaining tourism visitation because of political instability and a lack of a coherent tourism strategy.

Fiji

Tourism in Fiji... operates in two contradictory directions. It helps to alleviate problems derived from Fiji's colonial legacy. But tourism is itself a product of this colonial structure and acts to exacerbate many essential features of this original condition (Britton 1983: 201).

We get cyclones, fires, floods, tidal waves, so what's a couple of coups (resort manager in Coventry 1988: 91).

Fiji has been a tourism destination since the early twentieth century when it was a regular stopping point for trans-Pacific shipping. The economic potential of tourism was officially recognised in 1924 when the Fiji Publicity Board was established to run a tourist bureau at the behest of the White Settlement League. The terms of reference for the Board were 'to make recommendations with a view to popularizing the colony to tourists, to provide facilities to tourists to visit places of interest, and to consider the best suitable methods of providing funds for the objects it desired to attain (in Ministry of Tourism (Fiji) 1992: 1).

In 1937 Fiji received 1328 landing passengers, 6426 cruise visitors, and 13 923 through passengers (Ministry of Tourism (Fiji) 1992). The Second World War prevented further direct development of the tourism industry but it did serve to develop air connections between Australia, New Zealand and the USA. However, following the end of the war, government support for tourism was less than that of the 1930s and reflected the desire of many South Pacific governments to discourage tourism.

Tourism growth during the 1950s was slow, although the United States Department of Commerce (1961) report on Pacific tourism noted that Fiji had enormous potential for tourism and predicted that Fiji should be able to increase its tourist arrivals to 45 000 by 1968. Despite initial scepticism by the Fiji government, the report's predictions were to be greatly exceeded. In 1963, 31 000 tourists visited Fiji; in 1968 the number had grown to 66 467. The primary reason for the growth in visitor arrivals was the growth in long-haul aviation travel. However, the government also took steps to encourage visitation through the provision of duty-free shopping and through investment provisions for hotel construction. By the end of the 1960s, tourism had become a major economic activity in Fiji and accounted for 31 per cent of the country's total export earnings (Britton 1983).

As Fiji entered the 1970s, tourism had become a major factor in government economic thinking. In particular, tourism was regarded as a mechanism for alleviating Fiji's dependence on sugar by diversifying the economic base, increasing foreign exchange, and reducing the country's exposure to the vagaries of the international sugar market (Britton 1983: 23). In 1973 there were 173 000 arrivals and the industry was extremely buoyant with predictions of 600 000 visitors a year by 1980 (Atkinson 1989: 3). Despite high hopes for the potential benefits of tourism, visitor numbers only increased marginally between 1973 and 1983. Several reasons can be cited for this: the global energy crisis in 1973, the loss of aviation routes, the devaluation of the Australian and New Zealand currencies (Fiji's major markets), and the impact of cyclones both on tourism plant and the image of Fiji as a destination (Ministry of Tourism (Fiji) 1992). The loss of aviation routes is particularly significant and here, as with many other islands in the Pacific, Fiji is dependent on foreign carriers for the bulk of its tourists.

The 1987 coups and beyond

Tourism numbers to Fiji improved substantially between 1984 and 1986 but the 1987 military coup by Major Sitiveni Rambuka over Prime Minister Timoci Bavadra's democratically-elected government severely damaged the country's image in its main markets of Australia and New Zealand. Although tourists were not harmed in the coup, the storming of an Air New Zealand jet by Fiji's military did give an impression of danger to potential visitors. On 13 May 1987, tourism in Fiji was up 10 per cent on the same period for the previous year. On 14 May the industry collapsed as the newly elected Bavadra Government was overthrown. Japanese visitation was halved during June, and dropped further during July and August. Tourist arrivals from Australia, New Zealand and the USA were cut by almost 75 per cent. From the 85 000 visitors in April, arrivals fell to 5000 in June. The Australian and New Zealand Governments advised their nationals not to travel to Fiji and the occupancy rate in Fiji dropped to approximately 10 per cent (Armstrong 1988; Fiji Visitors Bureau 1988).

The immediate reaction of the Fijian tourism industry, aided by the devaluation of the Fiji dollar, was to slash holiday prices. By August 1987 there was an increase in Australian and New Zealand arrivals of 9.6 per cent, and by September these markets were up 40 per cent. Then on 28 September, the second coup occurred leading to a further 30 per cent drop in arrivals. The instability of Fijian politics was to continue to have a negative impact on tourist arrivals, with the 1986 visitor arrival total not being reached again until 1990 (Fiji Visitors Bureau 1992) (Table 7.1). Cut-price fares and accommodation were only a short term solution to the problems posed by the coups. As Armstrong (1988: 43) observed, tourists 'who spend $20 a day instead of $100 cannot make the country solvent'.

In the early 1990s, Fiji visitor arrivals are growing yet again. Fiji has made a number of promotional efforts to emphasise that it is a 'safe' destination (Keith-Ried 1989) and it has also been able to establish new air links with the rapidly growing Asian and Japanese markets. Fiji now has two direct flights to Japan and has enjoyed substantial inbound growth as a result. Competition from other Pacific Rim destinations such as Hawaii and Bali has made the promotion of Fiji to an increasingly cost-conscious Australasian market more difficult. Australia is still the major inbound market but as a proportion of all inbound travel its significance has decreased. Nevertheless, as Fiji's Ministry of Tourism (1992) recognises, industry growth still depends to a great extent on Australia and New Zealand.

The economic impact of tourism

Tourism and sugar provide the basis for the Fijian economy (Table 7.2 on p. 174). In 1990 tourism accounted for about 22 per cent of gross foreign exchange earnings, with net earnings estimated to be about 65 per cent of gross (Ministry of Tourism (Fiji) 1992: 7). Table 7.3 gives the gross tourism receipts for Fiji from 1980 to 1991. However, according to Fiji's Ninth Development Plan: 'About one quarter of the tourism receipts is directly spent on imported goods and services. In total about two-thirds of the gross receipts from the tourist industry eventually flows out of Fiji' (Central Planning Office 1988: 88). Based on 1990 figures, the hotel and restaurant sector accounts for about 4 per cent of GDP, although tourism expenditure through multiplier effects is estimated to contribute between 12 per cent and 15 per cent of GDP. Tourism is also the major source of paid employment in Fiji (22 per cent) and is estimated to directly and indirectly provide employment for 28 000 people, 90 per cent of which are full-time positions (Ministry of Tourism (Fiji) 1992).

Given the perceived economic development and employment generation opportunities of inbound tourism, the Fijian Government has openly encouraged foreign investment in the tourism sector, particularly following the effects of the 1987 coup on the Fijian economy (Pickering 1989). The most prominent government measure to attract foreign investment is the creation of tax free zones which offer investors a tax holiday and import duty waiver for thirteen years, freedom to repatriate profits and import specialist personnel, and 'an educated English-speaking, easily

Table 7.1: Visitor arrivals into Fiji by country of residence, 1982–1991

Country of Residence	1982	1983	1984	1985	1986	1987	1988	1989	1990	1991
Australia										
Number (000's)	95.46	85.03	101.40	89.46	86.29	65.38	75.26	96.99	103.54	86.63
% Change	17.98	-10.93	19.25	-11.78	-3.54	-24,23	15.11	28.87	6.75	-16.33
Share	46.88	44.37	43.11	39.21	33.47	34.44	36.16	38.71	37.11	33.40
New Zealand										
Number (000's)	28.30	24.05	26.80	19.54	22.72	16.20	21.51	28.13	29.43	30.63
% Change	-12.90	-15.02	11.43	-27.08	16.24	-28.70	32.78	30.79	4.64	4.07
Share	13.90	12.55	11.39	8.56	8.81	8.53	10.33	11.23	10.55	11.81
USA										
Number (000's)	23.21	25.64	37.29	49.56	69.71	47.04	42.14	34.43	36.93	31.84
% Change	-3.93	10.47	45.44	32.90	40,67	-32.53	-10.40	-18.32	7.27	-13.77
Share	11.40	13.38	15.85	21.72	27.04	24.77	20.25	13.74	13.24	12.28
Canada										
Number (000's)	13.70	13.04	16.52	18.91	23.65	16.82	16.88	16.54	18.44	15.24
% Change	-12.79	-4.82	26.69	14.46	25.06	-28.87	0.38	-2.06	11.50	-17.32
Share	6.73	6.81	7.02	8.29	9.17	8.86	8.11	6.60	6.61	5.88
Japan										
Number (000's)	18.03	14.4	14.86	12.6	11.8	5.49	3.43	13.84	21.62	27.80
% Change	69.93	-20.13	3.19	-15.20	-6.36	-53.5	-37.58	304.09	56.21	28.60
Share	8.85	7.51	6.32	5.52	4.58	2.89	1.65	5.52	7.75	10.72

UK										
Number (000's)	4.33	5.89	8.57	7.71	9.97	8.51	8.46	11.40	16.77	16.56
% Change	-9.98	36.03	45.50	-10.07	29.34	-14.62	-0.55	34.74	47.08	-1.31
Share	2.13	3.07	3.64	3.38	3.87	4.48	4.07	4.55	6.01	6.38
Continental Europe										
Number (000's)	6.11	8.33	11.28	12.67	15.08	14.73	20.50	23.92	27.21	26.23
% Change	-11.71	36.33	35.41	12.30	19.06	-2.35	39.20	16.67	13.78	-3.47
Share	3.00	4.35	4.80	5.55	5.85	7.76	3.85	9.54	9.75	10.13
Pacific Islands										
Number (000's)	9.97	10.59	13.18	11.94	12.81	11.22	14.22	18.06	17.53	16.23
% Change	3.64	6.22	24.46	-9.44	7.33	-12.44	26.76	27.04	-2.97	-7.43
Share	4.90	5.53	5.60	5.23	4.97	5.91	6.83	7.21	6.28	6.26
Other Areas										
Number (000's)	4.53	4.66	5.32	5.80	5.77	4.49	5.75	7.26	7.53	8.16
% Change	-3.62	2.87	14.16	8.97	-0.47	-22.18	28.08	26.24	3.75	8.39
Share	2.22	2.43	2.26	2.54	2.24	2.36	2.76	2.90	2.70	3.15
Total All Arrivals										
Number (000's)	203.64	191.62	235.23	228.18	257.79	189.87	208.16	250.57	279.00	259.35
% Change	7.21	-5.90	22.76	-3.00	12.98	-26.35	9.63	20.37	11.35	-7.04
Share	100.00	100.00	100.00	100.00	100.00	100.00	100.00	100.00	100.00	100.00

Source: Fiji Visitors Bureau 1992: 6

Table 7.2: Fiji foreign exchange earnings, 1989–1993

	1989	1990	1991	1992[1]	1993[2]
Tourist Arrivals	250 565	278 996	259 350	269 100	289 000
Estimated Average Length of Stay (days)	9.2	8.7	8.6		
Tourism Earnings (F$ million)	295.1	335.9	328.8	355.1	389.0
Sugar Earnings (F$ million)	208.2	221.8	220.4	220.0	230.0

1 Forecast
2 Target

Source: Statistics supplied by Fiji Visitors Bureau 1992

Table 7.3: Fiji gross tourism receipts, 1980–1991

Year	F$ million	Year	F$ million
1980	109.5	1986	185.4
1981	122.0	1987	145.7
1982	138.3	1988	181.0
1983	135.9	1989	280.0
1984	162.7	1990	335.0
1985	169.4	1991	329.0

Source: Ministry of Tourism (Fiji) 1992: 16

trainable and cheaper labour force' (Fiji Trade and Investment Board advertisement, *Pacific Islands Monthly*, June 1990: 41). The government has also made land available for industry and commerce in the 'tax free' zones (Writer 1988). Such is the enthusiasm for the Fijian Government measures that Gibson (1990: 35) was moved to declare that 'growth in the tourism industry will be sustainable given the [current] level of government commitment and the way the economy is developing'.

Fiji's tourism industry is dominated by foreign corporations. International transport links by both sea and air are controlled by external powers. International standard tourist accommodation is also dominated by foreign investors particularly from Australia and New Zealand (Britton 1983; Taylor 1987; Poole 1991), but since 1987 Japanese investment has also started to occur in earnest (Coventry 1988).

One of the most significant overseas tourism investments was that of EIE International Corporation of Japan on Denarau Island in the western area of Viti Levu, Fiji's main island. At an estimated cost of F$300 million, EIE International was developing Fiji's largest integrated resort which will eventually be able to cater for upwards of 5000 visitors. When completed, the complex will include five hotels with 1500 rooms, 618 townhouses, condominiums and villas, a marina, and an 18-hole golf course (EIE International Corporation 1989). According to EIE International (1989: 2), the project would contribute over 2000 jobs during construction, provide income-generation for traditional owners, and enhance Fijian participation in the economy in what is seen 'as a model for Japanese investment in the South Pacific' and 'a contribution to Japan's new world outlook' (see Chapter 2). In addition to the Denarau Island development, EIE also made other investments in Fiji, including The Regent of Fiji, the Sheraton Resort and a minority shareholding in Air Pacific, Fiji's national air carrier. The vertically integrated investments of EIE International were part of a wider strategy to maximise the growth in intra-Pacific tourism and in Japanese outbound tourism in particular. Although EIE International has been affected by the international recession and the lower growth in the Japanese economy, it has held on to many of its core tourism and leisure investments in the Pacific.

In its public statements in Fiji, EIE International has been at pains to stress that it wants to retain positive relationships with the community and emphasise the employment generated by the Denarau Project, and argues that it 'will help in the national effort to enhance participation by indigenous Fijians in the commercial economy' (EIE International Corporation 1989: 7). The limited amount of skilled personnel in Fiji has been a major constraint on tourism development and there has been substantial discontent over the low level of local participation in the tourism labour force, primarily by the indigenous Fijians who often fill unskilled positions (Rajotte & Crocombe 1980; Poole 1991). The tension between indigenous Fijians and Fijian Indians has also been exacerbated by the pattern of tourism employment. Generally, indigenous Fijians are employed in the service areas with direct customer contact while the Indians are often employed in back of house activities where there is little direct contact with tourists (Britton 1987b).

In post-coup Fiji, specific attention is being given to creating employment and business opportunities for indigenous Fijians. Large-scale investment projects such as those of EIE International are one mechanism for employment generation. However, the development of small-scale tourism business is also regarded as having significant employment potential (World Tourism Organization 1988a, b).

Poole (1991) argued that Fiji should 'devote greater energy to maximizing the internal returns of its tourism industry' in order to increase the level of local participation and control over its tourism industry. She went on to suggest that the primary mechanism for increasing local participation should be that of 'alternative' secondary tourism activities. Secondary tourism activities (STAs) are defined by the World Tourism Organization (1988b: 4) as 'all activities in which tourists (and recreating Fijians) may engage (and for which facilities may be provided on a commercial basis) which are not "mainstream" resort accommodation or transport operations, either in respect of their style, or location/area of operations'. Examples of STAs include scuba diving, yacht charters, surfing, sea kayaking, fishing, hiking and trekking, village tourism, and cultural activities. STAs are therefore similar to special interest tourism activities which are recognised to be one of the fastest growing travel markets (Weiler & Hall 1992). In particular, Poole suggested that secondary tourism accommodation ventures consisting of short homestays would be the most appropriate form of tourism as it would 'give local people the leadership role, and the chance to define the relationships between themselves and the tourists' (1991: 14).

A further factor in the development of business and employment opportunities for indigenous Fijians has been improvements in the linkages between tourism and other sectors of the economy. For example, Lunn (1988) proposed the establishment of a hotel buying co-operative to purchase produce from local farmers in order to improve the linkages between the agricultural and tourism sectors. Hotels and resorts have also been encouraged to buy local indigenous food products (Arndell 1990). However, while the development of secondary tourism businesses should provide an opportunity to maximise Fijian involvement in the tourism industry, the future direction of tourism in Fiji would appear to be determined primarily by foreign corporations.

The future

The Ministry of Tourism has set an ambitious growth target for Fijian tourism. The Fiji Tourism Masterplan has a target of 373 000 tourist arrivals by 1995, representing approximately a 9 per cent growth rate from the 1990 figure (in Ministry of Tourism (Fiji) 1992). In order to achieve this target, the Fijian Government is avidly encouraging foreign investment in the country as well as trying to diversify the availability of tourism product. The actions of the Fijian Government would appear to support Britton's (1983: 6–7) observation that 'immobile tourism plant in the periphery relies on foreign corporations to supply tourists. The flow of tourists is achieved by gaining the cooperation of foreign interests or by national bargaining power over factors affecting the profitability of these foreign investments.' To an extent Britton is correct; however, there are a number of factors which would appear to have a bearing on the ability of foreign interests to determine the supply of tourists. First, there is a slow but steady decrease in the dependence of Fiji on Australian and New Zealand markets and capital. Second, the increase in Asian and Japanese tourists should give Fiji greater diversity in marketing and promotion and provide for more consistent growth. Third, the emergence of Japan as a major investor and aid donor in the region has given the Fijian Government a greater range of development options. Fijian tourism is still dominated by foreign interests but the number of those interests has been extended, providing the Fijian Government with improved bargaining power.

Two major factors still need to be dealt with if Fijian tourism is to reach its 1995 target. First is the need for political stability. The coups of 1987 and the unstable political environment which has existed since, have done little to improve the country's image. Without political stability potential tourists, particularly from Japan, Australia and New Zealand, will be extremely wary of travelling to Fiji when other similarly priced South Pacific destinations are available. The second factor is the need to maintain aviation connections with the major tourism generating regions on the Pacific Rim. Although such connections generally lie outside the Fijian Government's control, without suitable aviation links Fiji will not be able to receive a supply of tourists. As the following case study of Vanuatu indicates, politics and air links are critical elements in determining the attractiveness of tourist destinations.

Vanuatu: a 'touch of paradise'?

While many countries in the South Pacific have been toying nervously with the idea of tourism development for decades, trying to decide whether the economic gains were worth the perceived socio-economic losses, Vanuatu has come to terms with tourism in a most straight forward manner—controlled development of tourism by highlighting Melanesian culture and tradition (Tourism Council of the South Pacific 1990b: 13).

As with many other islands of the Pacific, Vanuatu has placed great emphasis on tourism as a means of economic development and as a source of foreign exchange. 'The objective was to use the money so earned, for the development of domestic industries, especially those classed as agro-based, upon which the country's economic strength could be founded' (Tourism Council of the South Pacific 1990b: 1). Although this policy appeared to have success in the early 1980s, a string of natural and political disasters led to a dramatic reduction in tourist arrivals in the latter half of the decade (Hoon 1990). However, the 1990s has seen an improvement in tourist numbers with the tourism sector again playing a leading role in the nation's economy.

Since independence in 1980, the Vanuatu Government has given tourism priority status in the country's economic development strategy. The ruling Vanua'aku Pati policy was that tourism should continue as the infrastructure was already in place and stopping tourism would cause more economic and social disruption than allowing it to continue. It was proposed that tourism development should be kept in proportion with growth in other sectors of the economy in order prevent over-dependence. However, 'this policy is now being questioned as the general economy shrinks and pressure increases for more tourist development' (*Pacific Islands Monthly* 1989: 42).

In 1985 the government disbanded the Department of Tourism and established the National Tourism Office responsible for planning and development, marketing and promotion, providing tourist information, and liaising with industry, particularly the Vanuatu Hotels and Resorts Association also established in 1985. According to the Second National Development Plan (1987–1991) the goals of tourism development in Vanuatu are to:

1 maximise the economic benefits of tourism through increased local participation in the tourism industry and reduced leakages of tourist expenditure from the country
2 encourage the future expansion of tourism facilities in the preferred locations of Efate, Espiritu Santo and Tanna
3 develop Vanuatu and promote its image as a high class tourist destination, attracting visitors from the upper income groups from widespread tourist originating countries
4 plan and implement projects with explicit attention given to the conservation of fragile or vulnerable aspects of the country's environmental and cultural heritage (Tourism Council of the South Pacific 1990b: 2).

Tourism is an important element of the Vanuatu economy. Port Vila, the capital, is the centre for the nation's business and commercial activities and for the tourism industry. The economy of the rural areas, in which approximately 80 per cent of the population lives, is primarily subsistence-based agriculture and fishing, with copra and pigs being the main cash crops. The country's main merchandise exports are copra, cocoa, beef and timber. However, foreign exchange is gained mainly from the service sector, especially banking and financial services (Port Vila is a tax haven) and tourism. In 1988, 20 per cent of Vanuatu's foreign exchange earnings were from merchandise exports; 15 per cent from tourism, and 38 per cent from banking and trading services. However, the foreign exchange earnings from tourism increased substantially in the following year by almost 60 per cent due to a 36 per cent increase in visitor arrivals and a deterioration in the exchange rate (Tourism Council of the South Pacific 1990b).

Fluctuations in tourism

Visitor arrivals to Vanuatu have fluctuated substantially in the past two decades due to three main factors: aviation developments, natural disasters and political events. As with any island destination, visitor arrivals are dependent on the quality, regularity and routes of airline connections. Like many Pacific island states, Vanuatu has had difficulty in securing airline services. For example, in 1980 Japan constituted the third largest source of visitors to Vanuatu after Australia and New Zealand with 3721 arrivals. However, Japanese visitation to Vanuatu fell to a low of 438 in 1987 following the removal of direct connections to Noumea and the UTA services to Tokyo. Japanese arrivals have since doubled and show signs of a gradual increase, although the primary connecting service is now to Nadi (Fiji) and the Air Pacific connection to Tokyo. Similarly, the loss of a convenient airline connection to Noumea also affected the French market in 1981 (a decline of 50 per cent) and New Zealand in 1985 (a decline of 55 per cent) (National Tourism Office of Vanuatu 1992) (see Table 7.4).

Table 7.4: Vanuatu visitor arrivals, 1980–1991

Year	Total	Australia	New Zealand	Pacific	Japan	France	UK	USA	Others
1980	21 973	7 259	2 575	5 711	3 049	1 043	305	625	1 406
1981	22 092	9 638	2 621	4 621	2 463	432	272	545	1 435
1982	32 180	18 409	2 864	5 659	2 065	617	417	614	1 535
1983	32 374	19 361	2 420	5 724	1 501	695	368	536	1 769
1984	31 615	21 223	2 172	4 306	818	484	454	613	1 581
1985	24 521	14 933	1 210	4 627	574	554	409	569	1 645
1986	17 515	9 326	1 422	3 700	591	455	276	600	1 145
1987	14 642	6 617	1 486	3 393	438	324	342	729	1 313
1988	17 544	9 613	1 449	3 455	511	321	355	648	1 192
1989	23 864	13 921	2 004	4 245	694	354	362	693	1 547
1990	35 042	17 667	6 291	5 603	751	614	697	904	2 387
1991	39 784	21 401	7 296	5 617	721	634	609	1 121	2 106

Source: Tourism Council of the Pacific 1990b: 6, National Tourism Office of Vanuatu 1992: 26

Table 7.5: Hotel facilities and occupancy rates in the greater Port Vila area, 1936–1991

Year	Hotels	Rooms	Beds	Room-nights	Occupancy rate
1986	11	469	1 042	159 764	40.2
1987	8	449	1 028	120 049	45.3
1988	10	464	1 019	164 160	40.9
1989	11	517	1 110	173 396	51.6
1990	11	521	1 150	189 049	59.6
1991	12	536	1 150	186 734	63.5

Source: National Tourism Office of Vanuatu 1992: 20

In order to secure air services, the government established Air Vanuatu in 1981. For the first five years of its operation, Ansett Airlines of Australia was contracted to operate all its services. The immediate effect of this arrangement was a doubling of Australian arrivals between 1981 and 1982 and substantial growth for the remainder of this period, with Australian visitors making up 67 per cent of the total visitor arrivals in 1984. Nevertheless, the over-reliance on the Australian market was to have a number of severe implications for the development of the Vanuatu tourism industry and economy. During 1985 two events occurred which led to major reductions in the number of Australian visitors. First, Vanuatu become less competitive in Australia following the weakening of the Australian dollar against the vatu. Second, political unrest by the Kanaks who were seeking independence from France in neighbouring New Caledonia was associated with Vanuatu, 'Unfortunately, as very little image building had been done there was confusion in many tourism source countries over whether Vanuatu was or was not a part of New Caledonia and Vanuatu's tourism industry suffered accordingly' (National Tourism Office of Vanuatu 1990: 3). In 1986, arrivals from Australia were the lowest for nine years.

Difficulties with the Australian market were further exacerbated in 1986 following the non-renewal of the contract between Air Vanuatu and Ansett, and in 1987 by cyclone 'Uma' which hit Port Vila and damaged most of the capital's tourism accommodation and associated infrastructure, with almost half of the region's hotel rooms put out of service (Table 7.5). As a result, Australian tourist arrivals slumped to 4974 and total visitor arrivals slumped to a fifteen-year low of 14 642, with only 9201 as holidaymakers (National Tourism Office of Vanuatu 1992). Total tourist numbers declined by more than 50 per cent in two years, with cruise ship passengers visiting Vanuatu also falling markedly from 75 742 in 1985 to 49 381 in 1987 (*Pacific Islands Monthly* 1990). In 1988 the situation failed to improve as a result of political unrest which was widely reported in the two major markets of Australia and New Zealand. The media coverage of Vanuatu politics was perceived by local operators as the primary cause of the decline of local tourism, although the lack of a coherent marketing strategy meant that Air Vanuatu and the national government were unable to counter negative images in the media.

Recovery

The problems faced by the national flag carrier, Air Vanuatu, since it fell out with its original bed-mate, Ansett Airlines, have now been solved. For some time Air Vanuatu had most of the requirements of an airline—an office, a logo, a board of directors, overseas consultants on operations procedure, even discussions about an inflight magazine. What it didn't have was an aeroplane (*Pacific Islands Monthly* 1990: 38).

Recovery got under way in 1989 following the purchase of a Boeing 727 jet by Air Vanuatu, enabling the development of a new service to Melbourne,

Australia, and the launch of a A$1.5 million marketing and promotion campaign in Australia (*Pacific Islands Monthly* 1989, 1990). The aircraft was purchased from Australian Airlines with assistance from Canberra for use on weekend and Wednesday flights and then leased back to Australian Airlines for Australian domestic flights during the week. However, the initial success of the venture brought its own dangers as there was the prospect of a room shortage (*Pacific Islands Monthly* 1990). The Australian promotional campaign used the theme of 'Vanuatu the untouched paradise' and featured Australian musician's John Farnham's hit 'Touch of Paradise'. The campaign led to 'an immediate increase in visitors from Australia which showed very healthy increases in the second half of 1989' (National Tourism Office of Vanuatu 1990). However, according to the *Pacific Islands Monthly* 'sceptics may smile at both the originality and the accuracy of the slogan. Surely of all the Pacific's "paradise", Vanuatu has been touched more often than many? But the success of the campaign is beyond argument' (1990: 38).

The questioning of the success of the untouched paradise campaign raises a number of issues in terms of Vanuatu tourism development. Just how much does tourism benefit the country? Although the foreign exchange generation, noted above, is clearly important, there is little accurate information on actual tourism revenue. Although a review of the Vanuatu Development Plan does acknowledge that 'out of every VT100 spent by a tourist, only a small proportion is retained within the economy—the remainder flowing overseas, either as profits or payments for imported goods etc.' (in *Pacific Islands Monthly* 1990: 38). The Tourism Council of the South Pacific estimated that around 55 per cent of tourist expenditure in Vanuatu leaks out of the country to pay for direct and indirect imports required to service the tourist industry, although they did note that 'this import leakage ratio, although relatively high, compares favourably with countries placed in similar situations like Hong Kong, Hawaii, etc.' (1990b: 12). On this basis, the foreign exchange surplus out of the total tourist expenditure of VT1987.9 million in 1989, was estimated to be approximately VT877 million.

The generation of employment by the tourism industry is also hard to determine as the Vanuatu employment statistics do not distinguish between those employed in tourism and those in other wholesale/retail businesses. The Tourism Council of the South Pacific (1990b) estimated that tourism generated 1768 full-time equivalent jobs in 1989. In contrast, the *Pacific Islands Monthly* (1990) has estimated that as many as 5000 people are engaged in tourism-related activities.

Another economic issue in Vanuatu tourism development is the extent to which Ni Vanuatu (the indigenous population of Vanuatu) own or control tourism. In addition to Air Vanuatu, the government has acquired a major shareholding in a local tour and sightseeing operator, Tour Vanuatu, in order to maximise Ni Vanuatu participation in the tourism industry. A small number of accommodation and restaurant properties are also owned by Ni Vanuatu but the majority are overseas owned and managed. Government policy in the early 1990s has been to discourage the backpacking market, although the development of low-cost tourist accommodation in Port Vila and a small budget resort on Tanna by former cabinet minister Barak Sope will undoubtedly start to attract the backpacking segment (*Pacific Islands Monthly* 1990).

An important social dimension of Ni Vanuatu involvement in the tourism industry is the extent to which tourism affects local culture. For example, the National Tourism Office is explicitly required to not only encourage the greatest possible Ni Vanuatu participation in tourism but also 'to preserve and stimulate pride in the cultural heritage of Vanuatu, to as far as possible prevent developments harmful to the social and cultural right of the people and discourage development likely to disturb the daily life of the people or detract from their right to privacy' (1990: 6). The focus of culture also has substantial tourism benefits. According to Jack Keitadi, National Museum curator, 'in some places it's becoming very difficult to say whether culture on its own will survive without an infusion of cash in some form' (in Mangnall 1990: 19) and noted that tourism was acting to counter the missionary influence and encourage the performance of native dances in some of the hotels. An example of the influence of tourism is that the famous Pentecost land dives, in which men dive from wooden towers with vines around their legs to break their fall, are now scheduled on certain Saturdays at set locations. However, there is clearly concern over the demands of tourism on Ni Vanuatu culture, particularly as many cultural activities such as carving and weaving are traditionally undertaken in private.

Cruise ship visits to Mystery Island (Anaytiem) and Champagne Bay (Santo) are encouraged as they not only provide passengers an adventurous experience but, according to the National Tourism Office, 'the cultural shock of mass tourism on the life of the people is minimised as visitors stay for only a few short hours and leave only money and friends behind' (1990: 7). In particular, the short encounters are regarded by government as giving local people a chance to develop a knowledge of tourism at a comfortable pace.

The future

The future of tourism development in Vanuatu is, as it was in the past decade, inexorably tied to airline services, and, to a lesser extent now than in 1980, to political events (National Tourism Office of Vanuatu 1990: 8).

Stability is the key to the future development of tourism in Vanuatu. The events of the mid- to late-1980s had a dramatic impact on the Vanuatu tourism industry and hence on the economy. A period of stability would enable airline services to be expanded, tourism plant to be improved, and local people to become more involved in the industry. Foreign investment will be a vital ingredient in tourism development. Apart from a few strategic investments, neither the Vanuatu Government nor its people have the capital necessary for large-scale tourism development. Ni Vanuatu clearly have potential to develop special interest tourism enterprises in areas such as culturally oriented tours, home stays, and scuba diving. A major upgrading of Vanuatu's Bauerfield Airport is being supported by Australian and Japanese investors and will allow airlines to land bigger aircraft, therefore making air services to Vanuatu potentially more profitable. However, the airport upgrade has been described as 'cargo cult thinking' (*Pacific Islands Monthly* 1989: 42), as more planes will not necessarily mean more tourists unless accommodation and infrastructure are also improved.

Although the Second National Development Plan laid a framework for the short-term objective of achieving industry recovery in the late 1980s, the Tourism Council of the South Pacific reported that there was a 'lack of a coherent national tourism policy and a plan including an implementation programme... tourism development policy objectives, targets and programmes have been spelt out only in a fragmented manner' (1990b: 14). A new tourism strategy is therefore being developed, central to which will be the maintenance of the islands' culture. Nevertheless, economic realities will be a major driving force behind Vanuatu tourism. The decline in aid from Australia and New Zealand has resulted in a 'chronic shortage' of foreign exchange. 'Tourism, perhaps, offers the only hope of ameliorating this situation in the short to medium term, unless there is a guarantee of continued external assistance to finance the external payments gap' (Tourism Council of the South Pacific 1990b: 12).

Tourism development in the South Pacific: the search for new alternatives

Do a few persons in corporate boardrooms have the right to engineer major migrations from the mainland when need, beyond providing reasonable growth and shoring up agriculture, cannot be established—Farrell (1974: 206) in describing tourism in Hawaii.

The decline of tourism is understandable. Why should tourists who come to experience the warmth of aloha and the breathtaking natural verdure, the power of Pelè, the brilliant blue of our once pristine ocean, the rainbow of flora, and the heavenly aroma of our pikake, plumeria and pakalana, visit concrete jungles, sluggishly crowded roads, cutesy tourist traps with man-made lagoons and waterfalls, all of which are over-priced—resident of Aiea, Honolulu, quoted in Douglas and Douglas (1991: 47).

Hawaii is probably the most well-known tourist destination in the Pacific (Choy 1992). In 1991 Hawaii received 6.873 million visitors (Hawaiian Visitors Bureau 1992) with direct visitor expenditures exceeding US$10 billion. In many people's eyes, Hawaii is the great tourism success story. However, behind the growth of tourism in Hawaii is the story of a loss of indigenous Hawaiian's rights to United States mainlanders and, more recently, to foreign investors (Farrell 1982; Moriarty 1989; Long 1990; Douglas and Douglas 1991; Minerbi 1992). Farrell (1982) has carefully documented the development of mass tourism and the related loss of control by Hawaiians of their own land. Tourism is seen as bringing employment and visible wealth to Hawaii but it has also damaged the environment and impacted the indigenous culture.

In 1988 a statewide telephone survey of more than 3900 residents undertaken by the tourist branch of the Hawaiian Department of Business and Economic Development identified housing costs, traffic congestion, crime and the cost of food and clothing as the most serious perceived problems relating to tourism. Although 74 per cent of respondents felt that tourism brought more benefits than problems:

- 74 per cent felt that a hotel moratorium was needed on their own island
- 67 per cent felt that casino gambling was not appropriate to Hawaii
- 60 per cent felt that more jobs in tourism was not desirable
- 59 per cent felt that foreign investment should not be encouraged
- 43 per cent felt that tourism was at the expense of the local people (cited in Minerbi 1992: 9).

Similarly, a study by Matsuoka (1991) undertaken on the Kona Coast of the Big Island of Hawaii indicated that while 60 per cent of respondents recognised the economic and employment benefits of tourism, many also recognised a range of negative factors such as effects on family values and traditional lifestyles and customs.

Substantial opposition to further tourism growth and tourism *per se* is beginning to emerge in Hawaii, particularly with local people seeking to receive greater economic benefit from tourism and having greater control over tourism development. As throughout much of South East Asia, indigenous Hawaiians have protested about golf course and hotel development and their effect on agriculture, fisheries, and environmental quality (see Chapter 4). As Minerbi (1992: 9) observed, 'many resort communities imposed on local communities have run into oppositions at zoning and at shoreline management permit hearings, run into delays of years and have been stalled by law suits in the courts'. Trask, a native Hawaiian, has gone so far as to state 'If you are thinking of visiting my homeland, please don't. We don't want or need any more tourists, and we certainly don't like them. If you want to help our cause, pass this message on to your friends' (1991: 14).

According to Kent (1977: 182), 'For the working people of Hawaii, the widely acclaimed "age of abundance" has never materialised, tourism has only brought the same kinds of low-paying, menial, dead-end jobs that have always been the lot of the local workers'. Indeed, in a manner reflecting the above concerns over the potential for tourism to become a plantation economy, Kent described tourism as 'a new kind of sugar' in which the industry was dominated by large corporations (then from the United States mainland) who utilise a vertically integrated structure to maximise their economic returns, therefore leaving little prospects for secondary businesses run by local people.

The wheel of history spins full circle. In the same way that the old plantation aristocracy held workers in a state of feudal dependency through ownership of the houses they lived in, modern resorts will be able to threaten rebellious workers with outright eviction from their company-owned homes (Kent 1977: 193).

Is this the future for the islands of the South Pacific?

In one respect the picture painted by Kent is not quite as gloomy as it seems. The indigenous peoples of Hawaii have been seeking to redress the damage that tourism development and tourists have caused to sacred sites and the loss of traditional access and use of resources. For example, a native Hawaiian group, the Hui Alanui o Makena, filed six lawsuits against a Japanese resort developer, Seibu Hawai'i, because they had cut public access to the coast at a section of a traditional trail which had been built around the island of Maui in the sixteenth century. After three years, a set tlement was reached which bound the corporation and its successors to keep the trail open and restore, at its own expense, public access. 'In addition Seibu contributed half a million dollars for a community based corporation to perpetuate Hawaiian culture and dedicated 3 acres of land for a living cultural center' (Minerbi 1992: 52). Nevertheless, despite the success of Hawaiians in curbing some tourism development, the extent to which they have lost control over their own land to non-Hawaiians serves as a potential warning to other islands in the Pacific.

According to Minerbi (1992: 51), 'tourism is associated with loss of self-reliance skills and the diminishment of traditional ties to land and sea when people shift to hotel employment or when the resort cuts access to those resources.' However, the growth of nature-based and culturally oriented tourism would tend to indicate that this need not be the case. The safeguarding of traditional values and norms, cultural activities and folklore, is now a central tenet of the tourism strategies for a number of Pacific states. Attention is now being turned to the notion of 'controlled tourism' which 'would enhance and definitely preserve and enrich authentic culture and tradition... a cautious approach to tourism would... advocate the preservation and enrichment of authentic culture and tradition' (Ministry of Tourism (Fiji) 1992: 8).

Although the domination of aviation links by foreign carriers and hotel and resort development by foreign corporations will continue to be an unavoidable concern for Pacific island microstates, the development of special interest travel opportunities would appear to be a valuable alternative to mass tourism. The new strategy of secondary tourism activities (STAs) development in the South Pacific would appear to be a useful means of expanding and diversifying the tourism activities base and to involve indigenous people in the tourism industry. According to the Fijian Ministry of Tourism, the bottom line in conducting STAs is to ensure that:

1 it is viable and profitable
2 it supplements the villagers' subsistence economy
3 it enhances the preservation and enrichment of authentic culture and tradition
4 it enhances the sustainment of village stability both economically and socially
5 the initial investment does not exceed $10 000
6 it can be done and managed by locals only (1992: 11).

The notion of STAs would appear to offer a substantial contribution to the development of 'alternative' tourism businesses in the South Pacific. However, for 'controlled tourism' to be made effective it also requires two further mechanisms. First, the development of tourism businesses needs to be controlled by local people. In the case of the South Pacific, the concerns of traditional landholders and local communities must be addressed if tourism of a nature appropriate to those people's needs is to be developed. In the case of Hawaii, many problems emerged because the indigenous community lost control of their land and the political process. As Britton (1983: 2) observed 'because of the importance of foreign capital within island states, the introduction of new economic sectors such as tourism have usually occurred through initiatives shown by foreign capital, or through local political and commercial élites in close liaison with foreign capital'. Controlled tourism therefore means control by local landowners and discussion at the village level rather than the implementation of schemes by 'big men' or by Western aid agencies or conservation organisations without due approval by traditional landholders.

The second dimension of controlled tourism is that control should also mean the limiting of tourism numbers. For example, the Australian external territory of Norfolk Island has a limit of 24 000 tourists a year, while Lord Howe Island has set a limit of approximately 800 tourists at any one time on the island. In order to maintain socio-cultural and environmental resources, it becomes imperative for governments and local communities to ensure that resources are not unduly impacted by tourism. Controlling numbers therefore becomes a mechanism by which negative tourist effects are limited and the scarcity value of the tourist experience enhanced.

Is tourism the new plantation economy of the South Pacific?

Tourism is not an indigenous practice, but a way for large corporations to make as much profit as possible in manners usually incompatible with balanced island development. Its profit maximization orientation conflicts with the giving and sharing ethics of the island kinship system. Tourism planning tends to bypass the local people. (Minerbi 1992: 68)

In the present climate of international relationships tourism holds especially good prospects... as compared to other industries because it constitutes trade with the wealthiest countries in the world in a situation in which protectionism, which in this case would be the restriction of travel by North Americans and Europeans, is far more difficult to impose than it is to impose on visible exports from Third World countries. In the light of a reassessment of the long-term ability of the traditional exports to earn adequate foreign exchange... under declining terms of trade, tourism remains a vital element in the economic survival of these developing nations despite the social problems attached to it (Momsen 1986: 23).

As this chapter has indicated, in many ways the island nations of the South Pacific fit the microstate description as 'small economically underdeveloped tourism-dependent countries of the world periphery' (Husbands 1986: 176). However, to be realistic, what other development options are available to the microstates of the Pacific? With their limited opportunities for agricultural production, timber and fisheries, the development of service sector industries such as finance and tourism, with the latter offering substantial employment opportunities (Milne 1990b, c, 1991) (Table 7.6), would seem to be the best mechanism to avoid aid dependence.

Tourism changes the pattern of control over resources as different groups gain or lose ownership, access and use rights (Johnston 1990; Minerbi 1992). The loss of control to external powers is clearly a major concern for many of the national and provincial governments of the South Pacific. But lacking the capital to develop tourism accommodation and infrastructure themselves and requiring the air links to the tourist generating regions, foreign tourism investment becomes a necessity. For example, Tahiti is encouraging Japanese investment in order to be able to attract Japanese and United States tourists. EIE International was promoting a 'South Pacific Club concept' by which club members, mainly Japanese, would island hop from club to club within the EIE International hotel and resort chain (*Islands Business* 1990b). As Pollard (1987: 84) commented in the case of Kiribati, self reliance is 'little more than a ritual for exorcising the devil of dependence... foreign capital must be ritually humiliated while practically wooed.'

Britton (1983: 2) argued that 'as a product, and an extension, of metropolitan capital, the international tourist industry acts to extend [structural dependency] in those island tourist destinations where it operates.'

Table 7.6: Income and employment multipliers in various Pacific island tourist destinations

Country	Income Multiplier	Employment Multiplier
Cook Islands	0.43	0.96
Kiribati	0.37	0.88
Niue	0.35	1.00
Papua New Guinea	0.87	1.52
Tonga	0.42	1.42
Vanuatu	0.56	1.00

Source: Milne 1990b, 1991: 510

Although this may hold true if the international tourism industry were to behave as a single entity, the transformation of investment patterns within the Pacific Rim in recent years would tend to suggest otherwise. As noted in Chapter 2, the behaviour of Japanese transnationals is markedly different from those of North America and Europe. While a core-periphery relationship exists between Japan and the Pacific microstates, structural dependency is not a necessary outcome. The increasing range of foreign investment and tourism generating regions within the Pacific Rim therefore appears to be working to reduce microstate dependence on individual sources of metropolitan capital.

The interest in special interest travel activities is also working to the advantage of Pacific island nations. According to Britton (1983: 6), 'The reduction of the travel experience to relatively standardized products can put any one tourist destination into a marginal market position.' However, the tourism experience is becoming more not less diverse (Weiler & Hall 1992). The focus of many Pacific nations on the features which make them unique, especially cultural and environmental resources, is serving to prevent marginalisation of their product in the international market-place. The development of secondary business opportunities and 'controlled tourism' would appear to have substantial benefits for the maintenance of cultural and ecological diversity and for the provision of high quality visitor experiences.

Undoubtedly, tourism in the South Pacific does show a number of features of a plantation economy. The island nations do contain the resources and labour which allows tourism product and infrastructure to be developed. Overseas interests do also have a very large bearing on the supply of tourists, for example through aviation and cruise links and through the provision of capital for hotel and resort development. Control has also appeared at times to lie more in the hands of local élites or foreign corporations than in democratically elected representatives or the traditional village structure. However, the locus of initiative is increasingly being shifted back to the periphery, where changes in the nature of the tourism market are enabling several of the Pacific islands to redetermine the nature of their tourism product to meet local as well as visitor needs.

Suggestions for further reading

A wealth of information exists on the development problems of microstates, particularly in relation to tourism. For an overview on the subject of microstate development see Connell (1988) *Sovereignty and Survival: Island Microstates in the Third World*. For an introduction to issues of tourism development in the Third World, students should consult the following: de Kadt (1979), Bastin (1984), Britton & Clarke (1987), Cater (1987), Wilkinson (1987, 1989), and Harrison (1992). The last book also contains a number of other useful chapters on tourism development in the Third World. A valuable study of development difficulties with specific reference to a Pacific island microstate is Pollard (1987), which examines development issues in Kiribati.

Although somewhat dated a number of edited books have been published which outline problems of tourism development in the South Pacific and which remain very influential in terms of perceptions of tourism in the region, see Farrell (1977), Finney & Watson (1977), Rajotte & Crocombe (1980), and Rajotte (1982). Britton and Clarke (1987) also contains a number of chapters on South Pacific nations. For a detailed discussion of aviation issues in the region students should consult Britton & Kissling (1984), Kissling (1990), and Bywater (1990).

Several articles and mongraphs have been published in recent years which give a good account of contemporary development issues in the South Pacific, particularly with respect to environmental and social impacts, and the effects of new forms of tourism. In particular, students should refer to Arndell (1990) and Milne (1990a, 1992a). More critical accounts of the impacts of tourism development are to be found in Minerbi (1992) and Hall (1993).

A number of studies which focus on specific South Pacific island nations are also available. For Fiji refer to Britton (1983, 1987b). For a discussion of tourism in Vanuatu, particularly as it relates to customary land ownership and the powers of local 'big men' and politicians see de Burlo (1984, 1987, 1989). In addition, Milne (1990c) provides a useful account of general tourism development issues in the country. The most comprehensive work on tourism development in Hawaii is Farrell (1982) *Hawaii: The Legend that Sells*, but students should also refer to his earlier work (1974).

The prospects for tourism in Papua New Guinea have been discussed by Lea (1980) and, more recently, by Milne (1991). Milne has also produced useful papers on the economic impact of tourism in Tonga (1990b) and tourism development in Nuie (1992b). Students wishing to remain up to date with tourism development issues in the South Pacific should consult regionally-based journals such as *Pacific Viewpoint, Pacific Islands Monthly,* and *Pacific Islands Business.*

Discussion and review

Key concepts
Developing nations, indigenous capital, island microstates, dependency, foreign aid, foreign investment, tax havens, service sector, plantation economy, employment generation, leakage, foreign ownership, agricultural sector, cultural impacts, airport art, cruising, airline services, cross-ownership, hub and spoke, natural disasters, political instability, military coups, economic impacts, tourist expenditure, leakage, alternative tourism, secondary tourism activities, special interest tourism, income and employment multipliers, tourism periphery.

Questions for review and discussion

1 Is tourism a 'last resort' for the countries of the South Pacific?
2 To what extent is it true to say that tourism in the South Pacific exhibits the characteristics of a plantation economy?
3 Why are aviation issues of such concern to Pacific island nations?
4 How have cyclones and political unrest contributed to difficulties in tourism development in Fiji and Vanuatu?
5 Is Hawaii a model for tourism development in the South Pacific?

8 The future development of tourism in the Pacific: The Pacific era or a Japanese lake?

All the forecasts by the futurists converge to favour the Asia–Pacific region as the boom area for tourism in the year 2000. Long-haul travel, facilitated by improvements in aviation and lower oil prices, is becoming less and less a luxury dispensable in times of economic recession. Compared to many other long-haul destinations, the Asia–Pacific region offers the mature markets of Europe and America a varied and attractive product at exotic locations and at a competitive price... The Pacific Traveller will open the door to the 21st century. The challenge is to develop new marketing strategies based on continuing research on the different needs of the specific customer segments and their increasing sophistication (Chew 1987: 84-85).

The Asia–Pacific region is the world's fastest growing tourism region. The indications are that the Pacific will continue to experience above average rates of growth for the remainder of the century and beyond. However, as the previous seven chapters have indicated, there are a number of potential constraints on growth for both individual nations and regions and for the Pacific as a whole. In addition, tourism development has not been wholly positive and nations must increasingly give their attention to preventing the unwanted social and environmental impacts of tourism.

This final chapter examines the future potential for tourism in the Pacific Rim with specific attention to the value of tourism as a development mechanism, the role of the Japanese in tourism development, and the significance of tourism for enhancing the integration of Pacific nations within a Pacific Economic Community. The final section discusses the future of tourism in terms of economic, social, environmental and political factors and highlights the role of tourism in creating economic, political, and social interdependency between the nations of the Pacific Rim.

Tourism as a development mechanism in the Pacific

In most countries, the industry's health is assumed to be the best indicator of a successful policy. This is not so. A tourism policy in a developing nation, particularly, should be judged by its net impact on the economic, social, and political life of the people. Since net economic benefits, as opposed to overall receipts, and social and political factors are seldom considered quantifiable, in many countries they are simply left out of the policy equation (Richter 1989: 103).

Tourism has been a key factor in the economic development of the Asia–Pacific region. The tourist industry has been seized upon by governments at all levels as a development mechanism. Tourism is perceived as being a good source of foreign exchange because of the flow of inbound tourists, and an employment generator because of its labour-intensive nature (Minerbi 1992). Although the tourism multiplier may be no greater than other industries (see Pearce 1989), the apparent abundance of natural and cultural resources with which the nations of East Asia and the Pacific have been able to attract tourists and associated foreign investment have made tourism a leading component in national and regional development strategies. With the notable exceptions of Japan and Taiwan, tourism is one of the major sources of foreign exchange, a leading employer and one of the largest contributors to GDP for nearly all of the countries profiled in this book. Even developed Western nations at the edge of the Pacific Rim, such as Australia, New Zealand, the USA and Canada, who for much of the past three decades have been net generators of travel, believe that tourism offers the prospect for improving balance of payments problems and relieving unemployment.

One of the key factors in making tourism an attractive industry for the nations of the region has been the rapid economic growth of the Pacific Rim, and North East Asia in particular, since the Second World War. As the various national and regional case studies have indicated, the rapid economic growth of Eastern Asia has provided for increased disposable income, greater leisure time, and increased consumer expectations. Japan was only the first wave of outbound travel (Chapter 2). The second wave of Korea, Taiwan and Hong Kong commenced in the late 1980s (Chapter 3), while the third wave which will come from the ASEAN countries is only just getting underway (Chapter 4). The fourth, and probably largest, wave of outbound travel will occur around the turn of the century when the People's Republic of China has further expanded its rapidly growing market economy (Chapter 5). Since 1978 China has moved 'from a low-income to a middle-income economy, with per capita GNP in the range of $US1200–1300. If that is the case, China is already the fourth-largest aggregate economy in the world' (Goodman 1993: 18). Given China's current extremely high rate of growth, increasing per capita incomes leading to the creation of a sizable middle class, greater acceptance of individual wealth, and rising consumer demand, China appears set to become a tourist generating region on a massive scale in the next century.

Tourism development has not been without its costs. The economic contribution of tourism to national development has often been accompanied by severe environmental problems, such as inadequate sewage and water pollution at coastal resorts (as in Thailand) or through damage to historic sites and monuments by inadequately managed tourists (see Chapter 4). The environmental components of tourism are now being readily addressed by governments in the region because there is a realisation that many tourists are interested in environmentally sound tourism (however defined) and wish to have a more authentic experience with the culture and nature of the destination (Hall 1992a, b; Weiler 1992; Hall & McArthur 1993). For example, countries such as Malaysia and New Zealand are focusing on the nature-based market, Indonesia is promoting marine tourism, and Korea and Thailand are putting more emphasis on culturally oriented travel.

The social impacts of tourism development in terms of cultural change and modernisation have also been substantial, but the evaluation of the costs and benefits of social impacts are somewhat problematic. As Harrison (1992: 10) noted, 'ultimately tourism in less developed countries, *or anywhere else*, is justified by its many participants, "host" or "guest", according to the alleged benefits it brings'. Harrison, for example, goes on to use the example of Boracay Island in the Philippines (Smith 1988) which has been invaded by 'drifter' tourists which has increased the amount of pollution, depleted coral resources, and imported narcotics and prostitution onto the island.

> Yet the people of Boracay, like all rural Filipinos, would enjoy having the infrastructure that is needed to support tourism, because it would make their lives easier, pleasanter and safer. And they certainly want the income generated by tourism, in the form of cash with which to buy goods and services including better education for their children. They appreciate the employment that is enabling their young people to stay on the island, or to return home to Boracay from the squalor of big cities, and be with their families. In the eyes of most villagers, tourism has been very positive—and the sins of the 'drifter' tourists can be temporarily overlooked in the face of their largesse (Smith, V. 1988: 15-16).

As the previous chapter noted, for many of the Pacific island microstates there are currently few if any viable alternatives to tourism if those nations are wanting to create employment and economic development opportunities. The issue should therefore perhaps be more one of control over the development process rather than the process itself. If communities wish to gain the benefits of modernisation in the full knowledge of the potential cultural difficulties it may create, then why should outsiders, often academics, aid agencies and conservation organisations, be in a position to criticise or prevent them gaining their tourism development goals?

One of the major issues in terms of tourism development in the Pacific Rim has been that of foreign investment and the potential of destinations to become controlled by external corporations. As Chapter 7 indicated, the growth of intra-Pacific travel has meant that dependence on a single tourism generating region is becoming less likely. Similarly, Richter (1989: 108) noted, 'no single nation constitutes a critical source of tourists, as is often the case in many developing areas... In this respect South Asia is less prone to develop the sort of core-periphery dependency relationship that affects many other Third-World countries'. Nevertheless, concerns over foreign investment and of the Japanese in particular will be a major issue in Pacific Rim tourism in the coming years.

The role of the Japanese in tourism development in the Pacific

Japan is not only the industrial giant of Asia, it is potentially the leading economic power of the twenty-first century (Livingstone 1989: 39).

Japan has become a major or principal economic partner for almost all Pacific Rim countries (Wevers 1988; Garnaut 1990). 'Japan's economic prowess in the region is a reflection of its increasing importance with regard to trade, investment and economic development both internally and externally' (Bollard *et al.* 1989: 3). Japan is not only the largest tourist generating country for many of the destinations in the East Asia–Pacific region but is also a major provider of investment and aid. The growth of Japanese outbound tourism and increased Japanese overseas investment in tourism and leisure projects has led to substantial concern as to the potential for Japanese control over destination regions (see Chapter 6).

Undoubtedly, the lack of Japanese acknowledgement of some of the events of the Second World War, such as the Rape of Nanking and the forced prostitution of many Korean women for the Japanese military, has created a backdrop of distrust in some countries towards the Japanese which may flow over into attitudes regarding tourism. Questions have also been raised as to whether the Japanese are now attempting to achieve, by economic means, the goal of a sphere of 'co-prosperity' over the Pacific which was held by the Japanese prior to 1945 (Edgington 1990). Many of the negative reactions towards the Japanese are clearly a result of emotional hostility generated by the Second World War, entrenched racist attitudes and a fear of the unknown (Japan Advisory Committee 1981; Hall 1991). Nevertheless, there is clearly widespread concerns throughout the Asia–Pacific that the Japanese are aiming to exercise hegemony over the region.

Suzuki (1989) argued that the Pacific had already witnessed two hegemonic periods; the first that of the UK, the second that of the USA but noted that 'Pax Americana will not be replaced by Pax Japonica but rather by a multilateral, international coordination system, and Japan will have to consider supplying international public goods within this system' (Suzuki 1989: 5). The constitutional and structural constraints placed on Japan following the Second World War have made it extremely difficult for the country to exercise its will within the Pacific and on the international scene in general. Indeed, Japan is extremely sensitive to criticism from within the region. In addition, the pattern of foreign investment has generally not served to establish Japanese dominance, rather it has created a series of new markets for its products and services and has hastened the economic development of several of the countries of Eastern Asia. As Edgington commented 'Japan is strengthening the interdependence of the entire area as almost two thirds of Japan's overseas investment and more than half of its international trade remains in the Pacific region' (1990: 2). Rather than establish Japanese hegemony over East Asia and the Pacific, Japan has served to integrate the region economically. Therefore, 'the long term interest of Japan and her partners are likely to be best served by emphasis on economic multilateralism' (Wevers 1988: 57).

Free trade, tourism, and the development of a Pacific economic community

The experience and lessons of history show what happens when a newly emerged primary creditor country does not open its markets and does not think about its own economic and macro policy with the world economy in mind: confrontations between the new and old powers become stronger, wars and depressions occur, and the world separates into economic blocs based on protectionism (Suzuki 1989: 4).

Economic regionalism is a concept which is gaining increasing significance in East Asia and the Pacific Rim. The signing of the North American Free Trade Agreement (NAFTA) between Canada, Mexico and the USA; the removal of trading barriers between members of the European Community (EC); and the expansion in late November 1992 of the Economic Cooperation Organisation, consisting of Iran, Pakistan and Turkey, to include five Asian republics of the former Soviet Union, have all fuelled demands for greater regional economic co-operation.

The concept of regional co-operation is of course not new (see Chapter 1). The Association of South East Asian Nations (ASEAN) was established to encourage regional co-operation over twenty-five years ago. However, it was only in October 1992 that member countries decided to adopt the ASEAN Free Trade Area (AFTA) in order to implement a common effective preferential tariff scheme (CEPT) for processed agricultural and manufactured goods made and traded within the grouping. The goal of the scheme is to have a common tariff of 0–5 per cent on designated goods within fifteen years of its launch in January 1993 (Tiglao 1992).

AFTA is only a first step along the road to wider economic co-operation. Numerous combinations and permutations of regional groupings have been put forward. For example, the Bush Administration proposed that NAFTA might be extended to include Australia, New Zealand, Hong Kong, Singapore, and Taiwan, while Malaysian Prime Minister Datuk Seri Mahathir Mohamad has put forward a proposal for an East Asian Economic Grouping (Rowley 1992c).

The concept of an Asia–Pacific Economic Cooperation Forum (APEC) has been championed by Australian Prime Minister Paul Keating, winning support from the USA and Japan and favoured over the proposal by Malaysian Prime Minister Datik Ser Mahathir Mohamad for an East Asian Economic Caucus that excludes Australia, New Zealand and the USA. As Friedland (1992: 20) commented, 'The US and Japan have made it clear that they are happy to see Keating take the lead in promoting the free-trade oriented APEC at the expense of a more exclusive regional grouping'.

Morley (1987) identified three main conditions that are required to make the Pacific Basin concept work:

1 Each country in the Pacific community will have to be convinced that a significant number of the economic issues which concern it can be better handled in a multilateral context than by bilateral or bloc negotiations.

2 Either the United States or Japan, or preferably both, will have to be prepared to make a disproportionate share of the new concessions which greater interdependence may require.

3 The security implications of the Pacific movement will have to be resolved.

Although the three conditions are major obstacles, they are not insurmountable. The increased integration of the Pacific Basin economies and the end of the Cold War provide a framework within which the Pacific Basin can be made to work. As Chapter 1 noted, there are a number of sound economic reasons for establishing a Pacific Basin community: the increase of North American trade with South East Asian and North East Asian countries compared with Europe; the rapid growth of the newly industrialised countries (NICs) of the region and Japan compared to non-Pacific Rim NICs; the large population and the corresponding growth in consumer markets, particularly that of Japan; the high degree of intra-Asian trade; and the fact that regional organisations such as ASEAN are already well established (Shin 1989). All of these factors will clearly have a major bearing on tourism growth and development in the Pacific Rim. The reduction of trade, aviation, and investment barriers will have a direct flow on to tourism, while the growth generated by increased free trade will generate international travel for both business and pleasure.

The future

The plans and dreams of those who see the Pacific World as the economic giant of the next century can only be realised if there exists a healthy political environment (Delworth 1982: 9).

One of the major questions which this book poses to the student of tourism is for how long can above world average tourism growth in the Asia–Pacific region continue? The answer would seem to be at least for the rest of the decade and probably well into the twenty-first century.

The economic, environmental, technological, social and political factors which influence tourism are inextricably linked. Seventy per cent of the population of the region's fastest growing economies (Hong Kong, Indonesia, Malaysia, South Korea, Singapore, Taiwan, and Thailand) is under the age of thirty and the growing per capita disposable incomes has meant that the people have become avid consumers. Tourism has clearly become a major beneficiary of the growth of an Asian middle-class. For example, South East Asian tourists now spend more money per day than their Western European counterparts when they visit Hong Kong. As the general manager of the Hong Kong Tourist Association, Douglas J. King, commented 'Ten years ago, there was only a middle class in Hong Kong and Singapore. That's not the case anymore, and these people think part of being advanced is to see the world' (Taber 1992: 26).

Underlying both the prospects for future economic growth and the attractiveness of destinations for tourists is the level of political stability in the region. As several of the national studies in this book have indicated, political stability is a critical element for tourism growth. China, Korea, Thailand, the Philippines, and Fiji have all demonstrated the effect that political instability can have on tourism arrivals. Political stability is a concern both within and between nations. At a national level, a number of countries within the region, including those just mentioned, face significant obstacles in their search for sustainable democratic institutions. At an international level, a number of danger spots loom. One of the most critical of these will be the takeover of Hong Kong by the People's Republic of China in 1997. The clash of ideologies inherent in the union will have repercussions throughout North East Asia. Similarly, the attitude of Taiwan towards the mainland will also be important for regional stability.

The World Tourist Organization (1991) has estimated that by the year 2000 the East Asia–Pacific region will generate 17.9 per cent of worldwide international tourist arrivals, compared to the 1991 estimate of 11.5 per cent (Table 8.1). However, as noted above, the world has only witnessed the first two waves of outbound travel from tourism generating regions in East Asia and the Pacific. The first wave from Japan is still increasing despite a lower rate of Japanese economic growth than that experienced during the 1980s. Japanese outbound travel is expected to double from present levels by the end of the century (see Chapter 2).

The recent rapid growth in outbound travel from the newly industrialised economies of Korea, Hong Kong, Taiwan and Singapore can also be expected to continue through the 1990s. Intra-ASEAN travel is starting to reach significant levels and with maintained economic growth outbound travel from Malaysia, Thailand, Indonesia, and the Philippines will also start to have a marked impact on intra-Pacific Rim travel patterns. Finally, the economic development of China can be expected to sustain continued high rates of international tourist arrival growth far into the twenty-first century.

Travel growth in the Asia–Pacific region has been built upon a firm foundation of economic growth which has provided the disposable incomes, increased leisure times, and changes in consumer behaviour required for international tourism. Economic regionalism is increasing in its appeal in East Asia and the Pacific Rim. The reduction of trade barriers between ASEAN nations, the Closer Economic Relationship (CER) between Australia and New Zealand, and NAFTA all point towards the development of greater economic integration through both trade and investments, and regional trade agreements. The move towards tariff reductions demonstrated by the various trade agreements and the GATT negotiations on trade in services, augur well for the Pacific tourism industry and would appear to boost prospects for maintained economic growth in the region. Travel growth has also been generated because of increased access through improvements in transport technology. Although the major focus of these improvements for international travel in recent years has been in the aviation sector, improvements in road transportation will also be significant, particularly in South East Asia. For example, the completion of the bridge across the Mekong River between Laos and Thailand and the associated construction of sealed highway all the way from Singapore through to Beijing, will not only help unite the region economically, but will also open a new avenue for tourism development into the next century.

Table 8.1: Share of world-wide international tourist arrivals, 1991–2000

Region	1991 (est.) %	2000 (forecast) %
Africa	2.9	5.0
Americas	21.5	20.1
East Asia–Pacific	11.5	17.9
Europe	61.8	53.0
Middle East	1.6	3.5
South Asia	0.7	0.6
Total	**449m**	**637m**

Source: World Tourism Organization 1991

This book has provided an overview of tourism in the Pacific Rim. Tourism is a key element in the increasingly integrated economies of the Asia–Pacific region, although the role that tourism plays in the region is often ignored or underestimated by many commentators. Hopefully, this situation will occur less and less as the full economic, social, political and environmental dimensions of tourism come to be better understood.

Change is an inevitable consequence of tourism development. However, tourism development is intrinsically neither good nor bad, it depends on the perspectives, goals and objectives of governments, individuals and other stakeholders. Although tourism is not without its unwanted or negative impacts, for many communities in the region it is often one of the few, if not the only, avenues for economic development, employment generation, and the attainment of the benefits of modernisation. The challenge for the peoples of the Pacific Rim therefore is to maximise the undoubted benefits that tourism can bring while ensuring that cultural integrity is not sacrificed for the sake of the tourist dollar.

Suggestions for further reading

In addition to some of the recommended books on the economic development of the Pacific noted in Chapter 1, students should also refer to Scalapino (1989) for a discussion of some of the general economic and political issues facing the region. Forecasting the future is an extremely difficult business, the Economist Intelligence Unit (1990a) report on *Far East and Pacific Travel in the 1990s*, and the World Tourism Organization's report on *Tourism Trends Worldwide and in East Asia and the Pacific 1950–1991*, give some valuable insights into the overall growth of travel in the region; while the annual report of the Japan Travel Bureau (1991) provides a number of estimates on the growth of outbound travel by the Japanese by the year 2000 (see Chapter 2). Other useful forecasts relevant to the future of tourism in the pacific region include three articles in *Tourism Management* (1987, vol. 8, no. 2) by Chew (1987), Martin & Mason (1987), and Shackleford (1987). In addition, Choy (1992) makes some interesting comments regarding the potential long-term growth of tourism for certain Pacific destinations.

Discussion and review

Key concepts
Long-haul destinations, tourism as a development mechanism, environmental problems, social impacts, employment, economic development, dependency, racism, hegemony, interdependency, economic multilateralism, economic regionalism, political stability, economic growth, disposable incomes, increased leisure time, consumer behaviour, economic integration.

Questions for review and discussion

1 To what extent has tourism contributed as a development mechanism to the countries of the Pacific?
2 How crucial are the Japanese to tourism development in the Pacific?
3 According to Morley (1987) what are the three conditions required to make the Pacific Basin concept work?
4 What are the primary reasons for establishing a Pacific Basin community?

References

AMPO 1991, *AMPO, Japan–Asia Quarterly Review: Special Issue on Resort Development*, vol. 22, no. 4.

Ap, J., Var, T. & Din, K. 1991, 'Malaysian perceptions of tourism', *Annals of Tourism Research*, vol. 18, no. 2, pp. 321–3.

Ariff, M. (ed.) 1991, *The Pacific Economy: Growth and External Stability*, Allen & Unwin, North Sydney.

Armstrong, D. 1988, 'Tourism '88: challenges and opportunities', *Pacific Islands Monthly*, February, pp. 41–4.

Arndell, R. 1990, 'Tourism as a development concept in the South Pacific: an integrated approach under the South Pacific Regional Tourism Development Programme', *The Courier*, no. 122, July–August, pp. 83–6.

Asia Travel Trade 1989a, 'Inbound's full of woes', *Asia Travel Trade*, vol. 21, May, p. 41.

Asia Travel Trade 1989b, 'Five projects set for Taiwan provinces', *Asia Travel Trade*, vol. 21, October, p. 19.

Asia Travel Trade 1989c, 'Korea's Olympic windfall bodes well for tourism', *Asia Travel Trade*, vol. 21, February, p. 15.

Asia Travel Trade 1989d, 'The 2.5m arrivals goal', *Asia Travel Trade*, February, pp. 20–1.

Asia Travel Trade 1989e, 'The building up of Bali', *Asia Travel Trade*, March, pp. 32–3.

Asia Travel Trade 1989f, 'Garuda builds up its network', *Asia Travel Trade*, vol. 21, June, p. 13.

Asia Travel Trade 1989g, 'Wanted: 3.5 million visitors by 1993', *Asia Travel Trade*, June, pp. 30–3.

Asia Travel Trade 1989h, 'There's more than seaweed in "hazardous" waters off Pattaya', *Asia Travel Trade*, vol. 21, October, pp. 48–50.

Asia Travel Trade 1989i, 'Tourism still top earner although mid-year growth off', *Asia Travel Trade*, vol. 21, October, pp. 51–3.

Asia Travel Trade 1990a, 'Govt., industry set goals for growth', *Asia Travel Trade*, vol. 22, October, pp. 31–3.

Asia Travel Trade 1990b, 'Paying closer attention at home', *Asia Travel Trade*, vol. 22, October, pp. 42–4.

Asia Travel Trade 1990c, 'Japan at a glance', *Asia Travel Trade*, vol. 22, October, p. 45.

Asia Travel Trade 1990d, 'Agents say inbound volume worse than figures indicate', *Asia Travel Trade*, vol. 22, April, pp. 49–50.

Asia Travel Trade 1990e, 'PRC, Japan big winners in outbound boom', *Asia Travel Trade*, vol. 22, April, pp. 51–2.

Asia Travel Trade 1990f, 'Capacity increases may improve airline seat shortage', *Asia Travel Trade*, vol. 22, April, pp. 43–6.

Asia Travel Trade 1990g, 'Despite rampaging rates, demand still exceeds supply', *Asia Travel Trade*, vol. 22, April, pp. 47–8.

Asia Travel Trade 1990h, 'Agents face stiff competition', *Asia Travel Trade*, vol. 22, June, pp. 50–1.

Asia Travel Trade 1990i, 'THAI growth tied to privatization', *Asia Travel Trade*, vol. 22, November, p. 50.

Asia Travel Trade 1990j, 'Development, environment compete for top billing', *Asia Travel Trade*, vol. 22, November, pp. 46–9.

Asia Travel Trade 1990k, 'Economic boom bolsters travel', *Asia Travel Trade*, vol. 22, November, p. 45.

Asia Travel Trade 1990l, 'AIDS problem menaces tourism', *Asia Travel Trade*, vol. 22, November, pp. 56–7.

Asia Travel Trade 1990m, 'Expected hotel glut scares investors', *Asia Travel Trade*, vol. 22, November, pp. 53–5.

Asia Travel Trade 1990n, 'It's just natural', *Asia Travel Trade*, vol. 22, September, pp. 22–37.

Asia Travel Trade 1990o, 'Too many rooms, too few tourists', *Asia Travel Trade*, vol. 22, February, pp. 29–33.

Asia Travel Trade 1992, 'AFTA the coup', *Asia Travel Trade*, September, pp. 8–9.

Astbury, S. 1992, 'Quantity vs quality', *Asia Travel Trade*, vol. 23, no. 5, May, pp. 36–9.

Atkinson, B. 1989, Fiji: Riding the Crest or..., paper presented at the Fiji Tourism Convention, 14–16 June, The Regent of Fiji, Nadi.

Awanohara, S. 1991, 'Rich man, poor man', *Far Eastern Economic Review*, 3 October, p. 13.

Bastin, R. 1984, 'Small island tourism: development or dependency', *Development Policy Review*, vol. 2, no. 1, pp. 79–90.

Beijing Review 1987, 'More Chinese touring China', *Beijing Review*, 12 January, p. 31.

Best, L. 1968, 'A model of pure plantation economy', *Social and Economic Studies*, vol. 17, no. 3, pp. 283–326.

Blanco, S. 1989, 'Japanese visitors show a yen for luxury hotels', *Asia Travel Trade*, June, pp. 34–5.

Bollard, A., Holmes, F., Kersey, D. & Thompson, M.A. 1989, *Meeting the East Asia Challenge: Trends, Prospects and Policies*, Victoria University Press for the Institute of Policy Studies, Wellington.

Breen, M. 1990, 'South Korea's big spenders remain conspicuous', *Asia Travel Trade*, November, p. 5.

Breen, M. 1991a, 'Eastern wisdom', *Asia Travel Trade*, April, pp. 54–62.

Breen, M. 1991b, 'A development programme begins: Korea re-vitalises its prospects for tourism', *Tourism Asia*, May–June, pp. 40–52.

Brevetti, F. 1992, 'Honing in on Hong Kong', *Asia Travel Trade*, vol. 23, no. 7, July, pp. 25–9.

Britton, S. & Clarke, W.C. (eds.) 1987, *Ambiguous Alternative: Tourism in Small Developing Countries*, University of the South Pacific, Suva.

Britton, S. 1982b, 'The political economy of tourism in the Third World', *Annals of Tourism Research*, vol. 9, no. 3, pp. 331–58.

Britton, S. 1987b, 'The Fiji tourist industry: a review of change and organisation', in *Fiji: Future Imperfect?*, ed. M. Taylor, Allen & Unwin, Sydney, pp. 77–94.

Britton, S.G. & Kissling, C.C. 1984, 'Aviation and development constraints in South Pacific microstates', in *Transport and Communications for Pacific Microstates*, ed. C.C. Kissling, Institute of Pacific Studies, Suva, pp. 79–96.

Britton, S.G. 1982a, 'International tourism and multinational corporations in the Pacific: the case of Fiji', in *The Geography of Multinationals*, eds. M.J. Taylor & N. Thrift, Croom Helm, Sydney, pp. 252–74.

Britton, S.G. 1983, *Tourism and Underdevelopment in Fiji*, Monograph No. 13, ANU Development Studies Centre, Canberra.

Britton, S.G. 1987a, 'Tourism in Pacific island states, constraints and opportunities', in *Ambiguous Alternative: Tourism in Small Developing Countries*, eds. S. Britton & W.C. Clarke, University of the South Pacific, Suva, pp. 113–39.

Brokensha, P. & Guldberg, H. 1992, *Cultural Tourism in Australia*, A Study Commissioned by the Department of the Arts, Sport, the Environment and Territories, AGPS, Canberra.

Bromby, R. 1990, 'Soaring hope: a volatile aviation industry continues to turn', *Pacific Islands Monthly*, vol. 60, no. 8, pp. 23–5.

Bull, A. 1990, 'Australian tourism: effects of foreign investment', *Tourism Management*, December, pp. 325–31.

Burbury, R. 1991, 'Profile: Simon Baggs', *B & T*, 30 August, pp. 14, 21.

Bureau of Tourism Research 1991a, 'Visitors from Asia', *BTR Tourism Update*, *September Quarter*, pp. 5–6.

Bureau of Tourism Research 1991b, 'Potential growth in Asian tourism to Australia', *BTR Tourism Update*, September Quarter, pp. 5–6.

Bureau of Tourism Research 1992, *Australian Tourism Data Card*, Bureau of Tourism Research, Canberra.

Bywater, M. 1990, 'Airlines in the South Pacific', *EIU Travel & Tourism Analyst*, no. 1, pp. 5–28.

Cadiz, L.S. 1992, 'Beyond expectations', *Asia Travel Trade*, September, pp. 30–4.

Castle, L.V. & Findlay, C. (eds) 1988, *Pacific Trade in Services*, Allen & Unwin, Sydney.

Cater, E.A. 1987, 'Tourism in the least developed countries', *Annals of Tourism Research*, vol. 14, pp. 202–26.

Caulfield, M.D. 1978, 'Taxes, tourists and turtlemen: island dependency and the tax-haven business', in *The World as a Company Town: Multinational Corporations and Social Change*, eds. A. Idris-Soven, E. Idris-Soven & M.K. Vaughan, Mouton, The Hague and Paris, pp. 354–74.

Central Planning Office 1988, *Ninth Development Plan: 1986–1990, Policies, Strategies and Programmes for National Development*, Central Planning Office, Ministry for Economic Development, Suva.

Chamberlain, J. 1992, 'On the tourism trail', *North and South*, September, pp. 88–98.

Chew, J. 1987, 'Transport and tourism in the year 2000', *Tourism Management*, vol. 8, no. 2, pp. 83–5.

Cheyne-Buchanan, J. 1992, The restructuring of government involvement in tourism in New Zealand 1987–1992, unpublished Master of Business Studies report, Massey University, Palmerston North.

Chon, K. & Shin, H. 1990, 'Korea's hotel and tourism industry', *Cornell Hotel, Restaurant and Administration Quarterly*, vol. 31, no. 1, pp. 69–73.

Choy, D.J.L. & Gee, C.Y. 1983, 'Tourism in the PRC—five years after China opens its gates', *Tourism Management*, vol. 4, no. 2, pp. 85–93.

Choy, D.J.L. 1992, 'Life cycle models for Pacific island destinations', *Journal of Travel Research*, Winter, pp. 26–31.

Choy, D.J.L., Dong, G.L. & Wen, Z. 1986, 'Tourism in PR China', *Tourism Management*, vol. 7, pp. 197–201.

Clark, L. 1988, 'Planning for tourism in far north Queensland a local government response', pp. 77–88 in *Frontiers in Australian Tourism: The Search for New Perspectives in Policy Development and Research*, eds B. Faulkner & M. Fagance, Bureau of Tourism Research, Canberra.

Clifford, M. 1991, 'Working at leisure', *Far Eastern Economic Review*, 18 April, pp. 62–3.

Cohen, E. 1979, 'The impact on the hill tribes of northern Thailand', *Internationales Asienforum*, vol. 10, pp. 5–38.

Cohen, E. 1982a, 'Thai girls and farang men: the edge of ambiguity', Annals of Tourism Research, vol. 9, no. 3, pp. 403–28.

Cohen, E. 1982b, 'Jungle guides in northern Thailand—the dynamics of a marginal occupational role', *Sociological Review*, vol. 30, no. 2, pp. 234–66.

Cohen, E. 1988, 'Tourism and AIDS in Thailand', *Annals of Tourism Research*, vol. 15, no. 4, pp. 467–86.

Cohen, E. 1989, '"Primitive and remote". Hill tribe trekking in Thailand', *Annals of Tourism Research*, vol. 16, no. 1, pp. 30–61.

Collier, A. 1991, *Principles of Tourism*, 2nd edn, Pitman, Auckland.

Commonwealth Department of Tourism 1992, *Tourism Australia's Passport to Growth: A National Strategy*, Department of Tourism, Canberra.

Commonwealth of Australia and Government of New Zealand 1991, *Costs and Benefits of a Single Australasian Aviation Market*, prepared by a Joint Australia–New Zealand study team consisting of the Bureau of Transport and Communications Economics and Jarden Morgan NZ Limited (now CS First Boston New Zealand Limited), AGPS, Canberra.

Connell, J. 1988, *Sovereignty & Survival: Island Microstates in the Third World*, Research Monograph No. 3, Department of Geography, University of Sydney, Sydney.

Cook, D. 1989, 'China's hotels: still playing catch up', *Cornell Hotel Restaurant and Administration Quarterly*, vol. 30, no. 3, pp. 64–7.

Corben, R. & Robinson, G. 1990, 'What price, success?', *Asia Travel Trade*, vol. 22, June, pp. 16–21.

Corben, R. 1990a, 'High-yield incentive travel is Thailand's top priority', *Asia Travel Trade*, vol. 22, February, pp. 38–9.

Corben, R. 1990b, 'Report says Phuket is mismanaged by industry', *Asia Travel Trade*, vol. 22, April, p. 21.

Corben, R. 1990c, 'Thailand takes another step to curb AIDS', *Asia Travel Trade*, vol. 22, June, pp. 7–9.

Corben, R. 1990d, 'Traffic halts Bangkok's tourism growth', *Asia Travel Trade*, vol. 22, June, p. 9.

Corben, R. 1990e, 'Sobering times ahead', *Asia Travel Trade*, vol. 22, June, pp. 34–5, 37, 40.

Corben, R. 1990f, 'Japan grants Thailand another loan for tourism purposes', *Asia Travel Trade*, vol. 22, October, p. 8.

Corben, R. 1992, 'Thailand: tourism with dignity', *Asia Travel Trade*, vol. 23, no. 6, June, pp. 24–5.

Coventry, N. 1988, 'Japanese lead reawakening in Fijian tourism', *New Zealand Financial Review*, November, pp. 89–91.

Coventry, N. 1990, 'NZ/Australia tourism members press for one-entry concept', *Asia Travel Trade*, vol. 22, October, pp. 6–8.

Craik, J. 1991, *Resorting to Tourism: Cultural Policies for Tourist Development*, Allen & Unwin, Sydney.

Crean, J. 1988, 'Lifting the lid on outbound travel', *Asia Travel Trade*, July, pp. 30–1.

Crosbie, A.J. 1987, 'The changing political realities of the Pacific Rim', in *Geography and Society in a Global Context*, eds R. Le Heron, M. Roche, & M. Shepherd, New Zealand Geographical Society Series No. 14, Massey University, Palmerston North, pp. 154–9.

de Burlo, C. 1984, Indigenous response and participation in tourism in a southwest Pacific island nation, Vanuatu, unpublished PhD dissertation, Syracuse University, Syracuse.

de Burlo, C. 1987, 'Neglected social factors in tourism project design: the case of Vanuatu', *Tourism Recreation Research*, vol. 12, no. 2, pp. 25–30.

de Burlo, C. 1989, 'Land alienation, land tenure, and tourism in Vanuatu, a Melanesian Island nation', *Geojournal*, vol. 19, no. 3, pp. 317–21.

de Kadt, E. (ed.) 1979, *Tourism: Passport to Development?*, Oxford University Press, Oxford.

Delworth, W.T. 1982, 'Canada and the Pacific Rim: a political perspective', in *Politics of the Pacific Rim: Perspectives on the 1980s, Papers from an International Conference held at Simon Fraser University 15–17 April*, 1982, ed. F.Q. Quo, SFU Publications, Burnaby, pp. 3–9.

Densai, A.V. 1976, 'Small island economies: problems of external dependence', in *Co-operation and Development in the Asia/Pacific Region—Relations Between Large and Small Countries, Papers and Proceedings of the Seventh Pacific Trade and Development Conference held in Auckland, New Zealand, 25–28 August*, 1975, eds. L.V. Castle & F. Holmes, The Japan Economic Research Center, Tokyo, pp. 144–57.

Department of Trade and Industry 1988, 'Joint statement by the Prime Ministers of Australia and New Zealand on the occasion of the conclusion of the 1988 review of the Australia New Zealand Closer Economic Relationship', in Agreed Documents from the 1988 Review of ANZCERTA, Department of Trade and Industry, Wellington, pp. 1–6.

Dichen, G. & Guangrui, Z. 1983, 'China's tourism: policy and practice', *Tourism Management*, vol. 4, pp. 75–84.

Din, K. 1988, 'Economic implications of Muslim pilgrimage from Malaysia', *Contemporary Southeast Asia*, vol. 4, no. 1, pp. 58–72.

Din, K. 1989, 'Islam and tourism: patterns, issues and options', *Annals of Tourism Research*, vol. 16, no. 4, pp. 542–63.

Directorate General of Tourism 1992, *Statistics on Visitor Arrivals in Indonesia*, Directorate General of Tourism, Department of Tourism, Post and Telecommunication, Jakarta.

Do-sun, C. 1992a, 'In the balance', *Asia Travel Trade*, April, pp. 58–61.

Do-sun, C. 1992b, 'More than Seoul', *Asia Travel Trade*, September, p. 48.

Douglas, N. & Douglas, N. 1991, 'When things are hurtin': Hawaii's tourism tumbles, hit by war, recession and image fatigue', *Pacific Islands Monthly*, September, pp. 45–7.

Drysdale, P. 1988, *International Economic Pluralism: Economic Policy in East Asia and the Pacific*, Allen & Unwin, North Sydney.

Dunning, J.H. & McQueen, M. 1982a, 'Multinationals in the international hotel industry', *Annals of Tourism Research*, vol. 9, no. 1, pp. 69–90.

Dunning, J.H. & McQueen, M. 1982b, *Transnational Corporations in International Tourism*, United Nations Centre for Transnational Studies, New York.

Dwyer, L., Findlay, C. & Forsyth, P. 1990, *Foreign Investment in Australian Tourism*, Occasional Paper No. 6, Bureau of Tourism Research, Canberra.

Dwyer, L., Forsyth, P. & Findlay, C. 1990, Japanese investment in the Australian tourism industry: rationales and consequences, Paper presented at the Asian Studies Association of Australia 8th Annual Conference, Griffith University, Nathan, July.

Economist Intelligence Unit 1989, 'Foreign investment in China's hotel sector', *EIU Travel & Tourism Analyst*, no. 3, pp. 17–32.

Economist Intelligence Unit 1990a, *Far East and Pacific Travel in the 1990s*, Economist Intelligence Unit, London.

Economist Intelligence Unit 1990b, 'The travel and tourism industry in Japan', *EIU Travel & Tourism Analyst*, no. 5, pp. 93–9.

Economist Intelligence Unit 1990c, 'South Korea', *EIU International Tourism Reports*, no. 2, pp. 23–43.

Economist Intelligence Unit 1990d, 'Singapore', *EIU International Tourism Reports*, no. 2, pp. 68–91.
Economist Intelligence Unit 1990e, 'Australia', *EIU International Tourism Reports*, no. 4, pp. 64–83.
Economist Intelligence Unit 1990f, 'New Zealand', *EIU International Tourism Reports*, no. 2, pp. 44–67.
Economist Intelligence Unit 1991, 'Indonesia', *EIU International Tourism Reports*, no. 3, pp. 23–40.
Economist Intelligence Unit 1992, 'Prospects for international tourism in 1992', *EIU Travel & Tourism Analyst*, no. 6, pp. 77–93.
Edgington, D.W. 1990, *Japanese Business Down Under: Patterns of Japanese Investment in Australia*, Routledge, London and New York.
Edwards, K. & Murphy, D. 1992, 'Mixed blessings', *Time Australia*, vol. 7, no. 6, 10 February, pp. 32–41.
EIE International Corporation 1989, *The EIE Denarau Island Resort: Project Profile and Fact Sheet*, EIE International Corporation, Nadi.
Elliot, J. 1983, 'Politics, power and tourism in Thailand', *Annals of Tourism Research*, vol. 10, pp. 377–93.
Far Eastern Economic Review 1991, 'Editorial', *Far Eastern Economic Review*, 18 July, pp. 10–11.
Far Eastern Economic Review 1992b, 'Infrastructure: aims are high, funds are low', *Far Eastern Economic Review*, 12 November, pp. 44, 46.
Far Eastern Economic Review 1992a, 'Economic prospects', *Far Eastern Economic Review*, 24–31 December, p. 58.
Farrell, B.H. (ed.) 1977, *The Social and Economic Impact of Tourism on Pacific Communities*, Center for South Pacific Studies, University of California, Santa Cruz.
Farrell, B.H. 1974, 'The tourist ghettos of Hawaii', in *Themes on Pacific Lands*, eds., M.C.R. Edgell & B.H. Farrell, Western Geographical Series No. 10, University of Victoria, Victoria, pp. 181–221.
Farrell, B.H. 1982, *Hawaii: The Legend that Sells*, University of Hawaii Press, Honolulu.
Faulkner, H.W. & Fagence, M. (eds.) 1988, *Frontiers of Australian Tourism: The Search for New Perspectives in Policy Development and Research*, Bureau of Tourism Research, Canberra.
Faulkner, H.W. 1990, 'Swings and roundabouts in Australian tourism', *Tourism Management*, March, pp. 29–37.
Faulkner, H.W. 1991, 'Editorial: the role of research in tourism development', *BTR Tourism Update*, September Quarter, pp. 2–3.
Field, A. 1992, 'Aviation update', *Ministry of Tourism Newsletter*, no. 4, p. 2.
Fiji Trade and Investment Board 1990, 'Fiji Trade and Investment Board advertisement', *Pacific Islands Monthly*, June, p. 41.
Fiji Visitors Bureau 1988, *Statistical Report on Visitor Arrivals to Fiji*, Fiji Visitors Bureau, Suva.
Fiji Visitors Bureau 1992, *A Statistical Report on Visitor Arrivals into Fiji Calendar Year 1991*, Fiji Visitors Bureau, Suva.
Finney, B.R. & Watson, K.A. (eds.) 1977, *A New Kind of Sugar: Tourism in the Pacific*, Center for South Pacific Studies, University of California, Santa Cruz.
Forsyth, P. & Dwyer, L. 1991a, *Measuring the Benefits and Costs of Foreign Tourism*, Discussion Paper No. 248, Centre for Economic Policy Research, Australian National University, Canberra.
Forsyth, P. & Dwyer, L. 1991b, Foreign Investment in Australian Tourism, Paper presented at the Tourism Outlook Conference, 11 June, Sydney, Australian Tourism Research Institute—Bureau of Tourism Research, Canberra.
Frechtling, D.C. 1987, 'Key issues in tourism futures the U.S. travel industry', *Tourism Management*, vol. 8, no. 2, pp. 106–11.

Friedland, J. 1992, 'Meeting of minds', *Far Eastern Economic Review*, 1 October, p. 20.

Fujiwara, M. 1991, 'Resort Act: panacea for the construction industry', *AMPO, Japan–Asia Quarterly Review*, vol. 22, no. 4, pp. 37–40.

Garnaut, R. 1990, *Australia and the Northeast Asian Ascendancy*, AGPS, Canberra.

Gartner, W.C. & Shen, J. 1992, 'The impact of Tiananmen Square on China's tourism image', *Journal of Travel Research*, vol. 30, no. 4, pp. 47–52.

Gelston, S. 1989, 'The golden rule of enforcement', *Asia Travel Trade*, vol. 21, December, p. 57.

Geojournal 1990, Chinese Tourist Industry (special theme issue), *Geojournal*, vol. 21, no. 1/2.

Geojournal 1993, Antipodean Tourism Economy (special theme issue), *Geojournal*, vol. 29, no. 3.

Gibson, P. 1990, 'Cashing in on a boom industry', *Pacific Islands Monthly*, March, pp. 34–5.

Girvan, N. 1973, 'The development of dependency economics in the Caribbean and Latin America: review and comparison', *Social and Economic Studies*, vol. 22, pp. 1–33.

Goodman, D.S.G. 1993, 'A brand new China', *The Independent Monthly*, February, pp. 16–18.

Graham, M. 1990, 'Culture shock', *Asia Travel Trade*, vol. 22, February, pp. 24–6.

Guangrui, Z. 1985, 'China getting ready for new prospect for tourism development', *Tourism Management*, vol. 6, pp. 141–3.

Guangrui, Z. 1987, 'Tourism education in PR China', *Tourism Management*, vol. 8, no. 3, pp. 262–6.

Guangrui, Z. 1989, 'Ten years of Chinese tourism: profile and assessment', *Tourism Management*, vol. 10, no. 1, pp. 51–62.

Hail, J. 1992a, 'Blow to Thai tourism', *Asia Travel Trade*, vol. 23, no. 7, July, pp. 6–8.

Hail, J. 1992b, 'Thailand: a new approach', *Asia Travel Trade*, vol. 23, no. 5, May, pp. 24–31.

Hairui, L. 1987, 'PR China's tourism industry and its future development', *Tourism Management*, vol. 8, pp. 90–1.

Hall, C.M. & McArthur, S. 1993, *Heritage Management in New Zealand and Australia: Visitor Management, Interpretation and Marketing*, Oxford University Press, Auckland.

Hall, C.M. & Zeppel, H. 1990, 'Cultural and heritage tourism: the new grand tour?', *Historic Environment*, vol. 7, no. 3–4, pp. 86–98.

Hall, C.M. 1991, *Introduction to Tourism in Australia: Impacts, Planning and Development*, Longman Cheshire, Melbourne.

Hall, C.M. 1992a, 'Sex tourism in South–east Asia', in *Tourism and the Less Developed Countries*, ed. D. Harrison, Belhaven Press, London, pp. 64–74.

Hall, C.M. 1992b, *Hallmark Tourist Events: Impacts, Management and Planning*, Belhaven Press, London.

Hall, C.M. 1992c, 'Issues in ecotourism: from susceptible to sustainable development', in *Heritage Management: Parks, Heritage and Tourism*, Royal Australian Institute of Parks and Recreation, Dickson, pp. 152–8.

Hall, C.M. 1992d, 'Heritage, parks and tourism: the golden triangle?', in *Heritage Management: Parks, Heritage and Tourism*, Royal Australian Institute of Parks and Recreation, Dickson, pp. 202–12.

Hall, C.M. 1993, 'Ecotourism in Australia, New Zealand and the South Pacific: appropriate tourism or a new form of ecological imperialism?', in *Ecotourism—A Sustainable Option?*, eds. E.A. Cater & G.A. Lowman, Belhaven Press/Royal Geographical Society, London.

Hall, C.M., Mitchell, I. & Keelan, N. 1993, 'The implications of Maori perspectives for the management and promotion of heritage tourism in New Zealand', *Geojournal*, vol. 29, no. 3, pp. 315–22.

Hamdi, H. 1990, 'Too little, too late', *Asia Travel Trade*, vol. 20, May, pp. 26–30.

Hamdi, H. 1991, 'Growing pains for South Korea market', *Asia Travel Trade*, February, pp. 10–11.

Hamilton, J. 1988, 'Trends in tourism demand patterns in New Zealand: international and domestic', *International Journal of Hospitality Management*, vol. 7, no. 4, pp. 299–320.

Handley, P. 1991, 'Victims of success', *Far Eastern Economic Review*, 19 September, p. 44.

Handley, P. 1992, 'New rules but old attitudes', *Far Eastern Economic Review*, 29 October, p. 40.

Harrison, D. 1992, 'International tourism and the less developed countries: background', in *Tourism and the Less Developed Countries*, ed. D. Harrison, Belhaven Press, London.

Hart, J. 1990, 'China hoteliers masking post–Tiananmen blues with bravado', *Asia Travel Trade*, vol. 22, May, p. 14.

Hawaii Visitors Bureau 1992, *1991 Annual Research Report*, Market Research Department, Hawaii Visitors Bureau, Honolulu.

Hitchcock, M.J., King, V.T., & Parnwell, M.J.G. (eds.) 1992, *Tourism in South–East Asia*, Routledge, London.

Hollinshead, K. 1990, 'The powers behind play: the political environments for recreation and tourism in Australia', *Journal of Park and Recreation Administration*, vol. 8, no. 1, pp. 35–50.

Holmes, J.W. 1982, 'From sea to sea: Canada's move from the Atlantic to the Pacific', in *Politics of the Pacific Rim: Perspectives on the 1980s, Papers from an International Conference held at Simon Fraser University 15–17 April, 1982*, ed. F.Q. Quo, SFU Publications, Burnaby, pp. 11–23.

Hong Kong Tourist Association 1992, *Annual Report 1991–92*, Hong Kong Tourist Association, Hong Kong.

Hong, E. 1985, *See the Third World While it Lasts*, Consumers Association of Penang, Penang.

Hoon, Y.S. 1990, 'Vanuatu: Life's tough when you're small', *PATA Travel News*, September, pp. 66–8.

Hsü, I.C.Y. 1990, *The Rise of Modern China*, 4th ed., Oxford University Press, New York.

Husbands, W.C. 1986, 'Periphery resort tourism and tourist resident stress: example from Barbados', *Leisure Studies*, vol. 5, pp. 175–88.

Hwu, C.J. 1992, 'Of MICE & men', *Asia Travel Trade*, vol. 23, no. 8, August, pp. 12–13.

Industries Assistance Commission 1989, *Travel and Tourism*, Report No. 423, AGPS, Canberra.

Inoue, R. 1991, 'An army of Japanese Tourists', *AMPO, Japan–Asia Quarterly Review*, vol. 22, no. 4, pp. 2–10.

Islands Business 1990a, 'Flying through the crisis', *Islands Business*, November, pp. 31–42.

Islands Business 1990b, 'After Mururoa, tourism?', *Islands Business*, November, pp. 47–8.

Jaleco, B. 1992, Bullish outlook', *Asia Travel Trade*, vol. 23, no. 7, July, p. 33–5.

Japan Advisory Committee 1981, *Tourism from Japan: Prospects, Promises, Problems, Papers presented to a seminar of the Japan Advisory Committee 27–28 May, 1981*, Japan Advisory Committee and Asia Pacific Books, Wellington.

Japan Travel Bureau 1991, JTB Report '91: All About Japanese Overseas Travellers, *Japan Travel Bureau*, Tokyo.

Jeffrey, L. 1990a, 'The pitfalls of going Archipelago', *Asia Travel Trade*, vol. 22, October, p. 59.

Jeffrey, L. 1990b, 'Fighting back', *Asia Travel Trade*, vol. 22, pp. 24–47.

Jeffrey, L. 1991, 'Squeezed out', *Asia Travel Trade*, March, pp. 34–40.

Jeong, G-H. 1988, 'Tourism expectations on the 1988 Seoul Olympics: a Korean perspective', in *Tourism Research: Expanding Boundaries*, Travel and Tourism Research Association, Nineteenth Annual Conference Proceedings, Bureau of Economic and Business Research, Graduate School of Business, University of Utah, Salt Lake City, pp. 175–82.

Johnston, B. 1990, 'Introduction: breaking out of the tourist trap', *Cultural Survival Quarterly*, vol. 14, no. 12, p. 5.

Jones, M. 1986, *A Shady Place for Shady People: The Real Gold Coast Story*, Allen & Unwin, Sydney.

Kee, L.W. & Ghosh, B.C. 1990, 'Strategies for hotels in Singapore', *Cornell Hotel and Restaurant Administration Quarterly*, May, pp. 74–9.

Keith-Reid, R. 1989, 'Few question the new wave of optimism', *Islands Business*, vol. 15, no. 6, pp. 60–1.

Kelly, N. 1991, 'Counting the cost', *Far Eastern Economic Review*, 18 July, p. 44.

Kent, N. 1977, 'A new kind of sugar', *A New Kind of Sugar: Tourism in the Pacific*, eds. B.R. Finney & K.A. Watson, Center for South Pacific Studies, University of California, Santa Cruz, pp. 169–98.

Khan, H., Chou, F.S. & Wong, K.C. 1990, 'Tourism multiplier effects on Singapore', *Annals of Tourism Research*, vol. 17, no. 3, pp. 408–18.

Kim, R. 1987, 'Pacific Basin Cooperation: Problems and Prospects', in *New Tides in the Pacific: Pacific Basin Cooperation and the Big Four (Japan, PRC, USA, USSR)*, eds. R. Kim & H. Conroy, Greenwood Press, Westport, pp. 165–91.

Kim, R., & Conroy, H. 1987, 'Introduction', in *New Tides in the Pacific: Pacific Basin Cooperation and the Big Four (Japan, PRC, USA, USSR)*, eds. R. Kim & H. Conroy, Greenwood Press, Westport, pp. 1–9.

King, B. 1991, 'Tour operators and the air inclusive tour industry in Australia', *EIU Travel & Tourism Analyst*, no. 3, pp. 66–87.

Kissling, C. 1993, 'Factors affecting trans-Tasman air services', *Geojournal*, vol. 29, no. 3, pp. 291–8.

Kissling, C.C. 1990, 'Management issues in Pacific island aviation and tourism', in *Destination South Pacific: Perspectives on Island Tourism*, ed. C. Kissling, Centre des Hautes Etudes Touristiques, Aix-en-Provence, pp. 13–30.

Klieger, P.C. 1992, 'Shangri-La and the politicization of tourism in Tibet', *Annals of Tourism Research*, vol. 19, no. 1, pp. 122–5.

Korea National Tourism Corporation 1991, *Korea '90/'91 Travel Manual*, Korea National Tourism Corporation, Seoul.

Korea National Tourism Corporation 1992, *Korea 'Monthly Statistics of Tourism: 1992–10, October*, Korea National Tourism Corporation, Seoul.

Korporaal, G., 1991, 'Diplomacy in the air', *Far Eastern Economic Review*, 3 October, p. 58.

Kuji, T. 1991, 'The political economy of golf', *AMPO, Japan–Asia Quarterly Review*, vol. 22, no. 4, pp. 47–54.

Kuroda, Y. 1982, 'Japan's future in the Pacific and Asia: perspectives on the 80s', in *Politics of the Pacific Rim: Perspectives on the 1980s, Papers from an International Conference held at Simon Fraser University 15–17 April, 1982*, ed. F.Q. Quo, SFU Publications, Burnaby.

Lavery, P. 1989, 'Tourism in China: the costs of collapse', *EIU Travel & Tourism Analyst*, no. 4, pp. 77–97.

Lea, D.A.M. 1980, 'Tourism in Papua New Guinea: the last resort', in *Of Time and Place*, eds J.M. Jennings & G.J.R. Linge, Australian National University Press, Canberra, pp. 211–31.

Lea, J. 1988, *Tourism in the Third World*, Methuen, London.

Lee, T.C. 1989, 'Move over Bali, here comes Banten...', *Asia Travel Trade*, vol. 21, June, pp. 20–1.

Leiper, N. 1984, *The Japanese Travel Market & Its Potential for Australian Tourist Destinations*, QANTAS Airways, Sydney.

Lickorish, L. 1987, 'Trends in industrialized countries', *Tourism Management*, vol. 8, no. 2, pp. 92–5.

Lim, N.Z. 1992, 'Philippines: mastering the plan', *Asia Travel Trade*, September, p. 50.

Lin, M, 1990, 'Taiwan: magnet for Japanese tourists', *Cornell Hotel Restaurant and Administration Quarterly*, May, pp. 96–7.

Ling, C.Y. 1991, 'Malaysia: for only a select few', *AMPO, Japan–Asia Quarterly Review*, vol. 22, no. 4, pp. 32–3.

Livingstone, J.M. 1989, *The Internationalisation of Business*, Macmillan, Houndmills.

Lloyd, P. 1985, *CER—The Implications for New Zealand*, Government Publishing Agencies, Wellington.

Long, D. 1990, 'Yen investment on the ebb', *Asia Travel Trade*, August, pp. 38–9.

Lorenz, D. 1989, 'Intra-regional trade and Pacific cooperation: problems and prospects', in *Trends of Economic Development in East Asia, Essays in Honour of Willy Kraus*, ed. W. Klenner, Springer–Verlag, Berlin, pp. 65–74.

Lunn, G.E. 1988, *Proposal for Establishment of a Hotel Buying Co–operative*, Tourism Council of the South Pacific—Agriculture/Tourism Linkage Project, Fiji Hotel Association, Suva.

Mackie, V. 1992, 'Japan and South–east Asia: the international division of labour and leisure', in *Tourism and the Less Developed Countries*, ed. D. Harrison, Belhaven Press, London, pp. 75–84.

Mak, J. & White, K. 1988, 'Tourism in Asia and the Pacific', *Pacific Focus*, vol. 3, Spring, pp. 115–43.

Mak, J. & White, K. 1992, 'Comparative tourism development in Asia and the Pacific', *Journal of Travel Research*, Summer, pp. 14–23.

Malik, M. (ed.) 1991, *Asia 1991 Yearbook*, *Far Eastern Economic Review*, Hong Kong.

Mangnall, K. 1990, 'A new direction: Vanuatu changes course a decade later', *Pacific Islands Monthly*, vol. 60, no. 9, pp. 18–21.

Martin, W.H. & Mason, S. 1987, 'Social trends and tourism futures', *Tourism Management*, vol. 8, no. 2, pp. 112–14.

Massey, M. 1991, ''Rebirth' of Qld tourism axes 41 in fresh focus', *Australian Financial Review*, 31 July, p. 29.

Matsuoka, J. 1991, 'Differential perceptions of the social impacts of tourism development in a rural Hawaiian community', *Social Development Issues*, vol. 13, no. 2, pp. 55–63.

Matthews, H.G. 1978, *International Tourism a Political and Social Analysis*, Schenkman Publishing Company, Cambridge.

McCormack, G. 1991, The price of affluence: the political economy of Japanese leisure', *New Left Review*, no. 188, July–August, pp. 121–34.

McDermott Miller Group 1991, 'Destination South West Pacific', *Tourism FX: A Quarterly Analysis of New Zealand Tourism*, July.

McGahey, S. 1991, 'South Korea outbound', *EIU Travel & Tourism Analyst*, no. 6, pp. 45–62.

Migration Section, Department of Statistics 1993, *Short-term Departures of New Zealand Residents (on-line)*, Department of Statistics, Wellington.

Milne, S. 1990a, 'The impact of tourism development in small Pacific island states', *New Zealand Journal of Geography*, no. 89, pp. 16–20.

Milne, S. 1990b, 'The economic impact of tourism in Tonga', *Pacific Viewpoint*, vol. 31, no. 1, pp. 24–43.

Milne, S. 1990c, 'Tourism and economic development in Vanuatu', *Singapore Journal of Tropical Geography*, vol. 11, no. 1, pp. 13–26.

Milne, S. 1991, 'Tourism development in Papua New Guinea', *Annals of Tourism Research*, vol. 18, no. 3, pp. 508–10.

Milne, S. 1992a, 'Tourism and Development in South Pacific microstates', *Annals of Tourism Research*, vol. 19, no. 3, pp. 191–212.

Milne, S. 1992b, 'Tourism development in Nuie', *Annals of Tourism Research*, vol. 19, no. 3, pp. 565–9.

Minerbi, L. 1992, *Impacts of Tourism Development in Pacific Islands*, Greenpeace Pacific Campaign, San Francisco.

Mings, R. & Liu, W. 1989, 'Emerging tourism in China—the case of Xian', *Tourism Management*, vol. 10, no. 4, pp. 333–6.

Ministry of Tourism (Fiji) 1992, *General Information on Tourism in Fiji Its Past and Future and Impact on the Economy and Society*, Ministry of Tourism, Suva.

Ministry of Tourism (New Zealand) 1991, *Introducing the Ministry of Tourism*, Ministry of Tourism, Wellington.

Ministry of Tourism (New Zealand) 1992a, *Residents' Perceptions and Acceptance of Tourism in Selected New Zealand Communities: Key Findings*, Ministry of Tourism, Wellington.

Ministry of Tourism (New Zealand) 1992b, *The Resource Management Act: A Guide for the Tourism Industry*, Issues Paper No. 1, Ministry of Tourism, Wellington.

Ministry of Tourism (New Zealand) 1992c, *Tourism Sustainability: A Discussion Paper*, Issues Paper No. 2, Ministry of Tourism, Wellington.

Ministry of Trade and Industry 1986, *The Singapore Economy: New Directions*, Government Printers, Singapore.

Ministry of Transport, Japan National Tourist Organization 1986, *Tourism in Japan 1986*, Ministry of Transport, Tokyo.

Ministry of Transport, Japan National Tourist Organization 1991, *Tourism in Japan 1991*, Ministry of Transport, Tokyo.

Ministry of Transportation, Korea National Tourism Corporation 1992, *Annual Statistical Report on Tourism*, Ministry of Transportation, Korea National Tourism Corporation, Seoul.

Moffet, L. 1991, 'Tourism commission jobs to go', *Australian Financial Review*, 7 August, p. 24.

Molloy, L. 1993, 'Interpretation of New Zealand's Natural Heritage', in *Heritage Management in New Zealand and Australia: Visitor Management, Interpretation and Marketing*, eds. C.M. Hall & S. McArthur, Oxford University Press, Auckland.

Momsen, J.H. 1986, *Linkages Between Tourism and Agriculture: Problems for the Smaller Caribbean Economies*, Department of Geography Seminar Paper No. 45, University of Newcastle, Newcastle.

Moore, F. 1991, 'The last word', *Tourism FX: A Quarterly Analysis of New Zealand Tourism*, July.

Moriaty, M. 1989, 'Japanese investment alarms residents', *Pacific Islands Monthly*, vol. 59, no. 14, February, pp. 14–15.

Morley, J.W. 1987, 'The genesis of the Pacific Basin movement', in *New Tides in the Pacific: Pacific Basin Cooperation and the Big Four (Japan, PRC, USA, USSR)*, eds. R. Kim & H. Conroy, Greenwood Press, Westport, pp. 11–34.

Murakami, A. 1976, 'Japanese foreign investment—problems of the large home country', in *Co-operation and Development in the Asia/Pacific Region—Relations Between Large and Small Countries, Papers and Proceedings of the Seventh Pacific Trade and Development Conference held in Auckland, New Zealand, 25–28 August, 1975*, eds. L.V. Castle & F. Holmes, The Japan Economic Research Center, Tokyo, pp. 243–56.

Murphy, D. & Reid, B. 1992, 'A Tasman marriage of convenience', *Time International*, vol. 7, no. 37, 14 September, pp. 18–23.

National Tourism Administration of the People's Republic of China 1992, *The Yearbook of China Tourism Statistics*, National Tourism Administration of the People's Republic of China, Beijing.

National Tourism Office of Vanuatu 1990, *A History of Tourism in Vanuatu: A Platform for Future Success*, National Tourism Office of Vanuatu, Port Vila.

National Tourism Office of Vanuatu 1992, *Statistical Indicators, 2nd Qtr 1992*, National Tourism Office of Vanuatu, Port Vila.

New Zealand Tourism Board 1991, *Tourism in New Zealand: A Strategy for Growth*, New Zealand Tourism Board, Wellington.

New Zealand Tourism Board 1992a, *Market Brief 1992–1993: Japan*, New Zealand Tourism Board, Wellington.

New Zealand Tourism Board 1992b, *Tourism in the 90s*, New Zealand Tourism Board, Wellington.

New Zealand Tourism Board 1992c, *New Zealand Tourism News*, New Zealand Tourism Board, Wellington.

New Zealand Tourism Board 1992d, *Monthly Tourism Statistics: August*, New Zealand Tourism Board, Wellington.

New Zealand Tourism Board 1992e, *Market Brief: Asia*, New Zealand Tourism Board, Wellington.

New Zealand Tourism Department 1991a, *New Zealand Tourism and the Economy*, New Zealand Tourism Department, Wellington.

New Zealand Tourism Department 1991b, *Corporate Plan 1991/92*, New Zealand Tourism Department, Wellington.

New Zealand Tourism Department 1991c, *Tourism Facts, June 1991*, New Zealand Tourism Department, Wellington.

Orr, R.M., Jr 1990, *The Emergence of Japan as a Foreign Aid Power*, Columbia University Press, New York.

Oudiette, V. 1990, 'International tourism in China', *Annals of Tourism Research*, vol. 17, no. 1, pp. 123–32.

Pacific Asia Travel Association (PATA) 1992, *Annual Statistical Report 1991*, PATA, San Francisco.

Pacific Islands Monthly 1989, 'Pacific report', *Pacific Islands Monthly*, vol. 59, no. 17, p. 42.

Pacific Islands Monthly 1990, 'Vanuatu's revival as untouched paradise', *Pacific Islands Monthly*, vol. 60, no. 3, pp. 37–9.

Parker, J.K. 1992a, 'China syndrome', *Asia Travel Trade*, vol. 23, no. 4, April, pp. 46–8.

Parker, J.K. 1992b, 'Out of the deep freeze', *Asia Travel Trade*, vol. 23, no. 10, October, pp. 42–7.

Parker, J.K. 1992c, 'Lacklustre promotion may dull China's golden year', *Asia Travel Trade*, vol. 23, no. 10, October, pp. 49–51.

PATA Travel News 1991, 'Beat the cold, hit the ski slopes', *PATA Travel News*, April, pp. 68–9.

Pearce, D.G. 1989, *Tourist Development*, 2nd ed, Longman, Harlow.

Pearce, D.G. 1990, 'Tourism, the regions and restructuring in New Zealand', *Journal of Tourism Studies*, vol. 1, no. 2, pp. 33–42.

Pearce, D.G. 1992, *Tourist Organizations*, Longman, Harlow.

Pearce, D.G. 1993, 'Domestic tourist travel patterns in New Zealand', *Geojournal*, vol. 29, no. 3, pp. 225–32.

Pickering, D. 1989, Keynote Speech by the Minister for Tourism, Civil Aviation and Energy, Paper presented at the Fiji Tourism Convention, 14 June, The Regent of Fiji, Nadi.

Pollard, S. 1987, *The Viability and Vulnerability of a Small Island State: The Case of Kirabati*, Islands/Australia Working Paper No. 87/14, National Centre for Development Studies, Canberra.

Poole, K. 1991, 'Small scale secondary tourist accommodations: appropriate alternatives for Fiji's tourist industry', *Review*, vol. 12, no. 19, pp. 8–17.

Pravda [English Edition], 29 July 1986, p. 3.

Pye, E.A. & Lin, T.B. 1983, *Tourism in Asia: The Economic Impact*, Singapore University Press, Singapore.

Quo, F.Q. (ed.) 1982, *Politics of the Pacific Rim: Perspectives on the 1980s, Papers from an International Conference held at Simon Fraser University 15–17 April, 1982*, SFU Publications, Burnaby.

Rajotte, F. & Crocombe, R. (eds.) 1980, *Pacific Tourism as Islanders See It*, Institute of Pacific Studies, Suva.

Rajotte, F. (ed.) 1982, *The Impact of Tourism Development in the Pacific*, Environmental and Resource Studies Programme, Trent University, Peterborough.

Republic of China Tourist Bureau 1992a, *1991 Annual Report*, Tourist Bureau, Ministry of Transport and Communications, Taipei.

Republic of China Tourist Bureau 1992b, *Report on Tourism Statistics, 1991*, Tourist Bureau, Ministry of Transport and Communications, Taipei.

Reynolds, P. 1990, 'Tourism in China: is the honeymoon over?', in *Progress in Tourism, Recreation and Hospitality Management*, vol. 2, ed. C.P. Cooper, Belhaven Press, London, pp. 104–16.

Richter, L.K. 1983, 'Political implications of Chinese tourism policy', *Annals of Tourism Research*, vol. 10, pp. 395–413.

Richter, L.K. 1989, *The Politics of Tourism in Asia*, University of Hawaii Press, Honolulu.

Rix, A. 1990, *Japan's Aid Program: A New Global Agenda*, International Development Issues No. 12, Australian International Development Assistance Bureau, Canberra.

Robinson, G. 1989a, 'AIDS fear triggers Thai action', *Asia Travel Trade*, vol. 21, September, p. 11.

Robinson, G. 1989b, 'Boom, bust or burst?', *Asia Travel Trade*, vol. 21, pp. 34–45.

Robinson, G. 1989c, 'Thai developers face a tidal wave of protest', *Asia Travel Trade*, vol. 21, December, pp. 51, 53.

Robinson, G. 1990, 'Re-couping in the Philippines', *Asia Travel Trade*, March, pp. 18–20.

Roehl, W.S. 1990, 'Travel agent attitudes toward China after Tiananmen Square', *Journal of Travel Research*, vol. 29, no. 2, pp. 16–22.

Ross, D.A. 1982, 'Canadian foreign policy and the Pacific Rim: from national security anxiety to creative economic cooperation?', in *Politics of the Pacific Rim: Perspectives on the 1980s, Papers from an International Conference held at Simon Fraser University 15–17 April, 1982*, ed. F.Q. Quo, SFU Publications, Burnaby, pp. 27–55.

Rowley, A. 1992a, 'Asia above the gloom', *Far Eastern Economic Review*, 24–31 December, pp. 52–3.

Rowley, A. 1992b, 'Kinder, gentler Japan: Tokyo officials want people to work less hard', *Far Eastern Economic Review*, 9 July, p. 61.

Rowley, A. 1992c, 'Coming together', *Far Eastern Economic Review*, 17 December, p. 64.

Rurakdee, N. 1991, 'The impact of the Visit Malaysia Year on Thai tourism', *Bangkok Bank Monthly Review*, vol. 32, May, pp. 182–98.

Sargeant, D. 1988, 'Perspectives on tourism development—industry panel division', *Frontiers of Australian Tourism: The Search for New Perspectives in Policy Development and Research*, eds B. Faulkner & M. Fagence, Bureau of Tourism Research, Canberra, pp. 53–6.

Scalapino, R.A. 1989, 'Southeast Asia—which path ahead?', in *Trends of Economic Development in East Asia, Essays in Honour of Willy Kraus*, ed. W. Klenner, Springer–Verlag, Berlin, pp. 135–46.

Schollhammer, H. 1978, 'Direct foreign investments and investment policies of Japanese firms', in *International Business in the Pacific Basin*, ed. R.H. Mason, Lexington Books, Lexington, pp. 131–49.

Schrock, J.R., Adams, C.R. & Lung, J. 1989, 'China's need for tourism development', *Cornell Hotel Restaurant and Administration Quarterly*, vol. 30, no. 3, pp. 68–71.

Senate Standing Committee on Environment, Recreation and the Arts 1988, *The Potential of the Kakadu National Park Region*, Senate Standing Committee on Environment, Recreation and the Arts, The Parliament of the Commonwealth of Australia, AGPS, Canberra, November.

Shackleford, P. 1987, 'Global tourism trends', *Tourism Management*, vol. 8, no. 2, pp. 98–101.

Shin, T. 1989, 'The Pacific basin community and Korean economy', in *Trends of Economic Development in East Asia, Essays in Honour of Willy Kraus*, ed. W. Klenner, Springer–Verlag, Berlin, pp. 131–4.

Simmons, D. 1991, *Towards a National Tourism Strategy: A Background Paper*, Department of the Arts, Sport, the Environment, Tourism and Territories, Canberra.

Singapore Tourist Promotion Board 1992, *Singapore Monthly Report on Tourism Statistics December 1991*, Market Planning Department, Singapore Tourist Promotion Board, Singapore.

Singh, S. 1992, 'Tourism development of Huangshan Scenic area', *Annals of Tourism Research*, vol. 19, no. 3, pp. 592–3.

Smith, M. 1991, 'Lower fares in aviation free-up', *National Business Review*, 7 June, p. 1.

Smith, T. 1988, 'Hotel investors/operators—Australia', *The Tourism and Hospitality Industry*, ed J. Blackwell, International Magazine Services, Sydney, pp. 182–8.

Smith, V. 1988, Geographical Implications of "Drifter" Tourism: Borocay, The Philippines, Paper presented at the International Geographical Union Commission on Leisure and Recreation Symposium, Christchurch, New Zealand, 13–20 August.

Stuart, T., 1992, 'A yen for travel', *Asia Travel Trade*, August, pp. 27–31.

Suzuki, Y. 1989, 'Japan's role as a creditor nation', in *Trends of Economic Development in East Asia, Essays in Honour of Willy Kraus*, ed. W. Klenner, Springer–Verlag, Berlin, pp. 3–10.

Taber, G.M. 1992, 'Growing, growing…', *Time International*, vol. 7, no. 37, 14 September, pp. 24–8.

Tamao, T. 1980, 'Tourism within, from and to Japan', *International Social Science Journal*, vol. 32, no. 1, pp. 128–150.

Tasker, R. & Handley, P. 1991, 'The good neighbours', *Far Eastern Economic Review*, 18 July, pp. 36–42.

Taylor, M. (ed.) 1987, *Fiji: Future Imperfect?*, Allen & Unwin, Sydney.

Teh, S. & Masterton, A.M. 1990, 'Is there room for budget class hotels in Malaysia?', *Asia Travel Trade*, vol. 22, September, pp. 39–41.

Teh, S. & Wong, Y. 1989, 'Bursting at the seams', *Asia Travel Trade*, vol. 21, December, pp. 6–7, 10–11.

Teh, S. 1989a, 'Marine tourism: a new thrust', *Asia Travel Trade*, February, p. 22.

Teh, S. 1989b, 'Biting off too much too soon', *Asia Travel Trade*, June, pp. 6–7, 10–11.

Teh, S. 1989c, 'Funding shortfall hampering VIY 1991', *Asia Travel Trade*, vol. 21, December, p. 41.

Teh, S. 1989d, 'Rate rises likely in Jakarta hotels', *Asia Travel Trade*, vol. 21, December, pp. 42–5.

Teh, S. 1989e, 'Booming Bali poser for tour operators', *Asia Travel Trade*, vol. 21, December, pp. 47–8.

Teh, S. 1989f, 'Is outbound travel out of reach', *Asia Travel Trade*, vol. 21, December, pp. 49–50.

Teh, S. 1989g, 'The early campaign lures the tourist?', *Asia Travel Trade*, vol. 21, October, pp. 55–64.

Teh, S. 1989h, 'Environmental concerns make an impact in Malaysia', *Asia Travel Trade*, vol. 21, December, pp. 60–1.

Teh, S. 1990, 'Coming together', *Asia Travel Trade*, vol. 22, August, pp. 22–3, 26–7, 29–31, 33–5.

Teh, S., Blanco, S., Gocher, J. & Boyd, A. 1989, 'The mega resort comes to Asia', *Asia Travel Trade*, vol. 21, March, pp. 39–40.

Thai Airways International 1992, 'Discover Thailand's natural heritage' (advertisement), *Time International*, vol. 7, no. 37, 14 September.

Tiglao, R. 1992, 'On the launch pad: Asean ministers set countdown to freer trade', *Far Eastern Economic Review*, 5 November, p. 50.

Tisdell, C. & Wen, J. 1990, 'Investment in China's tourism industry: its scale, nature and policy issues for consideration', *Discussion Paper No. 49*, Department of Economics, University of Queensland, St Lucia.

Tisdell, C. & Wen, J. 1991, 'Foreign tourism as an element in PR China's economic development strategy', *Tourism Management*, March, pp. 55–68.

Toh, M.H. & Low, L. 1990, 'Economic impact of tourism in Singapore', *Annals of Tourism Research*, vol. 17, no. 2, pp. 246–69.

Tourism Commission of New South Wales 1985, *Annual Report February–June 1985*, Tourism Commission of New South Wales, Sydney.

Tourism Commission of New South Wales 1987a, *North Coast Region Tourism Development Strategy*, Tourism Commission of New South Wales on behalf of the North Coast Advisory Committee, Tourism Commission of New South Wales, Sydney.

Tourism Commission of New South Wales 1987b, *Tourism Development Strategy for New South Wales*, Tourism Commission of New South Wales, Sydney.

Tourism Commission of New South Wales 1988, *Annual Report 1987–1988*, Tourism Commission of New South Wales, Sydney.

Tourism Commission of New South Wales 1991, *Annual Report 1990–1991*, Tourism Commission of New South Wales, Sydney.

Tourism Council of the South Pacific 1990a, *Review of Museums and Cultural Centres in the South Pacific*, Tourism Council of the South Pacific, Suva.

Tourism Council of the South Pacific 1990b, *Tourism Sector Report: Vanuatu Evaluation and Development Needs*, Tourism Council of the South Pacific, Suva.

Tourism Working Group 1991, *Ecologically Sustainable Development Working Groups Final Report —Tourism*, AGPS, Canberra.

Tourist Development Corporation Malaysia 1991, *1990 Annual Report*, Tourist Development Corporation Malaysia, Kuala Lumpur.

Trask, H. 1991, 'Lovely hula hands: corporate tourism and the prostitution of Hawaiian culture', *Contours*, vol. 5, no. 1, pp. 8–14.

United States Department of Commerce 1961, *Tourism in the Pacific*, prepared by Checchi and Company, United States Department of Commerce, Washington DC.

Urry, J. 1990, *The Tourist Gaze: Leisure and Travel in Contemporary Societies*, Sage Publications, London.

Uysal, M., Wei, Lu & Reid, L.M. 1986, 'Development of international tourism in PR China', *Tourism Management*, vol. 7, pp. 113–19.

Vasil, A. 1992, 'Tourism Board lays off 40 staff', *The Dominion*, 27 February.

Wall, G. & Dibnah, S. 1992, 'The changing status of tourism in Bali, Indonesia', in *Progress in Tourism, Recreation and Hospitality Management*, vol. 4, ed. C. Cooper, Belhaven Press, London, pp. 120–130.

Wall, G. 1993, 'International collaboration in the search for sustainable tourism in Bali, Indonesia', *Journal of Sustainable Tourism*, vol. 1, no. 1, pp. 38–47.

Weiler, B. & Hall, C.M. (eds.) 1992, *Special Interest Tourism*, Belhaven Press, London.

Weiler, B. (ed.) 1992, *Ecotourism Incorporating the Global Classroom*, Bureau of Tourism Research, Canberra.

Westlake, M., 1991, 'Taiwan waits to take-off', *Far Eastern Economic Review*, 10 October, p. 76.

Wevers, M. 1988, *Japan, Its Future and New Zealand*, Victoria University Press for the Institute of Policy Studies, Wellington.

Wieman, E. 1989a, 'Mao speaks his mind', *Asia Travel Trade*, vol. 21, May, pp. 36–7.

Wieman, E. 1989b, 'Spectacular growth continues', *Asia Travel Trade*, vol. 21, May, pp. 43–4.

Wieman, E. 1989c, 'Short on rooms, high on rates', *Asia Travel Trade*, vol. 21, May, p. 44.

Wieman, E. 1990, 'Not much to cheer about', *Asia Travel Trade*, vol. 22, April, pp. 40–2.

Wieman, E. 1992, 'Taiwan on', *Asia Travel Trade*, pp. 36–8.

Wilkinson, P.F. 1987, 'Tourism in small island nations: a fragile dependence', *Leisure Studies*, vol. 6, no. 2, pp. 127–146.

Wilkinson, P.F. 1989, 'Strategies for tourism in microstates', *Annals of Tourism Research*, vol. 16, no. 2, pp. 153–177.

Wong, K.C. & Gan, S.K. 1988, 'Strategies for tourism in Singapore', *Long Range Planning*, vol. 21, no. 4, pp. 36–44.

Wong, Y. 1990, 'The missing links in product blueprint', *Asia Travel Trade*, vol. 22, May, pp. 34–5.

World Tourism Organization 1991, *Tourism Trends Worldwide and in East Asia and the Pacific 1950–1991*, World Tourism Organization, Statistics Section, Madrid.

World Tourism Organization 1988a, *Small Scale Indigenous Tourism Business Development in Fiji*, report to the Government of Fiji, United Nations Development Programme, Suva.

World Tourism Organization 1988b, *Secondary Tourism Activity in Fiji: Opportunities, Policies and Control*, Report to the Government of Fiji, United Nations Development Programme, Suva.

Writer, L. 1988, 'Backing a business recovery', *Pacific Islands Monthly*, May, pp. 32–4.

Xiyang, T. 1987, *Living Treasures: An Odyssey Through China's Extraordinary Nature Reserves*, Bantam Books/New World Press, New York/Beijing.

Yabsley, M. 1991, 'NSW Committed to Research', *Australian Financial Review*, 5 November.

Yacoumis, J. 1990, 'Tourism in the South Pacific: a significant development potential', *The Courier*, no. 122, July–August, pp. 81–3.

Yam, S. 1987, 'Training tomorrow's hotel managers in China', *International Journal of Hospitality Management*, vol. 6, no. 2, p. 56.

Yarmy, W.M. 1992, 'Growth potential of Korea's outbound tourist market to United States travel and tourism', *Journal of Travel and Tourism Marketing*, vol. 1, no. 1, pp. 89–94.

Yoo, P. 1989, 'Here come the Koreans', *Asia Travel Trade*, vol. 21, July/August, pp. 38–9.

Yu, L. 1992, 'Emerging markets for China's tourism industry', *Journal of Travel Research*, vol. 31, no. 1, pp. 10–13.

Zeppel, H. & Hall, C.M. 1992, 'Review: arts and heritage tourism', in *Special Interest Tourism*, eds. B. Weiler & C.M. Hall, Belhaven Press, London, pp. 47–68.

Zhao, J. 1989, 'Overprovision in Chinese hotels', *Tourism Management*, vol. 10, no. 1, pp. 63–6.

Name index

Place index

Subject index